MW00990679

OXFORD POLITICAL THEORY

Series Editors: Will Kymlicka, David Miller, and Alan Ryan

CIVICS BEYOND CRITICS
CHARACTER EDUCATION IN A LIBERAL DEMOCRACY

OXFORD POLITICAL THEORY

Oxford Political Theory presents the best new work in contemporary political theory. It is intended to be broad in scope, including original contributions to political philosophy, and also work in applied political theory. The series contains works of outstanding quality with no restriction as to approach or subject matter.

OTHER TITLES IN THIS SERIES

The Ethics of Immigration
Joseph Carens

Linguistic Justice for Europe and for the World
Philippe Van Parijs

Critical Republicanism
The Hijab Controversy and Political Philosophy
Cécile Laborde

National Responsibility and Global Justice
David Miller

Disadvantage
Jonathan Wolff and Avner de-Shalit

Levelling the Playing Field
The Idea of Equal Opportunity and its Place in Egalitarian Thought
Andrew Mason

The Liberal Archipelago
A Theory of Diversity and Freedom
Chandran Kukathas

The Civic Minimum
On the Rights and Obligations of Economic Citizenship
Stuart White

Reflective Democracy
Robert E. Goodin

Multicultural Citizenship
A Liberal Theory of Minority Rights
Will Kymlicka

Deliberate Democracy and Beyond
Liberals, Critics, Contestations
John S. Dryzek

Real Freedom for All
What (if Anything) Can Justify Capitalism?
Philippe Van Parijs

On Nationality
David Miller

Republicanism: A Theory of Freedom and Government
Philip Pettit

Inclusion and Democracy
Iris Marion Young

Justice as Impartiality
Brian Barry

CIVICS BEYOND CRITICS

CHARACTER EDUCATION IN A LIBERAL DEMOCRACY

IAN MACMULLEN

OXFORD
UNIVERSITY PRESS

Great Clarendon Street, Oxford, OX2 6DP,
United Kingdom

Oxford University Press is a department of the University of Oxford.
It furthers the University's objective of excellence in research, scholarship,
and education by publishing worldwide. Oxford is a registered trade mark of
Oxford University Press in the UK and in certain other countries

First Edition published in 2015
Impression: 1

Published in the United States of America by Oxford University Press
198 Madison Avenue, New York, NY 10016, United States of America

British Library Cataloguing in Publication Data
Data available

Library of Congress Control Number: 2014950160

ISBN 978–0–19 873361–4

Printed and bound by
CPI Group (UK) Ltd, Croydon, CR0 4YY

To my parents, Linda and Andy MacMullen

ACKNOWLEDGMENTS

My interest in civic character education was piqued by *Morse v. Frederick*, a quirky case that the Supreme Court of the United States decided in 2007. Five years earlier, a teenager in Alaska had been suspended from his public high school for displaying a banner that declared, "BONG HiTS 4 JESUS." This arresting but enigmatic phrase was interpreted by some observers—including, most consequentially, the school principal—as promoting illegal drug use. Although the ensuing litigation and commentary focused predominantly on issues of free speech, I saw the case as raising questions about the roles that public schools could and should play in shaping children's attitudes to the laws of their society. More generally, I became interested in the many ways in which civic education can go beyond teaching skills and knowledge to include the inculcation of character traits that help to determine a person's civic behavior. It took me a long time to formulate my positions on this topic while progressively (re)defining the parameters of my inquiry. During that time I incurred debts to a great many people.

My Washington University colleague Clarissa Hayward, in addition to providing excellent feedback and advice at various stages in my project, generously organized a two-day workshop on a draft of the complete book manuscript. I am grateful to all of the participants in that terrific workshop and especially to the six people who each took the lead in discussing a different chapter of the work: Harry Brighouse, Julia Driver, Kyla Ebels-Duggan, Roudy Hildreth, Frank Lovett, and Greg Magarian. I also benefitted greatly from written comments provided by two people who read the entire manuscript despite the fact that they were unable to attend the workshop: Eamonn Callan and Carl Wellman. The text underwent many revisions in the wake of the workshop, and still further changes were prompted by Michael Hand, Kevin McDonough, and Lucas Swaine, each of whom read and responded in writing to the penultimate version.

I would like to thank my research assistant, Leigha Empson, who read several early drafts of the manuscript and helped to improve the clarity and readability of the text in several places. And I owe a great debt to Ron Watson, whose close engagement with a complete draft led me to make many improvements before the manuscript was presented to the workshop. Special thanks are also due to Andrew Rehfeld and Anna Stilz, both of whom gave me the benefit of their sustained and critical attention to embryonic forms of several of the arguments in the book, and to Krista Galleberg for preparing the index.

When I approached Oxford University Press with this project, first David Miller and then Dominic Byatt were immediately enthusiastic and encouraging. Dominic guided me skilfully through the review process and taught me patience with his gentle humor and gift for understatement. David wisely prompted me to say a little more about the relationships between my theoretical arguments and the real worlds of educational policy and practice. I am also grateful to Lucy Metzger, whose judicious and sensitive copy-editing improved the text in many places.

Many other people have provided valuable input as I developed my thoughts on this topic. With sincere apologies to those whom I may have forgotten (for it has been a long and winding road), I thank Nate Adams, Mark Alford, Eileen Hunt Botting, Dillon Brown, Randy Calvert, Matt Chick, Bill Galston, Matthew Gill, Patricia Albjerg Graham, Amy Gutmann, Zach Hoskins, John Inazu, Alan Lambert, Meira Levinson, Eric MacGilvray, Jal Mehta, Anne Newman, Sunita Parikh, John Patty, Cristian Pérez Muñoz, Neil Richards, Laura Rosenbury, David Speetzen, Kenneth Strike, Brian Tamanaha, Simine Vazire, Kit Wellman, and Greg Whitfield.

Much of the foundational work for this book was done during a precious year when I was relieved of teaching and administrative responsibilities by virtue of a postdoctoral fellowship provided jointly by the Spencer Foundation and the National Academy of Education. I am very grateful for this support.

Some of the material in Part I was originally published in "Educating Children to Comply with Laws," *Journal of Political Philosophy*, vol. 21, no. 1 (2013). I thank John Wiley & Sons for permission to reproduce this material. Similarly, some of the material in Parts II and III was originally published in the *Journal of Politics*. Part II draws upon "Doing Without Love: Civic Motivation, Affection, and Identification," vol. 76, no. 1 (2014), and Part III draws upon "On Status Quo Bias in Civic Education," vol. 73, no. 3 (2011). I thank Cambridge University Press (the publisher) and the Southern Political Science Association (the copyright holder) for permission to reproduce the material in these two articles.

Perhaps I was always destined to be a political theorist, but that destiny would not have been realized without the input and guidance of my teachers and mentors. At Durham Johnston Comprehensive School, Joan Gibb and Rob Williams introduced me to the activity of parliamentary debating, which was immensely rewarding in its own right and also led me somewhat belatedly to see that I should focus my undergraduate education on philosophy and politics rather than on physics (as I had long intended) or on music (as I briefly but seriously contemplated). As I read Philosophy, Politics, and Economics (PPE) at New College, Oxford University, Liz Frazer, Jonathan Glover, and Alan Ryan taught me (how) to appreciate the academic disciplines of political theory and moral philosophy. And, as I followed Jonathan's advice by continuing my studies on a Frank Knox Fellowship at Harvard University, Nancy Rosenblum, Dennis Thompson, Glyn Morgan, and Arthur Applbaum guided me to become a producer as well as a consumer of scholarship.

I am fortunate to have two delightful children on whom to practice my educational philosophy. Being a father to Tobi and Luke is now my most important role in life, but their arrivals did not (save for a generous parental leave from Washington University in each case) reduce my professional responsibilities. Combining fatherhood with my job has not always been easy, especially given that my wife has been engrossed in surgical training for many years and the boys' grandparents live hundreds and thousands of miles away. If I have succeeded in combining these two roles, much of the credit belongs to our parenting support team here in St. Louis. We have leaned heavily on two dear friends in particular, each of whom agreed to be a godmother to one of our children: Jill Stratton for Tobi and Lauren Steward for Luke. And we are deeply indebted and grateful to the wonderful teachers and care-givers who have worked so beautifully with our boys at their "school": Martha Burton, Rhonda Coleman, Carla Jacobs, Laura Kurczynski, Patricia Miranda, Debbie Morgan, Fannie Parker, Pam Radtke, Requel Thomas, Chanda Tucker, and Chris von Weise. These ladies gave me not only the time but also the peace of mind to think and write.

Finally, and most importantly, I want to thank my parents, Linda and Andy, who provided by their example a model for child-rearing that is far superior to any that this book contains, and my wife, Lola Fayanju, who has supported me and provided the much-needed perspective of a wise outsider through all the many ups and downs of the research and writing processes.

CONTENTS

PART II: FOSTERING CIVIC MOTIVATION

PART III: STATUS QUO BIAS IN CIVIC EDUCATION

CHAPTER 1

Introduction: theorizing education for civic character

What are the proper goals of civic education in a liberal democracy? There is widespread agreement that they include the transmission of certain kinds of knowledge: citizens need to know their society's laws and understand its political institutions. It is also generally accepted that civic education should aim to cultivate certain skills that empower citizens to contribute to the democratic process.[1] But, in addition to imparting political knowledge and teaching political skills, would an ideal liberal democratic civic education shape its recipients' values, beliefs, preferences, habits, identities, and sentiments? In other words, is character formation a proper part of civic education in a liberal democracy?

Most contemporary political and educational theorists who address this question respond with a heavily qualified yes. Education for civic character is vital to the survival and flourishing of liberal democracy, they argue, but its content must be strictly limited to avoid compromising its recipients' ability to think and act as critically autonomous citizens. This limit is usually understood to mean that the shaping of character for civic purposes should amount to no more than inculcating the basic and universal moral values that constitute the ideal of liberal democracy itself. I call this position the "orthodox view" both because of its dominance in the theoretical literature and because of the uncompromising nature of its commitment to cultivating and preserving citizens' critical autonomy.

[1] Admittedly, there is considerable disagreement (grounded in differing conceptions of democracy and the proper political role of ordinary citizens therein) regarding exactly which skills should be taught.

In this book, I argue that the orthodox view is wrong to prioritize critical autonomy over three other valuable traits that have traditionally been fostered by civic education: law-abidingness, civic identification, and support for the fundamental political institutions of one's society. But the best alternative is not simply to reverse the priority. The goal of this book is to show how we can recognize the value of the kinds of character formation that civic education has traditionally involved without losing the portion of the truth that can be found in the orthodox view. To be clear, my claim is not that the existing *practice* of civic education, in the United States or elsewhere, is too focused on the promotion of critical thinking. The target of my critique is the orthodox *ideal* among contemporary theorists.[2] I argue that this orthodox ideal neglects character traits that, although commonly labeled "conservative," are realistically essential for the survival and flourishing of liberal democracies.

In this introductory chapter I begin by exploring the orthodox view. I analyze the portion of that view that strikes me as entirely correct, namely, its insistence on the necessity and legitimacy of some significant civic character education that is provided in part by the state. Although orthodox, this claim has been challenged in various ways, and I shall explain briefly why none of those challenges succeeds. I then turn to the orthodox view's uncompromising commitment to critical autonomy: while my goal in the rest of the book is to poke holes in this absolutist stance, in the present chapter I shall content myself with describing the position and demonstrating its dominance in the contemporary literature. I also note the important work of two theorists who have rightly challenged the emphasis on autonomy but whose positions err in the opposite direction by failing to acknowledge the partial wisdom of the orthodox view. In the last sections of this chapter, I specify the scope and limits of my project, explain the book's overall structure and strategy, and sketch the major arguments of each chapter.

[2] As I note later in this chapter, there is some important evidence that an ideal of critically autonomous citizenship underpins the *aspirations* of many educational professionals and policy-makers in democratic societies. But it is a further question to what degree these aspirations find suitable expression in actual educational practice. I cannot answer this question. Moreover, I rather doubt that the ideal of critical citizenship is as widely and unwaveringly endorsed by practitioners and policy-makers as it is by academic theorists and philosophers.

1.1. The orthodox view

What place, if any, should character formation have in liberal democratic civic education? There is a definite orthodoxy among contemporary theorists who have engaged with this question. That orthodox view can be broken down into five parts (most of which attract a small but vocal minority of dissenters, or at least doubters).

1) Liberal democracy depends on certain character traits among citizens.
2) These traits will not be sufficiently strong or widespread unless they are intentionally cultivated in citizens, especially during childhood.
3) These traits can be cultivated without undermining the capacity of citizens to legitimate their political institutions via suitably free and authentic consent.
4) It is both permissible and prudent for the state itself to engage in this cultivation of civic character (although some of the work can and should be done by non-state actors such as parents, private schools, religious groups, and other voluntary associations).
5) The content of civic character education should be strictly limited to avoid compromising its recipients' ability to think and act as critically autonomous citizens.

In the remainder of this section I aim to substantiate my claim that these five commitments jointly comprise the orthodox view among contemporary theorists of civic education, and I explore the dissents and doubts that attend each of the five. I shall argue that the orthodox view is correct in its first four commitments. The fifth commitment, as I have already indicated, strikes me as severely misguided: my overarching goal in this book is to show that it should be relaxed in many important ways.

1) Liberal democracy depends on certain character traits among citizens

The orthodox view evinces its highest degree of consensus on this first commitment. At the risk of boring the reader with a thousand different ways of saying the same thing, I shall illustrate the strength of this consensus via a chronologically ordered series of brief quotations from leading theorists in the field over the last quarter-century. In her landmark book *Democratic Education*, Amy Gutmann (1987, p. 49) claims that "moral character along with laws and institutions forms the basis of democratic government." Bill Galston (1991, p. 217) concurs: "the operation of liberal institutions is affected in important ways by the character of citizens (and leaders)." He continues: "at some point, the attenuation of individual virtue will create pathologies with which liberal political contrivances, however technically perfect their design, simply cannot cope. To an extent difficult to measure but impossible to ignore, the viability of liberal society depends on its ability to engender a virtuous citizenry." John Rawls likewise regards citizens' good character as necessary for a just society. In *Political Liberalism* he writes that "justice as fairness includes an account of certain political virtues—the virtues of fair social cooperation such as the virtues of civility and tolerance, of reasonableness and the sense of fairness;" he goes on to argue that these virtues support "the forms of judgment and conduct *essential* to sustain fair social cooperation over time" and therefore "characterize the ideal of a good citizen of a democratic state" (1993, pp. 194–195, emphasis added).

Both Patricia White and Eamonn Callan echo Galston's aforementioned observation that good institutions are insufficient for a durable liberal democratic society. "Institutions have to be worked and used by citizens in the right spirit. Certainly citizens need a very great array of knowledge and skills for life in a democracy, but they also need to be disposed to use their knowledge and skills democratically. They need democratic dispositions" (White, 1996, p. 1). "Virtue is no substitute for judicious institutional design. But neither is institutional design any substitute for virtue" (Callan, 1997, p. 7). And Thomas Spragens and Stephen Macedo both emphasize that democracies cannot flourish if the relevant virtues are confined to an elite. "To be successful, liberal democracies depend upon a wide dissemination of traits and capacities often thought to be the province of the few rather than the many" (Spragens, 1999, p. 231). "For a liberal democracy to thrive and not only survive, many of its citizens should develop a shared commitment to a range of political values and virtues" (Macedo, 2000, pp. 10–11).

It is frankly hard to find contemporary dissenters from the proposition that liberal democracy depends importantly on the character virtues of its citizens. Indeed, when proponents of this aspect of the orthodox view feel the need to engage with a sincere opponent (rather than a devil's advocate) they frequently reach back to the late eighteenth century and the writings of Immanuel Kant. The following passage from Kant's "Perpetual Peace" lives on as a punching-bag for contemporary liberal theorists:

> many contend that a republic must be a nation of angels, for men's self-seeking inclinations make them incapable of adhering to so sublime a form of government. But now nature comes to the aid of the revered but practically impotent general will, which is grounded in reason. Indeed, this aid comes directly from those self-seeking inclinations, and it is merely by organizing the nation well (which is certainly within men's capacities) that they are able to direct their power against one another, and one inclination is able to check or cancel the destructive tendency of the others. The result for reason is the same as if neither set of opposing inclinations existed, and so man, even though his is not morally good, is forced to be a good citizen. As hard as it may sound, the problem of organizing a nation is solvable even for a people composed of devils (if only they possess understanding).... it does not require the moral improvement of man.
> (Kant, 1795/1983, p. 124)

When a more recent dissenting view is wanted, the theorist most often pressed into service is Stephen Holmes, who earned this distinction by writing the following passage:

> Constitutional devices, such as checks and balances, are not meant simply to compensate for a deplorable but predictable lack of moral fiber; they are actually considered as superior to personal virtue and strength of character.... For liberal framers... to build political stability on the basis of collective virtue... would overburden individual conscience, force a character standardization on citizens, and deprive society of an extra-political variety of selves. (Holmes, 1995, p. 175)

This is certainly a vivid articulation of the position that liberalism does not need (and should positively eschew) civic virtue, relying instead on good institutional design to prevent self-interested behavior from leading to injustice or other bad outcomes. But, although Holmes is commonly treated as a proponent of this view, he articulates it in just one paragraph of a 300-page book, and (as can be seen in the passage quoted above) it is far from clear that Holmes is declaring his own position as opposed to describing a certain view of liberal constitutionalism. That view is now, I believe, comprehensively discredited, and it is doubtful that it has ever been widely held. It was certainly not James Madison's view. He asked the 1788 Virginia Ratifying Convention:

> Is there no virtue among us? If there be not, we are in a wretched situation. No theoretical checks, no form of government, can render us secure. To suppose that any form of government will secure liberty or happiness without any virtue in the people is a chimerical idea. (Madison, 1788)

2) The traits upon which liberal democracy depends will not be sufficiently strong or widespread unless they are intentionally cultivated in citizens, especially during childhood

If the consensus among contemporary theorists approaches unanimity on the first part of the orthodox view, this second part attracts a few more dissenters. As we shall shortly see, there are two main lines of dissent, neither of which is convincing. The first argues that children who are educated merely in critical reason will reliably use their rationality to discover and act on liberal democratic values; the second proposes that merely living in a society governed by liberal democratic institutions and (as an adult) participating in those institutions reliably suffices to cultivate the character traits on which the future of liberal democracy depends. But before identifying these dissenting positions I again want to illustrate via selected quotations the degree of consensus on this aspect of the orthodox view.

Bill Galston (1991, p. 245) approvingly quotes a 1987 statement from the American Federation of Teachers: "Devotion to human dignity and freedom, to equal rights, to social and economic justice, to the rule of law, to civility and truth, to tolerance of diversity, to mutual assistance, to personal and civic responsibility, to self-restraint and self-respect—all these must be taught and learned." And other theorists fall over themselves to agree that civic education—of one kind or another—is indispensable for the requisite formation of character. Callan (1997, p. 3) declares that "the vitality of the political order depends on an education that is dedicated to specific ideals of character." Richard Dagger (1997, p. 120) notes that, "Like the other virtues, civic virtue is a character trait or disposition that is not likely to thrive without encouragement and cultivation." Meira Levinson (1999, p. 102) cautions: "we cannot trust that children will 'naturally' develop appropriate characters and commitments without being specifically educated in the liberal civic virtues." And Stephen Macedo is especially concerned about the dangers of complacency. "There is no reason to think that the dispositions that characterize good liberal citizens come about naturally: good citizens are not simply born that way, they must be educated by schools and a variety of other social and political institutions" (Macedo, 2000, p. 16). In particular, he adds, we must not make "the libertarian mistake of assuming that liberal citizens—self-restrained, moderate, and reasonable—spring full-blown from the soil of private freedom" (Macedo, 2000, pp. 20–21). Finally, and most recently, Peter Levine (2007, p. xiv, emphasis added) nicely captures both the democratic and the liberal imperatives for character-forming civic education. "Citizens are made, not born: it takes deliberate efforts to prepare young people to participate effectively and wisely in public life. Good government requires widespread civic *participation* and *virtue*."

As I noted above, one way to contest the claim that the character traits of good citizens must be intentionally cultivated appeals to the notion that children who are well educated in the intellectual virtues can be expected to find their way to the moral virtues—including the politico-moral virtues required by liberal democracy—without needing to be steered to that destination. Jack Crittenden makes precisely such an argument in response to the following passage by Amy Gutmann:

> Children are not taught that bigotry is bad, for example, by offering it as one among many competing conceptions of the good life, and then subjecting it to criticism on grounds that bigots do not admit that other people's conceptions of the good are "equally" good. Children first become the kind of people who are repelled by bigotry, and then they feel the force of the reasons for their repulsion. The liberal reasons to reject bigotry are quite impotent in the absence of such sensibilities: they offer no compelling argument to people who feel no need to treat other people as equals and are willing to live with the consequences of their disrespect. To cultivate in children the character that feels the force of right reason is an essential purpose of education in any society. (Gutmann, 1987, p. 43)

Crittenden (2002, p. 99) responds: "Whereas Gutmann wants to 'cultivate in children the character that *feels the force* of right reason' (emphasis added [by Crittenden]), I want education to cultivate reason first and let that reason in part determine or lead character." He alleges disparagingly that "what Gutmann is offering is less an education in deliberation and more a catechism." It is important to "permit and encourage children to make up their own minds" rather than inculcating "feelings, character traits or dispositions, and even prejudices." We should "present the case of what a way of life is and what it represents and, then through criticism, [children will see] why it is bad."

Harry Brighouse (1998, p. 725) flirts with this same view—"Shouldn't teaching critical skills and encouraging their deployment suffice to get students to adopt true values?"—but quickly and wisely retreats from it: "The facts of developmental psychology do support Gutmann's view that some values must be taught before critical reflection is possible." And Warren Nord (2003, p. 146) echoes this concession to reality: "even if character education proceeds largely by way of socialization and training, this need not be a criticism. Children must be morally trained before they reach the elusive age of reason (an age some people, alas, never reach)."

It is wildly implausible to suppose that moral education is altogether unnecessary (or, to describe the same position differently, that moral education can and should consist of no more than exposing children to a variety of positions and encouraging them to "make up their own minds" with the use of "critical reason"). Ostensibly this faith in children's undirected reason underpinned the "values clarification" movement that was briefly popular in certain American educational circles and that has been the object of withering criticism (Gutmann, 1987, pp. 55–56; Macedo, 2000, pp. 123–24; Nord, 2003, p. 143). But it seems to me that what little appeal "values clarification" may have (had) as a method for *professional* educators depends upon the assumption that parents and other influential figures in children's lives will already have intentionally inculcated certain basic moral values in those children before they arrive in the "values clarification" classroom.

Many proponents of this second part of the orthodox view are quick to anticipate and dismiss the claim that the cultivation of reason renders moral character education unnecessary (and perhaps also illegitimate). In an oft-quoted passage, Galston (1991, pp. 243–44) argues that "very few individuals will come to embrace the core commitments of liberal society through a process of rational inquiry. If children are to be brought to accept these commitments as valid and binding, the method must be a pedagogy that is far more rhetorical than rational." Curiously, this passage is so often quoted because it is typically understood to be at odds with the fifth part of the orthodox view, namely, the commitment to cultivating and respecting the autonomy of future citizens. Arguably this is the correct reading of the passage when it is taken in context: Galston is about to defend the "noble lie" approach to teaching children about the history of their country. But one can also read the passage as a restatement of the conventional wisdom about basic (liberal) moral education, a generalization (to all liberal values) of Gutmann's observation about how we teach children not to be bigots. Galston may exaggerate when he asserts that "very few" people will arrive at liberal principles solely through the exercise of their reason. But he does not need to make such a strong claim. Liberal democracy needs many more than a "very few" citizens who support its foundational values. Mere cultivation of rationality will not deliver anything close to the widespread support that is needed.

So, as Geoffrey Vaughan (2005, p. 397) has documented, the leading contributors to contemporary theoretical debates about civic education—Gutmann, Callan, Macedo, and Levinson—all recognize that "the development of critical self-reflection, autonomy, is not sufficient to produce good and virtuous democratic citizens, the kind of citizens political education is supposed to prepare." But it does not strictly follow from this that intentional shaping of character is needed. The conclusion that logically follows is less determinate. Fred Greenstein expressed it well almost fifty years ago:

> Education, interpreting the term in its *broadest sense*, is a highly efficient (and, in fact, necessary) instrument of politics. Political behavior... is partially determined by the "objective" circumstances which surround men—for example, the political institutions of their society. But behavior also is the result of *learned predispositions*—the goals, preferences, conceptions of reality, and loyalties which citizens and their leaders acquire through *prior experience*. (Greenstein, 1965, p. 2, emphasis added)

Notice the care with which Greenstein specifies that politics requires education only in the "broadest sense" of that term. It is conceivable that the "prior experience" through which citizens acquire the "learned predispositions" requisite for liberal democracy need extend no farther than their living under (and participating as adults in) liberal democratic political institutions.

But does anyone truly maintain that this "osmosis effect" is sufficient to cultivate civic character, rendering intentional cultivation redundant and perhaps even objectionably heavy-handed? I have yet to find such a view unambiguously stated. Alexis de Tocqueville (1850/2006, pp. 236, 276, 304, 512–13) and John Stuart Mill (1861, Chapter 8) both famously celebrated the educative effects of popular participation in democratic institutions (such as elections, jury trials, and local government), and the good effects they identified certainly included the shaping of citizens' character, but neither Tocqueville nor Mill draws the radical conclusion that liberal democracies can thrive altogether without intentional efforts to foster good character. Judith Shklar (1989, p. 33) approvingly observes that "the experience of politics according to fair procedures and the rule of law do [*sic*] indirectly educate the citizens [into] habits of patience, self-restraint, respect for the claims of others, and caution," but she does not deny that direct and intentional educational efforts are needed if the next generation is to acquire the virtues that support liberal democracy (and, as Shklar would emphasize, avoid developing the vices that undermine it). As we shall shortly see, both Mill and Shklar are at pains to deny that *the state* should get involved in deliberately shaping the character of its citizens, but that is an answer to a very different question.

Jason Scorza (2007, p. 164) suggests that George Kateb represents the "osmosis is sufficient" position, but I think we would be unduly hasty to attribute that strong view to Kateb. He does indeed claim that merely living in a "constitutional representative democracy helps to foster certain traits of character" including a commitment to the "moral equality" of all individuals, but this does not amount to the claim that the intentional character-shaping function of civic education is unnecessary. Indeed, Kateb's own language strongly suggests that he does not endorse that position: "All I wish to claim is that the workings of representative democracy magnify certain sentiments and attitudes and thereby strengthen and enrich them" (Kateb, 1992, pp. 43, 41, 46).

So, although Greenstein's aforementioned analysis alerts us to the theoretical possibility that the education upon which liberal democracy depends could *all* be a byproduct of the ordinary functioning of liberal democratic institutions, it is more helpfully read as a reminder that *some* civically important educative effects are unintended (and also, of course, that a great deal of intentional education occurs outside of formal educational institutions). The orthodox view does not hold that intentional character formation is *sufficient* to foster the requisite types and degrees of civic virtue, only that it is *necessary*. And, although it is often implicitly (and sometimes explicitly) assumed that much intentional shaping of character will take place in schools, proponents of the orthodox view are typically happy to admit that informal education also has a vital role to play in shaping children for citizenship in a liberal democracy.

3) Liberal democratic civic character can be cultivated without undermining the capacity of citizens to legitimate their political institutions via suitably free and authentic consent

Barry Bull (2006, p. 21) notes that civic educators *could* "teach students about the civic ideals of their particular nation as a set of empirical facts, what the people of this particular place at this particular time happen to believe about the political and social roles of government and the obligations of citizens to that government and to one another." If the first two parts of the orthodox view are correct, as I think they are, any liberal democratic polity that adopted such an approach to civic education (both in schools and outside them) might well not be liberal or democratic for long. But could this be a risk that a liberal democratic society is constitutively committed to taking? A number of theorists have argued that, perversely, the very educational measures that would reliably produce liberal democratic virtues in the next generation of citizens would thereby also undercut the polity's credentials as a *bona fide* liberal democracy. In this section I shall present some leading statements of this view—most notably, Harry Brighouse's powerful argument from liberal legitimacy—before exploring how defenders of the orthodox position have argued—rightly, I believe—that liberal democracies are not in fact caught in this catch-22 predicament.

For Jack Crittenden (2002, p. 76), "democracy as the public exercise of autonomy is collective self-direction, and that must entail a self-critical distancing, at some point in the deliberations, from the values, ends, and practices of the polity itself to scrutinize those values, ends, and practices." If civic education inculcates an uncritical acceptance of the polity's ideals, even its democratic ideals, it thereby destroys the foundations for future democracy. For this reason, Crittenden maintains, Amy Gutmann's democratic credentials are fatally weakened when she says that her nonrepression principle, which prohibits "using education to restrict rational deliberation of competing conceptions of the good life and the good society," is "compatible with the use of education to inculcate those character traits, such as honesty, religious toleration, and mutual respect for persons, that serve as foundations for rational deliberation of differing ways of life" (Gutmann, 1987, p. 44).[3] Crittenden's verdict: "It is ironic, if not cynical, that Gutmann emphasizes the virtue of deliberation and yet is willing to suspend or deny discussion of those beliefs, values, ideas, and ways of life that run counter to democratic virtues" (Crittenden, 2002, p. 99).

In a similar vein, Richard Flathman (1996, p. 24) argues that liberal civic education is an oxymoron. "From a political perspective, liberal education is regime nonspecific. The qualities of character that it hopes to cultivate are not chosen to service the objectives of anarchism or libertarianism; of liberal, participatory, or other forms of democracy; of aristocratic, bureaucratic, or other authoritarian polities." If a truly liberal education serves any civic function, that function is to enable its recipients to stand back from and evaluate the political institutions of their society: "education to critical conversability in our political languages does the most and the best that education can do for politics, for governance, and for civility and humanity" (Flathman, 1996, p. 26). A truly liberal and democratic society is committed to educating children for critical autonomy despite the fact that this leaves the future of liberal democratic political institutions very much in doubt. "Being free,

[3] Gutmann must be working here with an understanding of rational deliberation that builds in a good deal of moral content, some version of what Rawls (1993, pp. 48–54) would call the "reasonable."

the autonomous individual is also unpredictable, capable of choosing (almost) any political commitments" (Vaughan, 2005, p. 395).

The most developed and powerful expression of this objection to character formation as an element of liberal democratic civic education is to be found in the work of Harry Brighouse. He writes:

> Something is puzzling about the idea that liberal states may regulate the educational curriculum by mandating a civic education aimed at inculcating the values on which liberalism is based and behaviors which sustain it. If the state helps form the political loyalties of future citizens by inculcating belief in its own legitimacy, it will be unsurprising when citizens consent to the social institutions they inhabit, but it will be difficult to be confident that their consent is freely given, or would have been freely given. (Brighouse, 1998, p. 719)

As this passage makes clear, Brighouse understands himself to be making an argument about *state-directed* civic education, but Callan rightly observes that nothing about the structure of the argument limits its applicability in this way. "If nonautonomous belief and preference detract from the authenticity of consent when the state is their source, how could the same outcomes be irrelevant to authenticity once concentrations of power other than the state are their source?" (Callan, 2000, p. 152). I think Brighouse should take *this* portion of Callan's response (although not other parts!) as a friendly amendment. Callan shows that Brighouse's critique is even more unsettling than it first appears: concerns about liberal legitimacy would not be allayed if the state recused itself from character formation and voluntary associations of concerned adult citizens took up the slack. The fundamental problem is that nonautonomous consent has no legitimating force: a society whose citizens have been successfully educated to nonautonomously subscribe to liberal principles will be stable and it may even be just, but it will not be legitimate and in that sense it will not truly be liberal.

Callan faults Brighouse's argument primarily for its failure to recognize the full implications of Brighouse's own observation that not one but two conditions must be met in order for a polity to pass the test of liberal legitimacy. Brighouse says that legitimacy requires not only widespread *actual* consent that is free and authentic but also the *hypothetical* consent of "reasonable" persons, where reasonableness is understood not in the amoral sense of simple rationality but in John Rawls's (1993, pp. 48–54) sense of a principled commitment to fair social cooperation. Even if the inculcation of liberal values detracts from the autonomy of citizens' actual consent to liberal institutions and thereby diminishes the legitimacy of the state on this dimension, it should also have another, legitimacy-enhancing effect. As we have seen, people are far more likely to subscribe to substantive liberal values if they have been taught those values rather than being educated according to strict Brighousean (2000, p. 81) standards of "character neutrality." And a democratic polity with many more citizens who are committed to liberal values can be expected to be more just and therefore a stronger candidate for the hypothetical consent of a reasonable person.[4] "A regime with realistic prospects of achieving liberal legitimacy by Brighouse's lights must count both authenticity and reasonableness among the ends of an education for legitimacy. Otherwise the prospects for reconciling actual authentic and hypothetical reasonable consent will be slight" (Callan, 2000, p. 147).

That is Callan's primary response to Brighouse, and it is a powerful one, but he also hints at an additional response that directly confronts Brighouse's claim that all educational shaping of character is a threat to autonomy and therefore to one important dimension of political legitimacy. Callan (2000, p. 150) calls for a "theory of legitimacy that acknowledges the necessity of autonomy *and [a sense of] justice* to the ability freely to consent to political authority" (emphasis added). Such a theory, if well-founded, would show that fostering liberal values in children contributes to the future legitimacy of the polity not only by increasing the chances that it will be just (and therefore worthy of hypothetical consent) but also by increasing the capacity of future citizens to give legitimating actual

[4] Perhaps Brighouse (1998, p. 733) has some version of this argument in mind when he acknowledges in a footnote that, although the requirements for an autonomy-facilitating education include teaching "neither Gutmann's virtue of civic respect nor Galston's of tolerance," "there may be reasons that children should be taught these virtues." When read alongside Brighouse's (1998, p. 725) aforementioned recognition that "some values must be taught before critical reflection is possible" and his statement that "civic education is permissible only if it includes elements that direct the critical scrutiny of children to the very values they are taught" (1998, p. 720), this suggests that Brighouse's position may be less radical than it initially appears and has generally been interpreted to be.

consent. Callan does not himself provide the requisite theory, but we can find a compelling candidate for the role in the work of Randall Curren.

Curren's (2000, p. 156) "argument from the foundations of corrective justice" is essentially a version of Brighouse's legitimacy principle: "to create legitimate law, and to justly enforce it, a state must have some public system for ensuring the provision to all of whatever education is required for informed and rational consent to law, and whatever education is essential to creating a reasonable likelihood of voluntary compliance with it." But whereas Brighouse argues that only a character-neutral education can meet these criteria (because all educational shaping of character detracts from the autonomy and, in that sense, the voluntariness of consent and compliance), Curren maintains that consent and compliance are only truly legitimating if they come from a person who appreciates the force of reason in moral demands. And character education is needed to foster this appreciation: "neither an acquaintance with the good, nor true moral beliefs, nor a capacity to guide oneself in accordance with reason are acquired spontaneously. They must all be cultivated" (Curren, 2000, p. 155). Following Aristotle, Curren (2000, p. 153) argues that the moral education needed to sustain the legitimacy of a state will be

> devoted to the development of appropriate tastes and dispositions, to cultivating a receptivity to reason, and to developing habits of correct action far enough to enable a person to be pleased rather than pained by doing the right thing, and not undermined in doing the right thing by the presence of seductive but less worthy competing pleasures or the specter of pain.

The vital point here is that character education is a way of cultivating the child's capacities for good (moral) reasoning and for acting in accordance with the conclusions of such reasoning. These capacities are not best developed—indeed, they may not be developed at all—by exposing children to multiple points of view and encouraging them to make up their own minds, as Crittenden proposes. Teaching children to reason well about moral matters is quite different from what Macedo (1990) calls "liberal socialization" (p. 65) or, more pejoratively, "promoting liberal false consciousness" (p. 66). As Gutmann emphasizes, children must be given the moral reasons to reject bigotry in addition to being taught to feel repulsed by it:

moral education includes both elements, albeit for developmental reasons the latter needs to happen first. If and only if children are shown the force and validity of the moral reasons underlying liberal principles and practices, their subsequent consent to liberal institutions will be legitimating.

Ajume Wingo (2003, p. 29), like Callan and Curren, rejects the idea that the autonomous consent needed for liberal legitimacy should be understood in ways that preclude all moral education: we should only accept Brighouse's (1998, p. 723) requirement that citizens consent "on the basis of their own reason alone" with the important caveat that children's own (capacity for moral) reason(ing) cannot be expected to exist and develop unless it is cultivated. In similar fashion we should reject Brighouse's (1998, p. 726) notion that actively encouraging children on moral grounds to participate in democratic politics undermines the autonomy of their subsequent decisions to do so: "It does not violate children's future autonomy to teach them not to free-ride any more than it violates their autonomy to teach them other moral virtues such as honesty, generosity, and sympathy" (Levinson, 1999, p. 106).[5] Crittenden's (2002, p. 195) assertion that children "should not be socialized or indoctrinated into valuing participation as part of what it means to be a good citizen" can be accepted if it means only that children must not be led to value participation without being taught the moral reasons to do so. But his claim should be rejected if, as Crittenden presumably intends, it means rather that the goals of civic education should not include helping children to see and feel the force of the moral reasons to participate.[6]

In short, we should reject impoverished views of autonomy and moral reasoning according to which the inculcation of values involved in basic moral education is a threat to autonomy. Someone who has received a good moral education and consequently sees the

[5] We shall later see that children's future autonomy might indeed be diminished by teaching them that political participation is a constitutive element of the good life for a human being, as distinct from introducing children to the moral reasons to contribute to one's polity and helping them see and feel the force of those reasons. But, as we shall see in Chapter 5, nonautonomous motives for political participation are most troubling when they also detract from the autonomy of the judgments that citizens express through that participation; nonautonomous beliefs in the intrinsic prudential value of participation typically will not have this further effect.

[6] I discuss the nature, strength, and origins of these moral reasons in Chapter 5.

force of the reasons to treat others with respect is not thereby less free or lacking in autonomy. And liberals therefore have no grounds to be conflicted about the educational task of promoting the kinds of good moral reasoning that underpin liberal values and principles.[7] A central "aim of a liberal civic order should be to promote patterns of belief and action that are supportive of liberalism, to transform people's deepest commitments in ways that are supportive of liberal politics" (Macedo, 2000, p. 205).

4) It is both permissible and prudent for the state itself to engage in cultivation of liberal democratic civic character (although some of the work can and should be done by non-state actors such as parents, private schools, religious groups, and other voluntary associations)

Given that liberal democracy is unlikely to flourish, and may not even survive in recognizable form, unless most children receive a certain kind of character education, and if I am right that such an education does not threaten (and may even be necessary for) the legitimacy of a liberal political order, should the liberal state itself play a role in delivering this education? The orthodox view rightly maintains that it should. Bill Galston goes even farther—arguably too far—when he asserts that the state has the *primary* role: he reports approvingly that "in most times and places . . . it has been taken for granted that young people must be shaped into citizens and that public institutions have both the right and the responsibility to *take the lead* in shaping them" (1991, p. 241, emphasis added). More moderately, Rawls (1993, p. 195) argues that "if a constitutional regime takes certain steps to strengthen the virtues of toleration and mutual trust . . . it is taking reasonable steps to strengthen the forms of thought and feeling that sustain fair social cooperation between its citizens regarded as free and equal." And, echoing Rawls's language, Macedo (2000, p. 15) insists that "if a democratic constitutional regime is to thrive, it must constitute citizens willing to observe its limits and able to pursue its aspirations."

[7] But, as we shall see in Chapter 7, Brighouse's legitimacy objection still has force against forms of character education that extend beyond the inculcation of basic moral values.

At the same time, liberals typically acknowledge and sometimes emphasize the dangers that arise when an entity as powerful as the state gets involved in shaping character. A few liberal theorists view these dangers as sufficiently grave that the safest and wisest course is for the state to play no role whatsoever in character education. For Judith Shklar (1989, p. 33), the liberal state can never have "an educative government that aims at creating specific kinds of character and enforces its own beliefs. It can never be didactic in intent in that exclusive and inherently authoritarian way." And for Flathman (1996, p. 15), taking his lead from John Stuart Mill, state involvement in delivering character education through schools unacceptably aggravates the already regrettable tendency of all formal schooling to impose a stifling homogeneity: "professional educators and state bureaucrats [are] allies in a war against freedom and liberal individuality." But I think Shklar's and Flathman's relentless (and mildly hysterical?) focus on the potential harms associated with state educational power is deficient in its failure to recognize the potential benefits thereof.

In particular, Shklar seems implicitly to assume that private actors can be relied upon to provide character education of all the kinds and to the full extent that a liberal democratic society needs.[8] This is a reckless assumption, especially given that education for civic character is a public good in the sense that its provision to one person is a benefit not principally to that person but rather to everyone else in the society whose interests may be affected by that person's future political behavior (or lack thereof) and especially a benefit to those who might suffer if that person develops political attitudes of intolerance and disrespect for difference. Justice is (and aggregate welfare may well be) best served by universal cultivation of good civic character in the next generation of citizens, but we should not trust that all parents will voluntarily and spontaneously play their part in achieving this desirable outcome. As is the case with other important social goods whose realization in a free market is threatened by private selfishness, neglect, and free-riding,

[8] Flathman cannot fairly be accused of making this assumption because, as we have seen, he rejects all character education as illiberal, regardless of the identity of the educational agent.

the state has a legitimate and vital role to play in providing, encouraging, and perhaps even mandating education for civic character.

Advocates of what I am calling the orthodox view all support a significant but limited (and certainly not exclusive) role for the state in cultivating civic character, a role whose size is determined by striking a balance between the risks and the benefits of state involvement. For example, Spragens (1999, p. 235) concludes that although "for reasons both of propriety and of practicality... the liberal virtues must be inculcated more by the institutions of civil society than by the state... it is... acceptable for public institutions involved in the socialization of the young to thematize and seek to foster the liberal civic virtues under the rubric of good citizenship." And Macedo (2000, p. 10) tempers his aforementioned espousal of a transformative agenda for the liberal state with the observation that "liberals are not wrong... to relegate somewhat to the background concerns with virtue, character, citizen education, and the like. Making the promotion of citizen's [*sic*] virtue and personal excellence the overriding ends of our politics will overturn the liberties that we have good reason to prize." Although there is no consensus on the exact size and scope of optimal state involvement in this domain, the orthodox view rightly identifies education for civic character as "the shared responsibility of schools, families, *political institutions*, the press, and communities" (Levine, 2007, p. xiii, emphasis added).

Having briefly both surveyed and defended the orthodox view's claim that the state should play a role in civic character education, I should note that my arguments in the rest of this book do not depend upon the truth of that claim. As I shall shortly explain more fully, my project is to identify the proper *goals* of civic education, not to identify its proper *agents*. This is not a book about the allocation of civic educational authority. For the reasons I have sketched above, I am strongly inclined to side with the orthodoxy by assigning a (limited) role to the state. But if it turns out that, in a particular polity at a particular time, intentional cultivation of civic character can and will reliably be performed to a sufficient degree without the state playing any role, this might well be the best option (given the admitted dangers associated with state power in this domain).

5) The content of civic character education should be strictly limited to avoid compromising its recipients' ability to think and act as critically autonomous citizens

As we have seen, the orthodoxy among contemporary political and educational theorists is that liberal democratic civic education should include some elements of character formation. But most theorists are so concerned to develop and preserve citizens' capacities and dispositions for critically autonomous engagement with political authority that they regard optimal character formation as strictly limited in both *degree* and *scope*. Brighouse's aforementioned insistence that children be equipped and encouraged to reflect critically on the liberal democratic values they have been taught is an especially pronounced example of a limit on the *degree* of character formation. Most other liberal theorists endorse some, usually weaker, version of this requirement that values should not be inculcated in ways that altogether bypass the recipient's rational capacities. But here I want to emphasize the other dimension on which the orthodox view holds that character formation for civic purposes should be limited: the dimension of *scope*.

For most theorists who prioritize the development and preservation of critical autonomy, this priority manifests itself in the form of strict limits on the scope of permissible civic character education: specifically, the traits to be cultivated in future citizens should be restricted to those moral commitments that are constitutive of liberal democracy. Although the knowledge and (to a somewhat lesser degree) the skills properly imparted by civic education will obviously need to be tailored to the particular regime, education for civic character would ideally be identical in every liberal democratic society.[9] Future citizens everywhere should simply be taught the values that jointly constitute the fundamental liberal commitment to treat each person as free and (morally) equal as well as the fundamental

[9] Flathman (1996, p. 11) maintains that, properly understood, "Liberal education does not implant doctrines or promote institutional arrangements specific to particular regimes." Now Flathman here means to rule out even the cultivation of generically liberal democratic virtues, which is (as I argued above, in support of the orthodox view) certainly a bridge too far, but the notion that the character-forming aspects of civic education should not differ between different liberal democratic regimes would, as we shall see, broadly be embraced by advocates of the orthodox view.

democratic value of widespread critical engagement in the project of collective self-governance.

Recall that Amy Gutmann's paradigmatic example of shaping civic character is promoting tolerance: teaching children not to be bigots, as she bluntly puts it. Gutmann is at pains not to endorse educational agendas that go beyond fostering such universal liberal democratic values and virtues. This minimalism about permissible character education finds expression in her aforementioned "principle of nonrepression," which prohibits "using education to restrict rational deliberation of competing conceptions of the good life and the good society" (Gutmann, 1987, p. 44). In particular, civic education should not systematically dispose children to favor the particular political arrangements they will inherit. "Children must learn not just to behave in accordance with authority but to think critically about authority if they are to live up to the democratic ideal of sharing political sovereignty as citizens" (Gutmann, 1987, p. 50).

Stephen Macedo's account of liberal civic virtues is typical of the orthodox view. Good citizens, he claims, are committed to the moral equality of all persons, respectful of individual rights, tolerant of ways of life that are different from their own, and opposed to violence and coercion except when such measures are needed to enforce liberal rights (Macedo, 1990, pp. 266–67). Besides instilling these substantive but abstract moral commitments in children, education for civic character should be limited to cultivating "a willingness to think critically about public affairs and participate actively in the democratic process and in civil society" and "a willingness to affirm the supreme political authority of principles that we can publicly justify along with all our reasonable fellow citizens" (Macedo, 2000, pp. 10–11). As with Gutmann, the message is clear: inculcation of anything more than the most basic and universal liberal democratic values and virtues unacceptably threatens what should be the principal goal of civic education, namely, the creation of "a citizenry of self-critical reason-givers" (Macedo, 1990, p. 78).

Meira Levinson (1999, p. 101) echoes this emphasis on critical reasoning when she insists that "the skills, habits, dispositions, and knowledge central to autonomy are to a large degree coextensive with those central to civic virtue." Sarah Stitzlein (2012, p. 77) argues forcefully that children, as future full citizens of a liberal democracy, "have the right to an education that cultivates the skills and dispositions of dissent." And Barry Bull (2006, p. 25) deftly captures the orthodox view's extreme reticence about inculcating substantive values: "Civic education [is not] adequately conceived as the enforcement on the young of an authoritative and determinate civic doctrine" because the principles and practices of a liberal society "are subject to constant reconsideration and modification." One should emerge from civic education understanding "the tentative status and justifiability of one's own nation's current political principles and policies" (Bull, 2006, p. 28), and children "must be encouraged to formulate their own judgments about the adequacy of [civic] principles" (Bull, 2006, p. 30). In summary, "The morality involved in civic education is concerned as much with citizens' commitment to the process of public and private reasoning from which an overlapping consensus emerges as it is with the substance of the principles that arise from it" (Bull, 2006, p. 26). Indeed, for many theorists in the contemporary orthodoxy this last proposition may be an understatement: these theorists are very wary of using civic education to dispose children to favor particular answers to political questions, especially when these are concrete questions about political institutions and practices as opposed to abstract questions about politico-moral values. Rather than prescribe or even encourage particular answers to concrete political questions, theorists who subscribe to the orthodox view merely want to shape the spirit and values with which citizens approach those questions.

Although my purpose in this book is primarily to engage with the prevailing orthodoxy among theorists and philosophers of education, it is worth noting that the stated goals of many civic educational practitioners and policy-makers in democratic societies bear a strong resemblance to the academic consensus. Take, for example, the heavy emphasis on promotion of critical thinking in the guidelines for teaching citizenship in the national curriculum of the United Kingdom. The study of citizenship, we are told, "equips students to engage critically with and explore diverse ideas, beliefs, cultures and identities and the values we share as citizens in the UK." The official attainment targets for "key stage four" (sixteen-year-olds) would not look out of place in an academic statement of the orthodox view of civic character education. Children should "challenge assumptions or ideas as they explore them" and "ask challenging questions to explore the ways in which justice, laws and governments operate in different places," all with a view to making and acting on their own informed judgments about "the kind of society they as citizens would like to live in" (UK Department for Education, 2013).

These attainment targets were inspired by the so-called Crick Report (1998), which was commissioned by the New Labour government and provided the impetus for mandating citizenship education in all UK state schools. The Crick report quoted approvingly the work of David Hargreaves, a prominent educational theorist: "Civic education . . . raises questions about the sort of society we live in, how it has come to take its present form, the strengths and weaknesses of current political structures, and how improvements might be made" (Hargreaves, 1994; quoted in Crick, 1998, p. 10). Aversion to status quo bias in civic education is not a mere academic preoccupation. Indeed, the Crick report (1998, pp. 56–61) contains a detailed discussion of the importance of and methods for avoiding bias whenever teachers broach issues "about which there is no one fixed or universally held point of view" (p. 56).

An especially clear non-academic articulation and endorsement of what I call the orthodox view is provided by the Citizenship Foundation, an influential UK organization that has strongly supported the inclusion and retention of citizenship in the national curriculum. "The most effective form of learning in citizenship education is *critical*: encourages young people to think for themselves . . . Citizenship education is about *enabling* people to *make their own decisions* and to *take responsibility* for their own lives and their communities. It is *not* about trying to fit everyone into the same mould, or about creating 'model' or 'good' citizens" (Citizenship Foundation, 2012, emphasis in original). Of course, one might ask (with a tone of skepticism, perhaps) how far the reality of citizenship education in UK schools conforms to and advances the ideals that are embodied in government policies and supported by such groups as the Citizenship Foundation. This is an empirical question that I cannot answer. But it is nonetheless striking that a vision of civic character education (and its limits) that is very similar to and evidently inspired by the academic orthodoxy has been formally adopted by the UK government and is supposed to guide the civic education of all children enrolled in state schools.

Beyond the UK, one readily finds evidence that some version of the orthodox view is widely endorsed by professional civic educators who are not also scholars of education. In the late 1990s, a landmark study by the International Association for the Evaluation of Educational Achievement (IEA) found that, in the twenty-eight countries studied, a plurality of teachers of civic education believe that their top priority should be the promotion of critical thinking (Losito and Mintrop, 2001, pp. 167–69).[10] And, in the United States, two recent position statements by the National Council for the Social Studies (NCSS), the country's largest association of civic educators, align closely with the academic orthodoxy concerning the scope and limits of appropriate education for civic character. The Association's 1997 statement, "Fostering Civic Virtue: Character Education in the Social Studies," advocates instilling many beliefs and values, but the long list strikingly contains only those abstract and universal commitments that are constitutive of liberal democracy.[11] In particular, there is no suggestion that American children should be taught in ways that dispose them to favor American political arrangements over other institutional embodiments of liberal democracy. And the NCSS's 2013 statement, "Revitalizing Civic Learning in Our Schools," repeatedly emphasizes the importance of critical thinking for citizenship, implying (naively, I shall

[10] Some other teachers of civic education report that they would like to focus primarily on inculcating values; it is not clear whether they aspire to do this in a way that would compromise children's development of autonomy. Many teachers say that they are in fact required to concentrate on the transmission of civic knowledge; complying with this requirement evidently exacts an opportunity cost in terms of promoting critical thinking, but it is unclear whether civic "knowledge" is being transmitted in ways that actually inhibit critical thinking.

[11] "The citizen must demonstrate a reasoned commitment to fundamental principles, such as popular sovereignty, rule of law, religious liberty, and the like. The citizen must also demonstrate a reasoned commitment to fundamental values, such as life, liberty, pursuit of happiness, equality, truth, and promotion of the common good. Students should both understand the nature of democratic principles and values and demonstrate a commitment to those values and principles in the daily routines of their private and public lives. Civic education is not complete until students possess a set of appropriate civic dispositions. Civic dispositions are those habits of the heart and mind that are conducive to the healthy functioning of the democratic system. Examples include civility, open-mindedness, compromise, and toleration of diversity, all of which are prerequisites of a civic life in which the American people can work out the meanings of their democratic principles and values." (National Council for the Social Studies, 1997)

argue) that none of the other appropriate goals of social studies education (such as encouraging civic participation) are in tension with the promotion of critical thinking.

We have seen that many practitioners and policy-makers are concerned to avoid status quo bias in civic education, but one might reasonably wonder whether their concern is as thoroughgoing as the position commonly held by professional theorists and philosophers of education. As we shall see in Chapter 7, the orthodox view among academics aspires to avoid not only those educational biases that directly and narrowly favor a concrete political institution but also any systematic privileging of a particular and contestable conception of the basic moral concepts that underpin liberal democracy. Our polity's prevailing conception of liberalism may be liberal egalitarianism, but civic education should not prejudge the choice between this view and a more libertarian conception of individual rights.[12] Similarly, our political culture may understand democratic rights as little more than "one person, one vote," but civic education should equip citizens to ask whether democracy demands more. Or less: as John Stuart Mill (1861, Chapter 8) noted, "though every one ought to have a voice—that every one should have an equal voice is a totally different proposition." To offer one last example, citizens should not be educated in ways that prejudice them against Lani Guinier's (1994) radical challenge to the dominant notion that democracy means some form of winner-takes-all majoritarian decision-making.

Although liberal democratic civic education properly teaches future citizens the moral reasons to participate in the civic and political life of their society, adherents of the orthodox view insist that it should not teach children to regard such participation as *intrinsically* valuable for the participant (Macedo, 1990, p. 272; Scorza, 2007, p. 54; Spragens, 1999, pp. 231–34), and it certainly should not promote civic humanism, the ethical doctrine according to which "taking part in democratic politics is seen as the privileged

[12] Roughly speaking, libertarians believe that rights are predominantly negative, in the sense that they set limits on interference (by the government or by other citizens) in an individual's activities, whereas liberal egalitarians recognize a more substantial domain of positive rights, i.e., obligations on the government to provide resources or opportunities rather than merely refraining from, and protecting individuals against, interference.

locus of the good life" (Rawls, 1993, p. 206). When Flathman excoriates those "political educationists" who would "tell us, and more particularly would teach our children, that subscription and fidelity to certain quite definite political beliefs and values are conditions of a full, satisfying, noble, or humane life" (Flathman, 1996, p. 23), he seems to think that he is assailing the orthodox view, whereas in fact the orthodoxy precisely disclaims such methods for encouraging participation in future citizens.[13]

Some advocates of the orthodox view, while rejecting the promotion of civic humanism, are willing to endorse the cultivation of patriotism as an educational strategy for boosting civic motivation. But such endorsements are typically heavily qualified by and sometimes in outright tension with the same theorists' abiding concern not to infringe citizens' capacity for critically autonomous thought and action. Eamonn Callan (1997, p. 96) suggests that civic education should try to create "liberal patriots," people for whom "the flourishing of a just community has become a central constituent of their own good." But he insists (1997, pp. 103–108) that we must take great care not to inculcate patriotism using sentimental methods that impair the capacity for critical thinking about one's country. And, more recently (Callan, 2006), he concedes that patriotism, as a form of love, always leads to some distortion of judgment.[14]

Although Amy Gutmann once claimed (with scant justification) that education should promote children's "*identification with* and

[13] Elsewhere in his provocative article, Flathman (1996, p. 22) does clash with the orthodox view. When he describes the "participatory ideal" as oppressive, decrying the way in which "those who find ruling—office holding and official duties, imposing and being imposed on by others—distasteful, diminishing, or merely distracting from preferred pursuits thereby become alien and threatening figures, enemies of the regime," Flathman (wrongly) opposes teaching children that there are important moral reasons for all citizens to participate in democratic politics.

[14] By continuing to advocate the cultivation of patriotism even after acknowledging that patriotism impedes critical judgment, Callan deviates from the orthodox view of civic education, although he remains optimistic that patriotism can both take a form and be cultivated in ways that pose only a relatively minor threat to the ideal of critically autonomous citizenship. In Chapter 5, I argue that civic identification poses (even) less of a threat and is therefore a superior solution to the civic motivation problem. And, in Chapter 7, I argue (*contra* Callan) that a sizeable degree of status quo civic educational bias will realistically be needed to arouse either patriotic love or civic identification in the widespread and robust form that would be needed to solve the civic motivation problem.

participation in the good of their family and *the politics of their society*" (Gutmann, 1987, p. 43, emphasis added), the new epilogue in the revised edition of her book seems to contradict this earlier position:

> Democratic education has the potential for being far more ecumenical and effective if it does not insist on teaching students that all moral beings must identify themselves in any single way, whether as citizens of the world, Kantian ends-in-themselves, Millean progressive beings, or cosmopolitan patriots... Democratic education welcomes all identifications that are compatible with pursuing liberty and justice for all. (Gutmann, 1999, p. 315)

Elsewhere in her book (1987, p. 62), Gutmann observes but does not evaluate the tendency for young children to acquire patriotic identification regardless of the intentions of their professional educators. Taking this phenomenon as a given, she later (1999, p. 316) argues that "schooling should make our particularistic cultural identification more well informed." Note that Gutmann's only prescription here concerns the transmission of knowledge, not the shaping of character.[15]

As we have seen, most contemporary theorists of civic education have grave concerns about character formation that extends beyond the vital but minimal task of instilling basic and universal moral values. Now that we have surveyed a number of these concerns, we can try to articulate the positive conception of critically autonomous citizenship that appears both to function as an ideal for these theorists and to underpin their opposition to many of the traditional goals of civic character education. Most theorists within the orthodoxy are less than perfectly clear and precise regarding the ideal of citizenship that informs their view, and this fact obviously makes it difficult to tell whether and how their (often implicit) normative visions differ from one another, but I believe that the following conception roughly captures the essential features that are widely shared by the theories I have discussed so far.

The ideal of critically autonomous citizenship: a person's behavior as a citizen should be directed by judgments she has made through a process of rational reflection that is both unimpaired and fully

[15] Like most theorists, Gutmann conflates civic identification and patriotic love. I argue against this practice in Chapter 4.

informed (by the relevant evidence and arguments, including the perspectives of other persons). As part of this ideal, the various pre-existing beliefs and values that contribute to the citizen's judgment in any particular case should themselves have been endorsed through a similar process of reflection (and should be re-examined if and when significant new evidence or arguments come to light).[16]

Needless to say, this ideal of critically autonomous citizenship is not fully attainable, even for an individual in the most propitious circumstances. But that fact should cause no embarrassment to the orthodox view's adherents, most of whom either explicitly acknowledge or implicitly accept that their normative theory, like many others, is utopian in the best sense of the term. Progress consists in reducing the distance between the unattainable ideal and the actual behavior of citizens. And such progress is unacceptably threatened by forms of civic education that diminish (or fail to develop) citizens' dispositions and cognitive capacities to critically evaluate the particular polities to which they belong; that selectively expose children to evidence and arguments that favor those polities' demands, actions, and existing institutions; that instill political beliefs that are contestable or straightforwardly false; or that manipulate children's preferences in ways that help to determine their behavior as citizens.

Critically autonomous citizenship is also threatened when children are habituated to perform particular civic actions. As I discuss in Chapters 2 and 3, the orthodox view does not condemn all habits of civic action. But it insists that habits, just like the beliefs and values that help to direct a person's civic actions, should have been endorsed by the person herself through autonomous and informed reflection. To be clear, the habits that I am discussing here as potential threats to autonomous citizenship are habits of action, *not* habits of reasoning. As we saw in Curren's defense of Aristotelian moral education, habits that support *good* reasoning promote rather than diminish autonomy. Adherents of the orthodox view therefore can and should support the use of education to form habits of attending and being responsive to the moral reasons that properly guide our actions. But it is a very different matter to engage in what

[16] For a discussion of the conditions under which an autonomous person initiates reexamination of her commitments, see MacMullen (2007, p. 75).

might be termed ordinary habituation, i.e., cultivating motives for action that function independently of the reasons for action that the agent perceives.[17]

Interestingly, Gutmann's *Democratic Education* does contain a solitary and passing reference (1987, p. 52) to the importance of "inculcation of habit" for securing compliance with laws, but the emphasis of her theory clearly lies overwhelmingly on the side of promoting critical moral reasoning rather than habituating compliance or any other kind of civic behavior. The "core political purpose" of education in a democracy is the "development of deliberative character," she tells us (Gutmann, 1987, pp. 50–52). Similarly, Macedo (1990, p. 278) asserts that "quiet obedience, deference, unquestioned devotion, and humility, could not be counted among the liberal virtues." Perhaps this is right. But if so, the argument of my book is that there are important and neglected virtues of the (liberal) citizen that are not liberal virtues!

Gutmann's transient references to patriotic identification and habits of compliance hint at a general response that advocates of the orthodox view may be tempted to give to some of the claims in this book. Although there are a few respects in which civic education should deviate slightly from maximization of critical autonomy, they might argue, there is no need to theorize, emphasize, or celebrate these minor deviations. Rather, such deviations can and should be taken for granted because they will reliably occur to at least the degree that is desirable even if (professional) educators aim solely to preserve and develop autonomy. But this complacent response would be wholly inadequate. It is only by articulating explicitly and precisely the many different ways in which civic education (both in schools and beyond) could and often does generate

[17] Lucas Swaine (2012) has argued that moral education properly includes significant elements of such ordinary habituation and thereby diverges significantly from education for autonomy. Swaine's ideal of moral education involves teaching children to see and feel the force of moral reasons, to be sure, but it also involves instilling certain (habitual) motives that can compete with perceived reasons for action and may even inhibit autonomous evaluation of particular "unthinkable" options, those that Swaine terms "extreme actions." My qualified defenses of habituation in civic education (forthcoming in Chapters 3 and 5) run in parallel to Swaine's defense of moral character education against unadulterated forms of education for autonomy.

nonautonomous beliefs and motives that we can begin to make informed and nuanced judgments about the malleability and desirability of these various effects. We certainly cannot assume that each of these effects will manifest at its realistically optimal level if, per the orthodox view, educators strive to avoid and eliminate all threats to the ideal of critically autonomous citizenship.

While the orthodox view treats the development and preservation of children's capacities and dispositions for critically autonomous citizenship as sufficiently important to rule out (almost) all shaping of character beyond the inculcation of basic liberal democratic values, two notable dissenters are willing to endorse much more conservative civic educational practices. Bill Galston's conceptualization and defense of civic education as distinct from (and in some ways opposed to) what he calls "philosophic education" is routinely invoked and rejected by theorists within the orthodoxy. According to Galston (1991, pp. 242–43), the purpose of civic education "is not the pursuit and acquisition of truth but, rather, the formation of individuals who can effectively conduct their lives within, and support, their political community. It is unlikely, to say the least, that truth-seeking activities will be fully consistent with this purpose." As previously noted, Galston goes on to argue that national history should be taught with an eye to instilling patriotism and that this purpose rules out complete candor: "civic education . . . requires a nobler, moralizing history: a pantheon of heroes who confer legitimacy on central institutions and are worthy of emulation" (Galston, 1991, p. 244). As Eamonn Callan (1997, pp. 101–115) has observed (with strong disapproval), this approach to teaching history is significantly at odds with the goal of preparing children to deploy critical reason in their future roles as full citizens.

More recently, Ajume Wingo has elaborated a thesis that is similar to Galston's. "Effective civic education," Wingo (2003, p. 130) writes, "demands that we stand with one foot in the world of reason, the other in the more primitive one of feeling, emotion, and sentiment." But this is precisely what the orthodox view denies. "The intelligent, well-informed citizen, reasons the liberal civic pedagogue, is a virtuous citizen of a liberal state; therefore, teaching rational deliberation and tolerance for alternative ways of life is *enough* to motivate citizens to act as required for a thriving, well-functioning liberal state" (Wingo, 2003, p. 108, emphasis added). On

Wingo's view, this is naïve, even utopian. "Modern liberals have typically failed to recognize the importance (indeed, the necessity) of the nonrational aspects of politics" (Wingo, 2003, p. 24). He argues that "we must clearly separate the task of justifying liberal political principles from that of motivating persons to act in accordance with them" (Wingo, 2003, p. 47), and he maintains that the latter task requires much more robust forms of character education than are countenanced within (what I call) the orthodox view.

Galston and Wingo are right to reject the orthodoxy's highly restrictive view of optimal character formation but, in their eagerness to embrace more traditional and conservative approaches to civic education, they fail to adequately acknowledge the costs and risks of these approaches and, correspondingly, the powerful reasons to value promoting autonomy in future citizens. In other words, Galston and Wingo have performed a vital service by showing that the orthodox view is one-sided, but (as is so often true in debates of this kind) they appear to have overreacted, throwing the proverbial baby out with the bathwater. And they certainly have not provided what this important debate needs, namely, a careful identification and treatment of the competing values, one that shows how best to strike a balance among them.[18] *Civics Beyond Critics* aims to meet this need.

1.2. Character, education, pluralism, polities, and authority

Before I describe the structure and sketch the arguments of the remainder of the book, I need to make a number of points to clarify the scope and limits of my project. First, when I say that my topic is

[18] Geoffrey Vaughan (2005, p. 389) argues that "Contemporary theorizing in political education is caught between incompatible ambitions [:] producing autonomous individuals, on the one hand, and deeply committed democratic citizens, on the other." In part, as we have seen, Vaughan's perception of a stark incompatibility between these ambitions derives from his insistence on conceptualizing autonomy as necessarily threatened by moral education. But, even when we adopt a more attractive conception of autonomy, there is still a tension between cultivating autonomy and fostering traditional civic virtues. The appropriate response to this tension is not, as Vaughan does, to declare melodramatically and unhelpfully that we are confronted with "incompatible ambitions" but rather to seek to identify and then to realize the optimal trade-offs among the competing values.

the formation of character as distinct from the teaching of political skills and knowledge, I certainly mean to include the foreseeable (and often intended) consequences of the latter for the former. It is difficult to teach someone a skill without affecting her beliefs, values, preferences, or habits. And, as I shall acknowledge throughout my analysis, decisions about which facts to teach and how to present them often have profound formative effects on children's character. For example, if children are presented with a stylized and somewhat idealized account of their polity's legislative process, or if they are exposed to concrete examples of policy-making that have been carefully selected to showcase the government's expertise, openness to diverse viewpoints, and attention to detail, the likely result will be to increase children's trust in their polity's legislative and executive acts. By contrast, if children are predominantly exposed to and informed about governmental incompetence and/or the seamier sides of democratic politics, such as corruption and the disproportionate influence of money and special interests, their resulting (partial) knowledge of how the sausages of law and policy are made will dispose them not to trust those laws and policies.

Second, throughout the book, when I refer to education I use the term in the broad sense that includes both formal schooling and the other elements of a child's upbringing, such as parenting. This is both important and difficult to remember because debates about civic education are usually focused more narrowly on schools; indeed, the debates are usually about public (i.e., state-run) schools and often even more specifically about the "civics" or "citizenship" courses taught in those schools. My focus is much broader: shaping of civic character can and does arise not only in schools (public, private, and home) but also throughout children's *informal* civic education, the many ways in which their politically relevant values, beliefs, preferences, habits, identities, and sentiments are shaped by non-school forces, especially parenting but also the media, popular culture, etc. As Murphy (2004) notes in reviewing the literature on political socialization, these non-school forces are often much more powerful than formal schooling. But the inclusion of these powerful forces in my conception of civic education is certainly not intended to suggest that they should be under state control. As we shall shortly see, I do not address the question of educational authority.

Even if we assume that parents should possess broad authority to direct and conduct children's upbringing, it remains important to recognize and reflect on the civic implications of the ways in which that authority is used. Civically responsible people will allow their parenting decisions to be guided by these implications. And all citizens, but especially professional educators and education policy-makers, will need to pay attention to the civic functions of upbringing in order to think contextually about schools as one force among many that shape civic character. If, as I shall argue, optimal civic education finds the virtuous mean between excessive and insufficient shaping of character at the expense of autonomy, anyone who contributes to children's civic education should be attentive to, and aware of the possible need to counterbalance, the other influences on those children's character. Civically responsible parents may need to push back against what their children learn in their civics classroom just as schools should complement (which does not necessarily mean reinforce) the informal civic education that children receive at home and in their communities.

Third, since my concern as a normative political theorist is with justifying educational ends rather than selecting the best means to those ends, I typically do not address the many important questions concerning how civic educational techniques and practices should vary with the age of children. My primary goal in this book is to identify the various ways in which people's character will ideally have been shaped by the time they emerge from childhood and acquire the legal rights and responsibilities of full citizenship in the polities of which they are members. Implementing my conclusions would obviously involve making a series of complex judgments about the effects of particular educational techniques and practices, including the ways in which those effects vary as children develop from infancy through adolescence. Although I will occasionally indicate my beliefs about such matters, especially when those beliefs strike me as relatively uncontroversial, I will not marshal systematic empirical evidence, and I am more than happy to revise my beliefs if and when it can be demonstrated that there are more effective ways of realizing the civic educational goals which I am advocating.

Furthermore, although I reiterate that the choice of educational tools is not my focus in this book, it is important to keep in mind that such tools should be judged not only according to their propensity to generate effects that are both intended and desirable but also by evaluating the unintended but foreseeable effects of using them (or approving their use). Concrete attempts to realize worthy educational goals will almost always have some undesirable side-effects, even when these attempts are broadly successful in achieving their intended effects. There are (at least) four reasons for this. First, most educational tools are somewhat crude: they affect children in multiple ways, some of which are often undesirable. Second, educators are only human and will therefore often make imperfect selections among and use of the tools available to them, thereby typically not only reducing the effectiveness of education in realizing its intended goals but also heightening and/or multiplying its undesirable side-effects. Third, the effects of any educational tool depend upon the child's nature and developmental state; these critical variables are often difficult and sometimes realistically impossible to gauge with a high degree of accuracy, so we are sure to make plenty of errors when we try to minimize or even eliminate unwanted side-effects by tailoring each child's education to her particularities. And fourth, even when educators possess (or could feasibly acquire) all the information that would be needed to customize a child's education in this manner, it is often impractical to do so (especially when, as in schools, children are educated in groups within institutions that cannot function effectively without uniform policies and procedures of various kinds).

As the preceding analysis makes clear, we should always be mindful of the unwanted but predictable side-effects of educational measures whose intended effects are salutary. When we compare two ways of pursuing the same educational goal, we may prefer the option that is less effective in realizing that goal if its negative side-effects will be significantly fewer and less severe. In extreme cases, we may even have to abandon pursuit of a desirable educational goal if there is no way to operationalize the pursuit without generating negative side-effects that outweigh the benefits of realizing the goal. But all of the misgivings I have identified evidently apply *generally* to the pursuit of educational goals; they have no special force against the goals I shall defend, and they certainly apply to the orthodox view's goal of cultivating critical thinking. It is one thing to advocate the ideal of critically autonomous citizenship, but it is quite another to confront the crude moral relativism, subjectivism, skepticism, or even nihilism that are often byproducts of well-intentioned efforts to cultivate critical thinking by presenting students evenhandedly with the best arguments for and against each of several incompatible political philosophies (Ebels-Duggan, 2014).

Fourth (in this list of preliminary remarks intended to make clear the nature of my project), readers should be warned that I am a "value pluralist" in the tradition of Isaiah Berlin (1958/2002, pp. 212–17) and Bill Galston (2002, pp. 4–7). Given the host of very different kinds of goods that can be advanced or stymied by education for civic character, it strikes me as absurd to imagine that normative analysis of the issue will reveal a set of lexically-ordered principles or even an algorithm to generate a uniquely correct solution to every decision problem. When we must choose a particular educational practice or policy, it will usually be the case that many of the options can be justified by some defensible weighting of the conflicting values at stake. Of course, there will often also be uncertainty about the empirical effects of different educational options. But my point is that the absence of a uniquely justified option is not due solely to this kind of empirical uncertainty. Even if (hypothetically) we knew all of the effects that each of our options would have, there would typically be value incommensurabilities that preclude identifying one option as objectively best. But the fact that reason rarely favors a single option over all others does not mean that it cannot provide some decisive and important verdicts. In particular, some civic educational strategies will be revealed to be indefensible because they cannot be reconciled with any reasonable weighting of the competing values.

As will be clear throughout the book, my value pluralist metaethics has especially important implications for my treatment of educational measures that would promote certain goods at the expense of individual autonomy. Autonomy does not function as a trump in such conflicts: it does not constitute an inviolable side-constraint on efforts to realize other goods. Autonomy is certainly important, and I shall strive both to acknowledge and not to undersell the many ways in which it is valuable, but its value can and sometimes will be outweighed. Having said that, one cannot specify the exact weight to be attached to autonomy. Trying to do so wrongly presupposes the general commensurability of values. There are powerful reasons to value critically autonomous citizenship. But some very important moral goods are best promoted by educational practices that sacrifice autonomy to a significant degree, and I shall argue that we should often be willing to make these trade-offs.

Fifth, civic education prepares children for (full) citizenship in the polities to which they belong, and those polities are not limited to states in the familiar sense of nation states, sovereign states, or countries: they include municipalities or regions that possess significant political autonomy, and they may also include supra-national polities such as the European Union. Most people are members of multiple polities, nested one within another. Except when I am directly analyzing other scholars' claims that are made in the language of "countries" or "states" I shall therefore use the more general term "polities."[19] In a geopolitical world long (and still largely) dominated by sovereign states (that are often also nation states), there are obviously good reasons to attend carefully to the ways in which education prepares people for citizenship in polities of this kind. But we should not forget that the questions I pose usually also apply at the sub- and sometimes also at the supra-national level. How should education affect Chicagoans' motives to comply with ordinances issued by their city? In what ways should the education of German children encourage them to participate in European Union elections? When children in Nebraska learn about their state's legislature, should they be taught in ways that dispose them to favor its unicameral structure over the bicameralism that characterizes the legislatures of the other forty-nine US states?

Sixth, and last, the various questions I address in this book all concern *how* children should be educated, not *who* should (decide how to) educate them. In other words, I am not asking who should have *authority* over children's education. Arguments about the legitimacy of authority are obviously of central importance both to normative political theory and to real-world politics, but I propose to bracket such second-order questions here in order to isolate the underlying first-order question: how should

[19] Note, however, that I shall (continue to) use the standard convention whereby "the state" refers generically to a polity, even if that polity is a municipality or a politically autonomous region.

education shape children's civic character?[20] I do not thereby mean to imply that the second-order question would be trivial if everyone accepted my first-order normative analysis. Far from it: even in the unlikely event that we achieved such a consensus on the first-order issues, the second-order question would remain extremely difficult. Should we seek to allocate educational authority so as to maximize the quality of the educational decisions that will be made? It will be very hard to know what allocation would achieve this goal because it is so difficult to gauge the competence and motivations of the various candidates for educational authority.

But we would also have to consider the position that claims to legitimate authority are not grounded (solely) in judgments about the ways in which that authority is likely to be used: the most appropriate question may not be "who is least likely to err in various ways?" but rather "given that errors will inevitably be made, who has the right to make them?" In answering this question, some will appeal to parental rights to control their children's education, others will invoke the professional autonomy of teachers, while still others will insist that the authority to make errors in civic education must ultimately reside in the people collectively via their democratic institutions. It could also be argued that some agents are entitled to direct a child's education in ways that *deliberately* diverge from the educational optimum: for example, parents may be permitted to pursue their own interests at some cost to the quality of their child's education. Besides which, children and their parents typically both benefit from sharing a familial life that is not micromanaged by some external authority (Brighouse and Swift, 2009): this benefit will surely be large enough to warrant granting parents authority over children's civic education in certain spheres—especially the most intimate aspects of a child's upbringing—even if the decisions of some other agent (the state, perhaps?) would accord better with

[20] Amy Gutmann (1987), by contrast, focuses her political theory of education heavily on the question of legitimate authority: she not only proposes that democratic authorities should be free to err within broad limits but also frequently declines to stake out a first-order normative position that would tell us when democratic decisions are (legitimate) errors.

the normative principles that should govern education for civic character.

Furthermore, we might value decision-making processes in part for their byproducts: for example, if deliberation about educational decisions is good for the deliberators and/or more broadly for society, this might warrant allocating educational authority in a way that will foster deliberation even if this allocation does not generate the best decisions.[21] Finally, we might also legitimately care about the speed with which decisions can be rendered by different agents, especially given that issues can arise suddenly and that delays in resolution may be costly. We may not want to vest initial authority in the agent that is most likely to decide correctly if the decision will come very slowly (although that agent might be the right locus for final authority via mechanisms such as appeals procedures, hierarchical oversight, or democratic accountability). As this (no doubt incomplete) list demonstrates, the problem of (civic) educational authority would be multi-dimensional and complex even in the unlikely event that everyone agreed on how (civic) educational practices and policies should be evaluated.

1.3. Preview of the arguments

My strategy in the remainder of this book is to identify and discuss in turn three conceptually distinct ways in which education for civic character has traditionally been understood to extend beyond inculcating universal liberal democratic values. Civic education has traditionally aimed to shape children's values, beliefs, preferences, habits, sentiments, and identities so as to create citizens who are more likely (than those educated in accordance with today's theoretical orthodoxy) to do three things with respect to a *particular* polity to which they belong: (I) comply with its laws, (II) contribute voluntarily to its flourishing, and (III) believe in the merits of its

[21] Versions of these two positions partially animate Amy Gutmann's (1987) support for broad democratic authority over education. Tocqueville (1850/2006, p. 275) offered an analogous argument for using juries in civil cases: "I do not know whether a jury is good for the litigants, but I am sure it is very good for those who have to decide the case. I regard it as one of the most effective means of popular education at society's disposal."

fundamental political institutions. I devote one part of the book to each of these three goals. In each part, I first identify (in one chapter) and then evaluate (in the subsequent chapter) the various methods that civic education could use to pursue the goal in question. And in each part I conclude that optimal civic education in a liberal democracy deviates significantly from the orthodoxy's call for maximizing future citizens' critical autonomy.

Part I makes the case for using education to cultivate nonautonomous motives for compliance with laws. I begin this task in Chapter 2 by proposing a typology of the many possible reasons to comply with a law. There are eight types of reason for compliance, I argue, because there are three independent and binary dimensions on which such reasons should be classified: moral or prudential, particular (to the law in question) or general (i.e., applicable to many different laws), and *in se* (i.e., a reason for action that would exist even in the absence of the law) or *prohibitum* (i.e., a reason for action that exists only because of the relevant law). After exploring the variety of *prohibitum* reasons for compliance, I use the typology to analyze the three fundamental ways in which education could cultivate reasons for compliance: instilling beliefs, including both *moral* beliefs (i.e., beliefs about the nature and extent of the consideration we owe to others) and *non-moral* beliefs (about the expected consequences of compliance and noncompliance); shaping prudential values; and inculcating trust (that the reasons to comply are often stronger and/or more numerous than the agent perceives). Finally, I discuss the important possibility that education could instill habits of (or other nonrational motives for) compliance.

Chapter 3 begins by arguing that autonomous motives by themselves cannot realistically be expected to generate the high rate of compliance with laws that is morally required in a reasonably just liberal democratic state. I explain how the various educational strategies identified in Chapter 2 promise major improvements on this dimension. But these benefits would not be costless, and so I propose a comprehensive theoretical framework for evaluating educational policies and practices by their effects on future decisions regarding compliance with laws. The principal task here is to identify the various ways in which compliance can be suboptimal despite being morally permissible. I focus especially on acts of compliance that are not morally required and that either fail to express the agent's own judgment or express a judgment that reflects inauthentic preferences or false moral beliefs. This analysis enables me to articulate the costs of cultivating nonautonomous motives for compliance. I conclude by arguing that, given the great moral importance of reducing the incidence of impermissible law-breaking, cost-benefit analysis will favor some educational strategies (of the kind identified in Chapter 2) for increasing levels of compliance by cultivating nonautonomous motives.

Part II argues that education should aim to boost civic motivation by instilling a sense of civic identity, despite the fact that identification with a polity impairs a person's capacity for critical judgment of that polity's actions and institutions. Chapter 4 lays the foundations for this argument by analyzing the various ways in which education could foster civic motivation. After identifying the independent roles that habits, tastes, and perceived moral reasons for civic action each can play in motivating people to contribute to the polities of which they are citizens, I focus on the vital and oft-neglected distinction between affection for and identification with a polity. Although the two attitudes are often conflated as "patriotism," I argue that civic identification can be separated from affection, both conceptually and psychologically, and I sketch an approach to civic education that promises to foster civic identification without unduly arousing patriotic love.

Chapter 5 introduces the normative analysis by identifying the important moral reasons for people to contribute to the democratic polities of which they are citizens. I argue that these reasons derive from the special opportunities that citizenship affords, rather than from any special moral relationship between co-citizens. Making good use of the distinctive opportunities afforded by her citizenship is a major component of what each person can do to best play her part in the effort to realize justice, legitimacy, security, and social coordination, both domestically and globally. This fact gives rise to weighty moral reasons for action. But, alas, perceived moral reasons for (civic) action are motivationally unreliable and often insufficient. And, although most people benefit from the survival and flourishing of the liberal democratic polities of which they are citizens, in a mass democracy narrow self-interest usually counsels free-riding whenever civic action is purely voluntary. I call this the civic motivation problem.

How can this problem be solved? Cultivation of suitable habits and tastes has an important role to play, as do coercion and positive incentives for civic action. But I suggest that, even in conjunction, these measures can only provide a partial solution. Patriotic love promises to make up the remaining motivational shortfall, but at a high price: love of one's polity impairs one's capacity to see that polity's weaknesses and faults. This price might be worth paying if patriotic love were the only available solution to the civic motivation problem. But, as argued in Chapter 4, civic identification is an alternative. And, I argue in Chapter 5, it is an *attractive* alternative because civic identification does not impair civic judgment as severely as patriotic love does, and robust civic identification does not depend upon the polity's having a highly exclusive ethno-cultural identity. Finally, I defend civic identification (as well as habits of and tastes for civic action) from the claim that all non-moral motives to participate in the civic life of one's polity constitute psychological barriers to morally appropriate reconfigurations of political space.

Part III offers a qualified defense of status quo biased civic education, which I define in Chapter 6 as education that encourages children's belief in the substantive merits of existing laws or institutions, where that effect does not derive solely from strengthening children's capacities and inclinations to engage in autonomous and informed evaluation. I distinguish between two (not mutually exclusive) forms of civic educational bias: children can be exposed to a biased selection of the available evidence and arguments for and against an existing institution, and children can be educated in ways that bias their judgment of whatever evidence and arguments they encounter. I note that it is much easier to make a case for educational status quo bias that is narrowly targeted to favor selected laws and institutions, but I argue that there are circumstances under which educators could be justified in cultivating a weak degree of trust in status quo arrangements generally. And I argue that, although status quo educational biases are often unintended and could not realistically be eliminated entirely, the range and degree of such biases are nonetheless very largely subject to human control.

Chapter 7 takes up the normative question: are status quo biases ever desirable features of civic education in a liberal democracy? Critics suggest that such biases are both a barrier to political progress and a threat to the state's legitimacy. Against these objections,

I show how and when adults' (admittedly fallible) beliefs about the substantive merits of existing political arrangements constitute compelling reasons for status quo educational bias. I also make the case that the values of stability, contentment, compliance, and civic identification underpin important auxiliary reasons for status quo bias: these are reasons that appeal *not* to the substantive merits of existing institutions but merely to the fact that those institutions are the status quo. The combined force of the multiple reasons I identify will sometimes outweigh the fallibility and legitimacy objections to particular instances of status quo bias, especially with respect to the fundamental institutions of a liberal democratic polity. If today's adult citizens want their polity to be a flourishing liberal democracy fifty years hence, their best strategy includes encouraging children's support for certain existing institutions that instantiate liberal democratic values in ways that are contestable and probably also imperfect. Therefore, I conclude, the best civic education will typically include significant elements of status quo bias.

Chapter 8 begins by succinctly restating the major findings of Chapters 2 through 7 and then abstracting from them to articulate my general conclusion. Critical autonomy is a great virtue of liberal democratic citizenship, but it sometimes conflicts with other important civic virtues and should not always be preferred in such cases of conflict. The civic goals of character education are therefore plural and exist in some tension with one another. The challenge for educators (broadly conceived) and for citizens more generally is to strike an appropriate balance between encouraging critically autonomous civic behavior and three other important goals: promoting compliance with the polity's laws, fostering motivation to contribute to its flourishing, and encouraging support for the fundamental political arrangements through which that polity seeks to realize the values of liberal democracy. Finally, I sketch what strike me as some likely practical implications of my view while reiterating the various reasons why the normative theoretical conclusions of this book do not constitute concrete prescriptions for educational policy or practice.

PART I

PROMOTING COMPLIANCE WITH LAWS

CHAPTER 2

Cultivating motives for compliance

Why do people comply with laws? In part, no doubt, they do so to avoid punishment by the state. If we emphasize this familiar explanation, it might seem that widespread compliance is best secured by establishing high levels of expected punishment for noncompliant acts, where expected punishment is a function of both the likelihood that law-breakers will be apprehended by the authorities and the severity of sanctions meted out to those who are caught. This deterrence strategy is an important component of any society's efforts to secure compliance with its laws, but it has significant drawbacks. Detection, prosecution, and punishment of law-breakers are all very costly, measured both in material resources and in other values (such as privacy and avoiding punishment of the innocent) that realistically must be compromised to maintain a vigorous system of law enforcement.

In addition to being costly, deterrence is not always effective. Increases in expected punishment may fail to reduce criminality if they have the unintended effect of changing citizens' attitudes and values. As incarceration rates go up, some citizens may see going to prison as normal, "no big deal." Citizens who perceive the state's laws to be unjust and/or its regime of punishment to be excessive may even react "defiantly" to any decision to ratchet up criminal sanctions, actually becoming *less* compliant (Sherman, 1993, pp. 445–73). This reaction is especially likely if incarceration comes to be regarded within particular communities not as a stigma but rather as a badge of membership or honor. Deterrence depends not only on citizens' beliefs about the probability and objective magnitude of sanctions for law-breaking but also on their attitudes to such "punishment," that is, the extent to which citizens are averse (or even favorably disposed) to different types and levels of sanction. These beliefs and attitudes may be causally related. And, of course, much depends on citizens' attitudes to risk.

So, *crude* deterrence strategies—those that rely exclusively on changing the *objective* expected pay-offs to noncompliance—can be very costly and are sometimes ineffective. A *sophisticated* deterrence strategy would attend also to *subjective* factors, by seeking ways to increase citizens' aversion to a given risk of incurring a given sanction. But, once we recognize that compliance can be promoted without changing expected pay-offs, we quickly see that enhancing the deterrent effect of unchanged criminal sanctions is only one among many such strategies. There are many beliefs, values, preferences, and habits that dispose citizens to compliance or noncompliance regardless of expected punishment.[1] Intentional shaping of these dispositions through education can be an effective tool in securing high levels of compliance with the laws. This statement is purely descriptive, but it invites normative questions. When and how are educators justified in using this potentially very powerful tool? Should children be educated to comply with the laws? These are the questions I aim to answer in this chapter and the next.

In a brutal dictatorship, education that cultivates a disposition to comply with the laws is objectionable both because it helps to sustain an unjust and illegitimate regime and because the law's demands are often outrageous.[2] In a polity whose laws are widely and routinely disregarded by its members, a disposition to comply with those laws often makes its possessor look ridiculous, unable to act in ways that are appropriately sensitive to realistic expectations about the behavior of others and prone to engage in senseless self-sacrifice. But what happens if we assume instead a well-functioning and reasonably just liberal democracy, whose population is effectively governed by a set of coercively-backed general rules that treat all members with roughly equal concern and respect; that rarely violate and often secure individual moral rights (even if they may be

[1] See Tyler (1990) for an important empirical study of the extent to which compliance is explained by citizens' moral judgments.

[2] Francis Schrag (2010, pp. 149–63) observes that dispositions suitable for favorable conditions may in unfavorable conditions expose *the possessor* to risks of serious harm. I would add that these dispositions may also expose *others* to such risks.

unwise, imperfect, and so on); and that are made using (or at least are subject to amendment by) a procedure that affords each adult member of the population an equal opportunity to influence the decision (on some account of "equal opportunity to influence" that is both practicable and normatively defensible)? In such realistically favorable conditions, which henceforth I assume to obtain, a disposition to comply with the laws has traditionally been regarded as a virtue that should be cultivated in children (Edmundson, 2006).

But any argument for cultivating a disposition to comply with the laws must be reconciled with the existence of cases in which it is morally permissible to break a law, even a just law in a democratic polity. There can be justified law-breaking, even under realistically favorable conditions, in each of four distinct categories of principled noncompliance: civil disobedience, conscientious objection, unreasonably demanding laws, and exceptional circumstances. *Civil disobedience* is defined by the public and strategic nature of the noncompliant act, which is intended to help effect a change in law, government policy, or the behavior of a non-governmental actor.[3] The remaining three categories of principled noncompliance, by contrast, are essentially private and nonstrategic actions. *Conscientious objection* refers to noncompliance that is motivated by the agent's belief that the action demanded by the law is morally impermissible both in this particular context and in most or all others. When an agent believes that her noncompliance is warranted by the *unreasonably demanding* nature of a law mandating action X, she maintains that X, although permissible (and perhaps even supererogatory), is not morally required (in this context as in most or all others), even given the existence of the law.[4] Finally, when an agent appeals to *exceptional circumstances*, she accepts that compliance with the law in question is usually required but maintains that in this particular case noncompliance is morally permitted (and may be supererogatory or even morally required).

Once we recognize the possibility of justified noncompliance in each of these four categories, it should be obvious that there can be

[3] It is important to remember that, when civil disobedience aims at changing a law, the law that is broken is often not the law to which the protester objects.

[4] I shall soon explore in detail the various ways in which the existence of a law can generate new reasons for performing the action that the law mandates.

no simple answer to the question of how we ought to shape children's motives for compliance both with law in general and with particular laws. Compliance is not always morally required, and it does not always serve the agent's interests (or anyone else's, for that matter). We must therefore take seriously the worry that education will produce *excessively* compliant citizens. But, at the same time, we obviously must continue to give enough weight to the opposite and more familiar danger.

The appropriate normative theoretical question is therefore not *whether* but rather *in what senses* and *to what extent* children should be educated to comply with the laws of their society. This complex question does not permit a "one size fits all" answer. What is needed, and what I aim to provide in this pair of chapters, is a conceptual and normative framework within which one could analyze and answer the question in the context of a particular society and, where appropriate, on a case-by-case basis. This framework should guide us—citizens, teachers, parents—as we decide whether to educate children in various ways that would discourage them from breaking *controversial* laws by, say, having a late-term abortion, drinking at age twenty, riding a motorcycle without wearing a helmet, dodging the draft, jaywalking, or smoking marijuana. It should also inform the ways we shape children's motives for complying with relatively *uncontroversial* laws, which they might be tempted to break as an act of civil disobedience[5] (consider laws against trespass and obstruction of a highway), or because of exceptional circumstances (consider routine traffic laws, such as speed limits and the obligation to stop at red lights), or in an unprincipled fashion (vandalism or petty theft, for example).

But I shall also argue that, although the exact prescription will vary greatly with social and political circumstances, optimal education for compliance will realistically always involve significant cultivation of nonautonomous motives for compliance. By rejecting all such strategies, the orthodox view of civic education either severely

[5] Most professional educators are, I suspect, comfortable talking with students about the moral case for civil disobedience only when the conversation is firmly in the past tense. As Joseph Kahne and Joel Westheimer (2003, p. 64) observe, Martin Luther King is typically presented to children as "a hero to be respected (but not necessarily emulated)." It may be easier to see the justification for civil disobedience with hindsight, but schools must prepare children to make decisions in the moment.

underestimates the value of widespread compliance with laws or exhibits a wildly unrealistic faith in the capacity of individuals' autonomous reasoning to generate the very high rate of compliance that is morally required in a reasonably just liberal democratic state. Chapter 3 advances this normative argument while also articulating precisely the costs associated with nonautonomous compliance.

In the current chapter I lay the groundwork for the subsequent normative argument by conceptualizing the various ways in which education could promote compliance with laws. The analysis proceeds in four main steps. First, I argue that there are eight types of reason for compliance because there are three independent and binary dimensions on which such reasons should be classified: *moral* or *prudential*, *particular* (to the law in question) or *general* (i.e., applicable to many different laws), and *in se* (i.e., a reason for action that would exist even in the absence of the law) or *prohibitum* (i.e., a reason for action that exists only because of the relevant law). Second, I explore the rich variety of *prohibitum* reasons for compliance and offer an example to demonstrate how reasons of all eight types can simultaneously exist to comply with a particular law on a particular occasion. Third, I use the typology of reasons for compliance to analyze the three fundamental ways in which education could cultivate such reasons: instilling beliefs, including both *moral* beliefs (i.e., beliefs about the nature and extent of the consideration we owe to others) and *non-moral* beliefs (about the expected consequences of compliance and noncompliance); shaping prudential values; and inculcating trust (that the reasons to comply are often stronger and/or more numerous than the agent perceives). Fourth, I discuss the important possibility that education could instill habits of (or other nonrational motives for) compliance.

Before I develop my typology of reasons to comply I should note that I use the concept of compliance to refer to behavior in accordance with the demands of the law, regardless of how that behavior is explained. Obedience, as I shall use the concept, refers only to instances of compliance that are explained by the fact that the compliant agent takes the law itself directly to be a moral reason for action.[6]

[6] I address the issue of philosophical anarchism later in this chapter and again in Chapter 3.

I shall assume for the sake of simplicity that it is clear and uncontroversial what action(s) the law requires or prohibits in a given case. I do not consider cases in which the text of a law and/or the circumstances in which it is to be applied introduce the possibility of more than one reasonable interpretation *and* in which there has been no procedurally correct judicial pronouncement on the case. On my view, it is simply incoherent to talk about compliance with law in such cases. It might still make sense to describe someone's actions as noncompliant if they are not consistent with any reasonable interpretation of the law. But, after a judicial decision has been issued and for so long as that order remains in force, compliance with the law means compliance with that order, even if one believes in good faith that the text of the law is being misinterpreted or misapplied. The law during that time interval is what the designated judge says that it is. Although some superior authority (a higher court, perhaps, or the legislature) may subsequently act to clarify the law's meaning in a way that contradicts the original judicial interpretation, this should not be understood to be retroactive in the sense of entailing that a party who refused to comply with the lower court's order was actually in compliance with the law and, conversely, that a party who did as the lower court instructed was noncompliant with the law.[7]

But what about cases of gross incompetence or corruption in the judiciary? Does compliance with the law mean complying with the order of a judge who has clearly misinterpreted the law and may indeed have done so deliberately? There are two different questions we can ask about such cases. The first is purely conceptual and descriptive: does noncompliance with the judge's order constitute breaking the law? I think the answer is yes, although this is not without a hint of paradox. The second question is normative: ought one to comply with the judge's order (even as that order is being appealed to a higher authority by oneself or others)? As should

[7] The situation is different, of course, after a higher court has stayed the lower court's order. But, before or in the absence of a stay, one's failure to heed the lower court's decision in the period before one's appeal is decided is not retroactively transformed into an instance of law-abiding behavior by the higher court's reversal of that decision. It would be wholly consistent with the rule of law to prosecute someone in these circumstances, although one might sometimes criticize on other grounds any such decision to prosecute.

become clear later in this chapter, the case for noncompliance in cases of this sort is strengthened to the extent that familiar types of reason for compliance fail to apply. A lot may depend on whether the judge's outrageous decision succeeds in changing people's expectations about the conduct of others. The mere fact that compliance with the judge's order is, as a descriptive matter, legally required does not settle the normative question as to whether such compliance is morally required. Even if there is (*contra* the so-called philosophical anarchists) a general duty of obedience to laws, that duty is only *prima facie*.

2.1. A typology of reasons to comply

Although we should not neglect the important educational strategy of *habituating* children to comply with laws, which I shall discuss at the end of this chapter, most education for compliance will presumably take the form of leading children to perceive *reasons* for compliance. What types of reasons could those be? And how could education increase the number of reasons for compliance that people perceive and/or the strength that they perceive those reasons to have? The principal task of this chapter is to answer these two basic questions. To address the first, I offer a conceptual typology of reasons to comply, and I explore at some length the complex ways in which the existence of a law can generate new reasons for action. Then, later in the present chapter, I address the second question by exploring the three fundamental ways in which education can cultivate (perceived) reasons for compliance: instilling beliefs, shaping prudential values, and inculcating trust.

There can be many different reasons to comply with a particular law. To avoid overlooking any of these reasons, it helps to know in advance the different *types* of reason that *could* exist. I shall therefore propose a conceptual scheme for categorizing reasons for compliance. According to this scheme, there are three independent and binary dimensions on which a reason is classified; therefore, there are (2 × 2 × 2) eight types of reason. (Later in this chapter I provide both a table displaying the eight types of reason and an example designed to show how a reason of each type can exist to comply with one and the same law.)

Three preliminary remarks are in order. First, as we just saw with regard to the supposed general duty of obedience, a reason to comply need not be conclusive; it may be outweighed or merely counterbalanced by one or more reasons not to comply. Prudential reasons to comply may be outweighed by (prudential or moral) reasons favoring noncompliance. And the moral reasons to comply with a particular law in particular circumstances may be relatively weak—they can certainly be defeated or merely counterbalanced by other moral reasons or by certain claims of self-interest.[8] For example, even in cases when civil disobedience is justified there are usually some significant moral reasons to comply with the law, but those reasons are outweighed or at least counterbalanced by the moral reasons to engage in the protest.

A second preliminary remark: all eight types of reason for compliance must be conceptually distinguished from nonrational habits of compliance. Not all motives are rational: I address the nature and cultivation of habits of compliance later in this chapter, where I also explore the difficulties that can arise in determining whether a particular motive is a (perceived) reason or a habit. Third, in all that follows, X is a placeholder for an action that is required by the law in question, and Y stands in for an action that is prohibited by that law.

On the first dimension of my typology, a reason for compliance is either *moral* or *prudential*. A moral reason is categorical, in the Kantian sense that it applies regardless of the agent's desires or preferences, but it is not necessarily thereby conclusive (as I note above). Moral reasons are typically grounded in the consideration owed by each of us to other persons (and perhaps also to nonhuman animals), but I do not want to deny by mere stipulation that moral reasons might sometimes be grounded in the consideration owed to oneself or to a god.[9] Prudential reasons for compliance, by contrast, are reasons of self-interest, whether of the type that are commonly called selfish ("interests in the self") or of the

[8] As we shall see in Chapter 3, even when there are moral reasons to comply and only prudential reasons for noncompliance, the moral reasons may not be conclusive: compliance may be supererogatory rather than morally required. And some such acts of self-sacrifice strike us as generous but wrong-headed!

[9] I obviously cannot here provide a lengthy discussion of the precise nature of moral reasons!

type we normally consider altruistic or spiteful ("interests of the self" that concern the well-being of others) (Gauthier, 1986). Unlike moral reasons, prudential reasons for compliance are hypothetical imperatives in the Kantian sense: they exist if and only if the agent has preferences that would be satisfied by compliance.[10] But, of course, an agent may not be *motivated* by the prudential reason she has to comply: she may not be aware that compliance will satisfy one of her current preferences, or she may not stop to think about the ways in which noncompliance today will diminish her prospects for preference-satisfaction in the future.[11]

On the second dimension, a reason for compliance is either *particular* (to the law in question) or *general* (i.e., applicable to many different laws). A particular reason for compliance cannot be articulated without identifying the action that the law mandates or prohibits. A general reason, by contrast, invokes only the existence of the law and, perhaps, the sanctions for noncompliance; the reason can be stated in a way that renders it intelligible to someone who does not even know what conduct the law governs.

On the third dimension, a reason for compliance is either *in se* or *prohibitum*. An *in se* reason is one that would exist in the absence of the law, whereas a *prohibitum* reason exists only because of the existence of the law. It may appear that the independence of the three dimensions breaks down at this point: some readers may suspect that *in se* reasons are always particular. There is a sense in which this is true, but the important thing to observe is that the existence of a law may provide grounds for *believing* that there is some (unknown by the agent) *in se* reason for doing X. Whenever I comply with a law because I trust that the demands of the laws track the actions that I would have most reason to perform in the absence of those laws, I am acting on a general *in se* reason.[12]

[10] Note, therefore, that according to my typology, if it would be (*prima facie*) wrong for an agent to neglect certain interests in or of herself, then the fact that noncompliance with the law would damage those interests may underpin the existence of both moral and prudential reasons for compliance.

[11] Just as I cannot offer a full account of the nature of moral reasons, I cannot here fully explicate or defend a theory of well-being that would justify analyzing prudential reasons solely in terms of (current and future) preference-satisfaction.

[12] To be precise, one might say that I have a general reason to believe that there is an *in se* reason for compliance.

2.1.1. Prohibitum *reasons, expectations, and social coordination*

It is worth spending some time to identify the various forms that *prohibitum* reasons for compliance can take. This task is important not least because, as I shall soon discuss in more detail, there is some doubt about the existence of what many people regard as a centrally important *prohibitum* reason, namely, a general *prima facie* duty to obey the law. I believe that invocations of this supposed duty are often better understood as appeals to other moral reasons for compliance, reasons whose existence is not in doubt. And some of these other reasons are *prohibitum* reasons of a type, which I call "expectation-based," that we shall need to devote some time to understanding.

Before I begin the task of analyzing expectation-based reasons for compliance, I should briefly note two more familiar types of *prohibitum* reason. One important prudential general *prohibitum* reason for compliance is to avoid the (risk of) penalties that society imposes on law-breakers, whether formally through the legal system or informally through the private behavior of individuals and groups.[13] And there is also a familiar moral *prohibitum* reason for compliance when impressionable others are watching, namely, that noncompliance may be contagious. An act of noncompliance that would be unobjectionable if unobserved may nonetheless be faulted if it risks increasing the number of future impermissible and/or imprudent acts of noncompliance.[14] A witness to my unlawful act may engage in "retaliatory" law-breaking because she is angered by what she (wrongly, ex hypothesis) believes to be my straightforwardly unjustified conduct: "why should I play by the rules that I disagree with when he apparently feels free to break the ones that inconvenience him?" she may think to herself. Other witnesses may, conversely, believe that my action was justified and seek to follow my example, but if they have

[13] If John Stuart Mill's (1859/1989, p. 8) assessment is correct, fear of social stigma, disapproval, and avoidance by one's peers is often a more powerful motive for compliance than is fear of formal punishment by the state.

[14] We should also note the possibility that an act of noncompliance, even if unobserved, objectionably weakens the agent's own salutary (general and/or particular) habit of compliance. I discuss such habits at the end of this chapter.

misunderstood that example or for some other reason misapply it, they may break laws when they ought to comply.[15]

But there are other important *prohibitum* reasons for compliance, and these take the following form: you should do X given that the law leads other people to expect you to do X and leads you to expect others to do X.[16] Such expectation-based *prohibitum* reasons for compliance may be prudential or moral. For an example of the former, the expectations generated by an area's being legally off-limits may underpin a prudential reason to comply with the prohibition: lest I break my leg and find myself unable to walk, I should steer clear of areas where there are unlikely to be passers-by to discover and assist me and in which search parties will not readily think to look for me. For an example of the latter, the expectations aroused by a sign saying "do not throw stones over the cliff edge" add to my *in se* moral reason not to hurl the pebble in my hand: people are more likely to be walking on the beach below precisely because they know of the sign's existence and consequently expect to be safe from projectiles.

Expectation-based reasons for compliance appeal to the instrumental values of coordination, order, and predictability, the efficiency benefits that result when individuals and groups (including the state) devise and execute plans based on the true assumption that people will generally comply with laws that are adequately promulgated and therefore widely known. Legally enforced conventions are a way to resolve various coordination problems, that is, situations where the action that each person has most reason to perform

[15] This kind of *prohibitum* reason presupposes that the copycats will misunderstand and/or misapply the example of the person that they imitate. But they may instead be inspired to apply the example appropriately, following the original criminal's lead precisely by breaking only that particular law and doing so only in sufficiently similar circumstances. Consider, for example, a group of Americans who observe a newly-arrived European jaywalking after she checks carefully to make sure that there is no traffic anywhere nearby. If these witnesses are influenced to change their future behavior as pedestrians, why should we assume that they will start recklessly trying to cross busy streets in unauthorized places? If and when one has reason to believe that one's witnesses will be attentive to the context and nuance of one's proposed act of noncompliance, one may conclude that one's influence, if any, may be a force for good. In addition to one's prudential reasons for noncompliance, one now has moral reasons!

[16] Jeremy Waldron (1999) emphasizes reasons of this type. I assume for the sake of simplicity that the law in question mandates the same action for all persons.

depends upon the actions performed by other people. If a particular law establishes a coordinating convention that I expect others will follow and/or that others expect me to follow, those expectations will typically provide me with a reason to comply with that law.

It may be instructive to observe that expectation-based *prohibitum* moral reasons for compliance parallel the normative arguments for the rule of law. In general, the value of the rule of law (without making any assumption about the wisdom or justice of the laws) is that it enables each of us to plan her life on the basis of certain reliable assumptions about the actions of others. Accounts of the rule of law typically focus on the actions of government agents—the police and judges will proceed only according to the promulgated law—but my discussion of the expectation-based *prohibitum* reasons for compliance should remind us that we also care that the actions of private persons should be predictable in various ways. It is certainly helpful to know in advance that doing Y makes me liable for punishment by the state, but it may also be helpful to know that my neighbors will (most likely) not do Y. One person's particular act of noncompliance often imposes costs on others whose plans misfire because of frustrated expectations. And if, in a given society, compliance with law breaks down to the point where it is no longer expected, planning becomes harder and even, in some instances, impossible, severely impairing people's ability to achieve their goals. One has moral reasons not to impose these costs on others; therefore one often has moral reasons for compliance.

Of course, it is sometimes the case that the marginal costs to others of one person's noncompliance are negligible (or even zero): it would be bad if many people did not comply, but my noncompliance does not do significant (or even any) harm. But each of us may nonetheless have a moral *prohibitum* reason to comply in such cases because it would be unfair to free-ride on others' compliance. There is a moral reason to do one's fair share in sustaining a scheme of social coordination that delivers significant goods to others; that fair share often consists precisely in complying with the law oneself (Wellman, 2005, pp. 30–53; see also Lefkowitz, 2007, pp. 210–11).

Wellman (2001) argues convincingly that prudential considerations cannot coherently be combined with the moral value of fairness to generate a moral obligation not to free-ride (as is attempted by so-called fair-play theories of political obligation, according to which I ought to comply with the law because it would be disastrous for me if everyone decided not to comply).[17] These attempts at hybrid arguments fail because 1) there is no obligation to receive benefits from the political community and 2) one has not freely consented to receive the benefits and thereby acquired an obligation (of reciprocity) to do one's share to enable others to benefit.[18] In general, therefore, prudential reasons to comply with the law have to be composed *exclusively* of considerations of self-interest; appeals to fairness are out of place in such prudential reasoning. But this still leaves plenty of scope for prudential expectation-based *prohibitum* reasons to comply: if I (and only I) drive on the "wrong" side of the road, the marginal expected cost to me of that noncompliance is high.[19]

Conventions established and/or reinforced by laws are often especially effective coordination mechanisms; they enhance the predictability of actions because the threat of punishment by the state incentivizes compliance. But note two important caveats. First, when laws are not effectively enforced they may (but need not) cease to be widely followed, in which case the coordination reasons for compliance are diminished. Second, although the state typically claims and indeed may have a monopoly on the legitimate use of violence to enforce punishment for noncompliance with conventions, the state is emphatically not the only source of effective social coordination. Legitimate non-governmental actors often create conventions that are widely followed, at some times because of the reputational costs of noncompliance, at others because participants voluntarily enter into binding contracts (that the state will enforce), and in some cases entirely without the threat of punishment for noncompliance. And, of course, criminal organizations using credible threats of violence can establish and maintain conventions that exist alongside, and sometimes contradict and compete with, those conventions that are established by the law: some version of the mafia is alive and well in most societies!

[17] For classic versions of such a theory, see Hart (1955, p. 185) and Rawls (1964).

[18] The classic statements of this position are Nozick (1974, pp. 90–95) and Simmons (1979).

[19] Of course, in this case there are also clear *moral prohibitum* reasons for compliance that do not rely upon the moral argument against free-riding.

In an important subset of cases, expectation-based *prohibitum* reasons for compliance take the following form. Each person in a group has *in se* reasons to perform one of a set of discrete actions of type A, but that action could be A1, A2, or A3. For each person, which of these actions she has most reason to perform depends upon the actions performed by the other people in the group: the value of each person's action will be significantly greater if the actions are coordinated in some fashion. (Perhaps it is best for everyone to do the same thing, or perhaps the optimal coordination involves each option being enacted by a particular fraction of the population.) In a so-called pure coordination game, expectations about other people's choices provide the only reasons for each person's choice among the three options. In an "impure" game (such as the infamous "battle of the sexes"),[20] there are other reasons, but each player nonetheless has decisive reasons to value all the coordinated solutions more highly than any of the uncoordinated outcomes. If a particular law establishes a coordinating convention that I expect others will follow, then I have reason to comply with that law, even if I regard the legally established convention as suboptimal.[21]

To give a familiar example, I have *in se* moral reasons to support those less fortunate than myself, but I could do this by giving my time or money to one of any number of charities. However, given the existence of a (legally established) convention that we all pay money (taxes) into a central pot and then make collective decisions about how to distribute it among the needy, there may be strong coordination reasons for me to comply with that convention. In particular, widespread compliance makes it less likely that needy persons will be missed than if we all made private decisions about which charity to benefit with our money (or time), the likely result of which would be some form of maldistribution. In particular, in the absence of coordination, we might expect charities that help cute

[20] Waldron (1999, p. 103) calls these "Partial Conflict Coordination" games.

[21] In the impure game, if the coordinating law tells me to perform A2, it may not be in my self-interest to comply: my *in se* prudential reason to perform A1 may outweigh the *prohibitum* prudential reason to perform A2. But my moral reasons will take into account the cost to others of my noncompliance. And, even if the marginal cost of my noncompliance is negligible, considerations of fairness should underpin a moral reason to comply rather than free-ride, as discussed above.

kids to get lots of donations while rehabilitation of serious criminals languishes underfunded.[22]

The strength of these expectation-based *prohibitum* reasons to comply with the law will vary a great deal with the particular law and the particular circumstances. Sometimes it is of great (moral or prudential) value to coordinate our actions and expectations. But sometimes it is of little value, in which case such *prohibitum* reasons ought to be quite easily outweighed, and in other cases there may be no value whatsoever in coordination. The problem is that the coordination benefits of compliance can be hard to estimate. Specifically, they are often underestimated: we have *general* expectation-based reasons for compliance precisely because of our tendency not to perceive (the full force of) *particular* expectation-based reasons. It is, as we shall see, both prudent and morally appropriate to trust that the coordination benefits of compliance (to oneself and to others) are often greater than one perceives in the particular case.

Finally, having explored the important phenomenon of expectation-based reasons for compliance as well as the more familiar pair of *prohibitum* reasons grounded respectively in fear of penalties and the concern that noncompliance can be contagious, it may be instructive to examine a category of cases in which important *in se* reasons for compliance are commonly misperceived as *prohibitum* reasons. This category is best identified via an example. If I am deciding whether to smoke marijuana in a society wherein doing so is illegal, one prudential reason to abstain is uncertainty about the safety and quality of the product that is available to me. Of course, one can have similar doubts about a tobacco cigarette or any other object that one is legally permitted to consume, but the grounds for concern are typically stronger when one's action would be illegal. It might seem that this extra risk commonly associated with illegal consumption simply constitutes a *prohibitum* reason for compliance. But a narrow focus on the reasons generated by the legal prohibition fails to capture a major source of the risk.

[22] Simmons (2005, p. 154) makes a similar point. Alas, some maldistribution of this kind will often occur even when pooled resources are allocated via collective decisions, but the problem is likely to be much less severe than it would be in the absence of such a coordination scheme.

The fact that marijuana is illegal does indeed generate some special reasons to doubt that the product I buy will be safe and of high quality. Dealers in illegal drugs know that their customers will think twice before complaining to the state if they get sick after smoking a joint or if they discover that the "marijuana" they bought is actually dried spinach. Compared to providers of legal goods and services, drug dealers therefore lack one important incentive to deliver on their promises. But it is important to note that, at least in most advanced economies, many goods and services that are legal are regulated by the state in ways that extend far beyond minimal laws against false advertising and poisoning one's customers. The existence of such regulation further reduces uncertainty about the quality of the product. And it is the absence of state regulation as distinct from the legal prohibition that underpins some of the most powerful prudential reasons to comply with laws against marijuana.

To see this, consider a libertarian society in which the production, distribution, and use of marijuana are not only legal but also free from mandatory state regulation. The government of this society grants its seal of approval to those producers and distributors who voluntarily submit to and pass various government inspections and random tests. Consumers who buy and use marijuana that is not state-approved do so legally (and more cheaply) but largely at their own risk.[23] This increased risk is a reason not to use marijuana that has not been approved by the state, and *the very same reason* exists in a society that prohibits marijuana. The reason in question is not affected by marijuana's legal status. Therefore, when marijuana is illegal, the fact that its production and distribution are not regulated by the state underpins an *in se* reason for compliance.[24] And this reason may well be more powerful than the aforementioned *prohibitum* reason that is similarly grounded in concerns about the quality of the product.

[23] I say "largely" because the libertarian society still prohibits false advertising and poisoning one's customers.

[24] Of course, regardless of marijuana's legal status, there will typically be non-state organizations that "guarantee" the quality of their product. If marijuana is illegal, these guarantees will not be legally enforceable. If marijuana is legal, the guarantees will be enforceable only if they constitute legally-binding contracts.

2.1.2. Eight types of reason to comply: an example

Now that we have explored the important phenomenon of expectation-based *prohibitum* reasons for compliance, and before I proceed to examine educational strategies, it may be worth pausing to review the eight types of reason for compliance by showing via a concrete example how there could be a reason of each type to comply with a particular law. Imagine that you are hiking in Hawaii with a friend and you come to a large field of volcanic rocks. There is a sign stating: "By Order of the State of Hawaii, No Climbing on the Rocks!" Your friend has not seen the sign, and she runs towards the rocks, clearly intending to climb on them. What reasons might you offer in an effort to convince her not to do so? I label each of the eight types of reason with a letter using the scheme in Table 2.1.

If you decide to offer a reason of type A or B, you need not call your friend's attention to the sign. The particular *in se* reasons that you perceive are precisely those reasons that you would have perceived in the absence of the law. If you tell your friend that the rocks look slippery and that it's not worth taking the risk of a painful fall, you have offered a reason of type A. By contrast, if you tell her that these rocks are a valuable environmental feature and that it would be wrong to damage them, you have offered a reason of type B.

If you do draw your friend's attention to the sign, you may do so because you believe that the law's existence is good evidence that there are *in se* reasons not to climb on the rocks. You may say to your friend, "That looks like a safe and easy climb to me, but the sign makes me think that there are probably some hidden dangers," in which case you have offered a reason of type C. Or you may say, "I don't see anything special about those rocks, but if they've passed a law against climbing on them they're probably worth protecting," which is a reason of type D.

Alternatively, you may draw your friend's attention to the sign not as grounds to believe that there are *in se* reasons not to climb on the

Table 2.1 Types of reason to comply with a law

	Particular		General	
	Prudential	Moral	Prudential	Moral
In se	A	B	C	D
Prohibitum	E	F	G	H

rocks but to alert her to the expectations aroused by that sign. Thus you might offer a reason of type E: "I agree that the rocks look like a safe and easy climb, but no one else is going to be climbing on them because of this sign, so if you were to fall and injure yourself, there wouldn't be anyone to find and help you." Or you might offer the following type F reason: "Although this is not one of the best volcanic rock fields in Hawaii, it is one of the few that the government has decided to protect. It's important to preserve some volcanic fields: the best ones are very likely to be damaged because they're not legally protected, but this one stands a much better chance because the law has singled it out for protection, so we should comply with this scheme of social coordination (even though it is not the optimal scheme)."

Just as type C and D reasons for compliance may consist in invoking the sign as evidence for the existence of type A and B reasons respectively, so type G and H reasons may invoke the sign as evidence for the existence of unperceived type E and F reasons respectively. But, as I have discussed, there are other kinds of general *prohibitum* reasons. If you point to the sign and warn your friend that she may be caught by the park rangers and fined, you offer her a reason of type G. Or, if you point to the sign and then to some impressionable children who are just behind you on the trail, you are implicitly offering a type H reason: these kids may be influenced by her example to disregard signs in future instances when there are in fact compelling reasons for compliance with the posted instructions.

2.2. Cultivating reasons to comply

Now that we have systematically identified and explored the various types of reason for compliance with laws, it is time to focus on the question of education. How could education increase the number of reasons for compliance that people perceive and/or the strength that they perceive those reasons to have? Or, to state the same question more succinctly, how could education cultivate reasons to comply?[25] When I ask this, I mean to pose a philosophical question

[25] At the end of the chapter I explore the option of fostering habits of compliance as distinct from cultivating any type of reason.

about educational goals rather than an empirical question about the effectiveness of different techniques for realizing those goals. In other words, I am concerned with educational strategies but not with tactics.[26] There are three fundamental educational strategies to cultivate reasons for compliance. The first strategy is to instill beliefs, including both *moral* beliefs (i.e., beliefs about the nature and extent of the consideration we owe to others) and *non-moral* beliefs (about the expected consequences of compliance and noncompliance). The second strategy is to influence children's preferences by shaping their prudential values (including their tastes and their conception of the good). The third strategy is to inculcate trust (that the reasons to comply are often stronger and/or more numerous than the agent perceives). I shall explore each of these three strategies in turn, drawing on my typology of reasons to comply and especially on my exploration of *prohibitum* reasons to highlight the many different forms that each strategy can take.

2.2.1. Instilling beliefs

I shall assume without extensive argument that education should not promote compliance by instilling false beliefs that are expected to persist into adulthood, even if these false beliefs would improve the profile of the holder's compliance decisions. On this point I agree with the orthodox view. Adult citizens have many important decisions to make besides whether to comply with laws; not the least of these decisions are whether to retain, revise, or repeal those laws. False beliefs will systematically reduce the quality of those other decisions. As John Stuart Mill (1859/1989, pp. 25–26) famously argued, there is no long-run conflict between truth and utility that would justify preserving or reproducing false beliefs. At a minimum, this rules out educational strategies that encourage compliance by teaching children to believe propositions that we know or strongly suspect to be false when we also expect (and perhaps intend) that these beliefs will persist beyond childhood.

[26] For example, it may be that trust reasons for compliance are cultivated in children more effectively by fostering positive interactions with a diverse range of their fellow citizens than by making any explicit reference to the polity or its laws (Flanagan, 2013, p. 187). I acknowledge this possibility merely to illustrate the kind of interesting empirical/developmental question that is *not* my concern.

Some lies may well be justified as short-term expedients for promoting young children's compliance with the law. "If you eat stolen candy, your tongue will fall out." With older children who are unlikely to believe such a preposterous claim, it may even be justifiable for adults deliberately to exaggerate the risks of noncompliance by, for example, misrepresenting the scientific evidence about the harmful effects of an illegal drug or arousing the false belief that there are many hidden surveillance cameras that enable the police to catch law-breakers. Educational strategies of these kinds promise to increase rates of compliance by children. They may also be ways of inculcating habits of compliance that persist after the false beliefs have been discarded. But when the belief that is inculcated is known to be false, it must not be allowed to persist beyond childhood.

Matters get more complicated when we contemplate promoting compliance by teaching children to believe a proposition that we adults believe to be true while nonetheless recognizing a real possibility that it is false. To be clear, the issue is whether to educate children in ways that *encourage* formation of the belief as distinct from evenhandedly exposing children to the strongest arguments and evidence both for and against.[27] At this point I part company with the orthodox view. If holding the belief would improve the profile of the holder's compliance decisions, that benefit counts in favor of encouraging the belief in children, and it may outweigh the risk that the belief is false. I make an argument of this form in Chapter 7 when considering educational strategies that encourage children both to support and to comply with a particular law. The argument is even stronger for using education to instill contestable beliefs that constitute particular reasons for compliance but *not* for supporting the law in question; we shall shortly see some examples of such strategies. And the same basic argument can be made for teaching children to believe a contestable proposition that constitutes a fully *general* reason to comply with laws. This is especially important because many people take for granted that this proposition should be taught to children, and they do so precisely because they fail to recognize that the proposition is contestable. Let me explain.

[27] I explore this important distinction at much greater length in Chapter 6.

It is commonly thought that, at least in a reasonably just liberal democracy, there is a general duty to obey the law. On this view, the law has direct, albeit finite, moral force: the fact that X is legally required constitutes a significant (albeit not necessarily decisive) moral reason for action. But this view has been vigorously contested by the so-called philosophical anarchists (Simmons, 1979, pp. 93–196; Smith, 1973, pp. 950–76; Raz, 1979). How could citizens come to have such a general (albeit only *prima facie*) obligation, to obey all laws in all circumstances? Social contract theorists claim that a general obligation to obey the law arises from the duty to keep one's freely-made promises, but the anarchist observes both that very few citizens ever actually consent to obey the laws and that those who do so are often situated in conditions that render their consent insufficiently free for a binding moral obligation to result. One might think that the duty to obey the law is an example of a genuine obligation that is not voluntarily undertaken, but liberal principles greatly limit the extent of such obligations: a general duty to obey the law might appear to exceed these limits, especially given that there are cases in which my compliance would yield no benefit to others (or even to myself).

Philosophical anarchists need not and typically do not deny that there are often sufficient moral reasons to act as the law directs. Sometimes these are *in se* reasons for compliance: in favorable political conditions, the demands of the law reliably (albeit imperfectly) track those actions that we have sufficient pre-existing moral reasons to perform. But often the reasons are expectation-based *prohibitum* reasons of the kind I discussed earlier: given the importance of social order and coordination, many powerful moral reasons for action exist only because of the existence of particular laws. What morality asks of us in such cases is simply that we act in ways that are appropriately sensitive to people's (including our own) expectations about the behavior of others: laws may arouse such expectations, but, the philosophical anarchist maintains, it is only the expectations and not the laws themselves that are relevant inputs to this kind of moral reasoning in favor of compliance.[28]

[28] However, as I discuss in Chapter 3, these moral *prohibitum* reasons for compliance are weakened to the extent that the laws are (collectively or individually) unjust.

It is not my intention here to comprehensively review, let alone propose a resolution to, the important and ongoing debate about philosophical anarchism. I do believe that the anarchist position is often rejected because important trust-based and expectation-based moral reasons for compliance, which the philosophical anarchist can and should recognize, are wrongly conflated with the notion that there is a *prima facie* obligation to obey the law, which the anarchist rejects. The initially shocking claim that there is no duty to obey the law often turns out to involve a redescription rather than a repudiation of familiar reasons to comply. M.B.E. Smith (1973, p. 975) claims that this is *always* the case: on reflection, he asserts, "there is nothing startling in what I am recommending, nothing that in any way outrages common sense."[29]

But most people remain unconvinced that philosophical anarchism can accommodate all the genuine moral reasons to comply with the law. And so the question arises whether education for compliance should include instilling the belief that there is a *prima facie* general duty to obey the law. Given that, as I shall argue in the next chapter, 1) motives for compliance are rarely too strong and often too weak and 2) the philosophical anarchist's complex account of the moral reasons to comply is likely to be less motivationally efficacious than a simple belief in a general duty to obey the law, educators may well be justified in teaching children to believe in such a duty notwithstanding the non-trivial possibility that they are thereby leading children into error.

Having reviewed the possibility of promoting compliance by teaching children to believe propositions that are either known to be false or reasonably contested, I should acknowledge the important and essentially uncontroversial educational strategy of encouraging

[29] *Contra* Wellman (2005, p. 28), philosophical anarchists need not also be political anarchists, "in the streets throwing bricks and bottles in an attempt to overthrow the state." One can believe that sufficiently just and democratic states have the general moral liberty right to coercively enforce their laws without believing that citizens of such states have a general duty to obey those laws. Philosophical anarchists can recognize that, in favorable political conditions, a regime for general enforcement of the laws may be justified on balance: although there are some regrettable instances in which citizens are either deterred from or punished for performing morally permissible noncompliant actions, these costs are outweighed by the benefits of substantially decreasing the incidence of morally impermissible noncompliance. See also Simmons (2005, p. 192).

compliance by teaching children to believe propositions whose truth is not in doubt. Education should supply children with merely descriptive and true information about the possible adverse consequences for themselves or others of acts of noncompliance: "*x* Americans died from cocaine use last year," or "running a stop sign carries a $*y* fine," or "people who are hit by cars traveling at thirty-five miles per hour have a *z*% chance of dying." No doubt the selection of true information to present and the mode of its delivery both have the potential to shape children's moral beliefs: witness the intense controversy concerning how children should learn "the facts" about abortion. Descriptive information can also be imparted in ways that predictably influence the recipients' prudential values, as I shall discuss below. But it is nonetheless vital for children to learn the nonmoral facts that enable them to make informed compliance decisions.

Similarly, education should instill certain basic moral beliefs that constitute particular moral reasons for compliance with various existing laws, and doing so need neither detract from the cultivation of children's autonomy nor run the risk of inculcating false beliefs.[30] But when the shaping of moral beliefs to promote compliance goes beyond fostering the prerequisites for good moral reasoning to inculcate values that, even if they are overwhelmingly and emphatically endorsed by the adult citizens of the polity in question, can be the subject of reasonable disagreement, this will (by definition) detract from the cultivation of autonomy and introduce legitimate concerns about propagating false beliefs.[31] As I argued above, these concerns will not always constitute decisive arguments against

[30] I defended this claim in Chapter 1 with respect to the moral commitments that jointly constitute the ideal of liberal democracy: respect for the equal moral status of all persons, toleration of diverse ways of life, etc. I suspect that this ideal, properly understood, includes all the commitments that are prerequisites for moral reasoning about the treatment of persons. But the ideal of liberal democracy does not include any analogous prerequisites for reasoning about treatment of non-human animals. I assume that there are some basic moral values of this kind: for example, I do not think one compromises the cultivation of a child's autonomy by teaching her that it is wrong to inflict pain on animals solely for the pleasure of doing so.

[31] There is often reasonable disagreement about the existence and strength of moral reasons to perform (or refrain from) an action that is *certain* to have particular *known* effects on the agent's *contemporaries*. And the scope for reasonable disagreement expands even further when we consider actions whose effects are *probabilistic*, *contested*, and/or will be felt by *future generations*.

the educational strategy in question, but they must be considered alongside an assessment of the strategy's expected impact on future compliance decisions.

In some cases, instilling beliefs that constitute particular moral reasons for compliance will also encourage children to believe that the laws in question are good laws. I explore the conceptual and normative issues surrounding such status quo educational biases in Chapters 6 and 7. But, for our present purposes, it is important to see that educators can cultivate moral reasons for compliance with a particular law without necessarily thereby encouraging children to believe that it is a good law. It is obviously possible, and may often be appropriate, to tell children both that they have moral *prohibitum* reasons to comply with a particular law and that there are strong arguments that the law ought to be revised or repealed. "When the law restricts traffic to fifty miles per hour, the expectations thus aroused ground significant moral reasons not to exceed that speed, although it might be better to have a seventy mile per hour limit or even to abolish the speed limit altogether, as on the German Autobahns."

But there are other ways—besides invoking *prohibitum* reasons—to instill moral beliefs that favor compliance with a particular law without thereby encouraging support for the law. One could teach children that there are strong *in se* moral reasons to act as a particular law directs but that the law is (or may be) a bad one because it (arguably) demands supererogatory behavior. (This would be one approach to teaching children about a military draft or about European so-called Good Samaritan laws, that is, "duty to rescue" laws that mandate assisting others in certain circumstances, not the American type that merely limit the liability of those who voluntarily try to assist.) Or one might tell children that although doing Y is indeed *in se* morally prohibited, the law (arguably) oversteps the bounds of legitimate political authority. (Consider, for example, a law against adultery.) In general, since one can have strong *in se* moral reasons to comply with a particular law that one vehemently opposes, one can cultivate those reasons in children without encouraging their support for that law.

That being said, it may sometimes turn out that important reasons for compliance are, purely as a descriptive psychological matter, less motivationally efficacious for people who do not support the law (either because they think it is imperfect or because they think there should be no law on the matter). Consider a badly designed military draft that is rushed through the legislature to enable the prosecution of a just and vital war. Teachers will (ex hypothesis) minimize the number of draft-dodgers if they teach their high-school seniors to support the law and defend it against criticism, rather than merely teaching them that there are strong *in se* and *prohibitum* moral reasons to comply. When widespread compliance is of great moral importance, should we suspend the goal of teaching children to be critical of the laws? This is one of the classic questions of civic education in wartime or other emergency conditions. In Chapter 7 I shall explore and evaluate the various ways in which status quo biases in civic education can generate both rational and nonrational motives for compliance.

2.2.2. Shaping prudential values

Theorists of political obligation are rightly quick to dismiss prudential reasons for compliance as irrelevant to their task. If one's goal is to ascertain whether and when citizens have a *duty*, whether *prima facie* or all things considered, to obey the law, it is beside the point that considerations of self-interest may favor compliance in some, perhaps even in many, circumstances. But as one moves beyond the specific issue of political obligation, one discovers important normative theoretical questions about prudential reasons for compliance. One such question concerns the extent to which states should depend upon prudentially motivated compliance: Hobbes (1651/1994, p. 88) famously offered an answer to that question when he argued that, in politics, "the passion to be reckoned upon is fear" rather than any kind of moral motivation. And when we direct our attention to education, we avoid the mistake of treating as beyond our control the prudential values and resulting preferences that may dispose citizens to compliance: we illuminate important normative questions about educational practices that create and/or strengthen prudential reasons to comply with laws.

Educating children so as to provide them with particular prudential reasons for compliance is not simply a matter of giving them true descriptive information about the expected consequences of compliance and of noncompliance. Of course, as discussed above, this is a proper part of the educator's task: children ought to be given scientific evidence on the effects of drug use, for example. This essentially uncontroversial function of education merely alerts children to preexisting prudential reasons to comply. But we should also attend to the many ways in which education can change recipients' reasons (and the strength of their preexisting reasons) by shaping their prudential values, their tastes, and their conception of the good. An educational program that tells children "it's uncool to do drugs" and portrays the pleasures of drug use as debased is cultivating prudential *in se* reasons for compliance with anti-drug laws.[32] So, interestingly, is a program that conditions children to dislike the smell of marijuana.

Other common ways to cultivate prudential reasons for compliance include trying to influence the child's risk-preferences or time-preferences in particular domains.[33] Messages such as "it's not worth taking the chance that your marijuana will be contaminated" or "don't take these drugs because they'll shorten your life expectancy" go beyond presenting children with factual information about the possible effects of noncompliance to urge a particular attitude to those effects. But one can certainly cultivate prudential reasons for compliance, intentionally or otherwise, without explicitly recommending compliance. Educators cannot present students with *all* the facts that are relevant to compliance decisions; the particular subset that is presented, and the manner of presentation, may predictably have the effect of shaping children's preferences. For example, by emphasizing and graphically describing cases in which illegal abortions carried out in underground clinics have gone horribly wrong, educators predictably alter children's risk-preferences in this area and thereby cultivate prudential reasons for compliance with anti-abortion statutes.[34]

[32] As in the case of promoting compliance by instilling moral beliefs, one can cultivate prudential *in se* reasons of this kind without encouraging children to support the law in question. One might raise a child to believe in the prudential superiority of a drug-free life while also teaching her that existing anti-drug laws are unacceptably paternalistic.

[33] In the language of formal political and economic theory, risk-preferences are typically modeled as the way in which preferences over lotteries are a function not only of each lottery's expected utility but also of its variance, and time-preferences are typically modeled as the rate at which future goods and bads are discounted.

[34] Admittedly, it is not always easy to predict the ways in which particular knowledge (and the method by which it is transmitted) will affect children's preferences.

A similar analysis applies to teaching about criminal sanctions. Simply providing descriptive information about the chances of getting caught dealing drugs and the size of the legal penalties will alert children to preexisting prudential reasons for compliance, but it need not change their prudential values. Things get much more interesting for the normative theorist if this descriptive information is selected and presented in a way that encourages children to be risk-averse and/or to fear prison. We should also consider educational techniques that promote compliance by cultivating conformism, heightening the child's sensitivity to the disapproval of her fellow citizens or her discomfort with violating social conventions.[35]

Finally, as we shall see in Chapter 4, an education that arouses patriotic love and/or civic identification shapes its recipients' preferences in ways that can generate prudential reasons for compliance. Loving a polity (typically) involves regarding its well-being as an interest of the self; such love therefore constitutes a prudential reason for any act of compliance that would enhance the polity's well-being. Identifying with a polity means being susceptible to pride and shame at its actions: such identification therefore constitutes a prudential reason for any act of compliance that would increase the likelihood that the polity will act well and/or decrease the chance that it will act poorly.[36] Moreover, citizens who have been raised not only to love and/or identify with their polity but also to see compliance

[35] Educational strategies that promote conformism differ from those that would cultivate a sense of *shame* at being exposed as a law-breaker. The promotion of conformism shapes the child's conception of the good but *not* her moral beliefs. By contrast, since shame is presumably understood here in its moral sense as an appropriate response to wrong-doing, teaching children to feel ashamed when their noncompliance is made public is usually part of an effort both to instill a moral belief and to strengthen the motivational force of that belief. (If children are taught to feel shame when their noncompliance with *any* law is exposed, this is usually part of a strategy to teach them that there is a general duty to obey.)

[36] Why does identification generate *prudential* rather than *moral* reasons for compliance? Although a feeling of (moral) shame is always a response to an action that one regards as morally wrong, it does not always express the belief that one is responsible for that wrongful act. Admittedly, when one feels ashamed of *one's own* wrongful act one typically also believes that one is responsible for it, but we shall see (in Chapter 4) that it is perfectly common to feel ashamed of *one's polity's* wrongful act without believing that one bears any responsibility for that act.

with its laws as *expressive* of that affection and/or identity[37] can be understood as having an additional educationally-cultivated prudential reason to comply (Raz, 1986, pp. 54–55).[38]

2.2.3. *Inculcating trust*

Cultivating particular reasons for compliance is by its very nature an educational strategy whose effects are limited in scope. The behavior it encourages will not perfectly track the *changing* demands of the laws over a lifetime. And educators cannot address all the various existing laws about which children may have to make future compliance decisions. General reasons, by contrast, are (for better and for worse) both comprehensive in scope and durable. We have already identified several educational strategies for cultivating general reasons for compliance: teaching children to believe that there is a *prima facie* duty to obey the law; shaping their prudential values to enhance the deterrent effect of criminal sanctions and/or public disapproval; and fostering patriotic love and/or civic identification as a source of expressive reasons to comply. But there is another way in which educators can cultivate general reasons for compliance, one that does not involve instilling moral beliefs or shaping prudential values.

Even if (as philosophical anarchists claim) the fact that X is legally required is not itself a moral reason to do X, it is often a reason to *believe* that there are (unperceived) *in se* moral reasons to do X. The underlying belief is that the demands of the law somewhat reliably (albeit always imperfectly) track the actions that one has *in se* moral reasons to perform. And, although philosophical anarchists seem less keenly attuned to this possibility, there is also a corresponding category of *prohibitum* moral reasons: I believe that there are moral reasons to do X that follow from the expectations aroused by the law, although I do not perceive those reasons. In each case I *trust*

[37] In Chapter 4 I explore parallel claims about civic identification and patriotic love as sources of expressive motivation for civic actions that are *not* legally required.

[38] Elsewhere, Raz (1979, pp. 259–60) proposes that someone who identifies with a political community may thereby have not a *prudential* reason but rather an *obligation* to comply with its laws. This seems mistaken: the mere psychological fact that I identify with a community cannot affect what I owe to it and therefore cannot ground a moral reason to comply with its laws. In Chapter 4 I make an analogous argument against Yael Tamir's claim that loving a polity generates special moral reasons to contribute to its well-being.

that there are moral reasons to comply (and/or that I have not grasped the full force of the moral reasons for compliance that I do perceive). And, analogously, I may also trust that there are (*in se* or *prohibitum*) *prudential* reasons to comply; in other words, I may believe that compliance is likely to benefit me in ways that (ex ante) I either underestimate or altogether fail to see.

Prohibitum trust reasons for compliance typically do not involve trusting the law: rather, one might say that they involve trusting compliance itself. Just as I may *see* social coordination reasons to comply with a law that I regard as misguided, so may I *trust* that there are such (unseen) reasons for compliance with a different law that I similarly oppose. But *in se* trust reasons for compliance do involve trusting the law, that is, believing that its demands track the actions that I would have most reason to perform in the absence of the law. *In se* trust reasons for compliance are suggested by a well-known passage in Rousseau's *Social Contract* that explains why a citizen's freedom need not be diminished when he is compelled to comply with a law he voted against. In a well-functioning direct democracy, Rousseau (1762/1987, p. 206) tells us, if I was in the minority that opposed a law, I should assume that I was mistaken. "When . . . the opinion contrary to mine prevails, this proves merely that I was in error." In the simple case where the controversy over a legal prohibition concerns only the *in se* permissibility of the prohibited action,[39] I should trust that there is in fact a sufficient *in se*

[39] In more complex cases there are other mistakes I could have made in voting against a law that prohibits Y. I may know that Y is *in se* impermissible (or very imprudent) but have been wrong to believe that a legal prohibition on Y constitutes an illegitimate or otherwise inappropriate use of state power. Or perhaps the contested issue was not the *in se* permissibility (or prudence) of Y but rather the efficiency and fairness of solving a particular social coordination problem in a way that involves prohibiting Y: I could have been wrong in my judgment on these matters. When the contested issue is not the *in se* permissibility of Y, I often do not need to trust that I made a mistake by opposing the law in order to see good reasons for compliance (over and above the reason that is provided by the threat of state coercion). But, on Rousseau's view, when I comply for *prohibitum* reasons I have suffered a loss of freedom unless I was in fact wrong to oppose the law. It is not so clear how Rousseau would analyze the case of illegitimate use of state power to enforce an *in se* moral duty. Would he even recognize the coherence of this description? If so, is there any loss of freedom involved when the law improperly requires me to do what I already had a decisive moral reason to do? I shall have to leave these questions for Rousseau scholars to answer!

moral reason to abstain from that action, albeit I fail to perceive that particular reason (or, at least, I fail to perceive its sufficiency).[40]

In Rousseau's ideal theory, my trust in the democratic sovereign's decisions should be absolute, at least when the majority is so overwhelming as to approach unanimity, which is the sign that the citizenry remains uncorrupted. In David Estlund's (2008) terms, I should attribute "epistemic authority" to majoritarian decisions made under appropriate conditions. As we shall see in the next chapter, it seems most unlikely that any children should be taught to have absolute trust in the laws created by real-world political institutions with their many imperfections. But trust can be defeasible rather than absolute, and there is certainly often a case for using education to inculcate the former, weaker variety. As I noted in Chapter 1, children who are primarily exposed to examples of their government working at its best will tend to assume that there is wisdom congealed in its laws, whereas children whose education focuses on defects in their polity's legislative process are unlikely to develop any trust in its products.

2.3. Habits and habituation

All the preceding ways of educating for compliance involve shaping children's perceptions of the reasons that should guide their actions. People may use such perceived reasons on a case-by-case basis or by adopting a rule of thumb, a heuristic to guide their decisions about compliance. But we must also consider the nonrational motives of habit that educators could instill in children,[41] habits of complying with the law in general and/or with particular laws.[42]

[40] And, Rousseau would add, that reason is *mine*, i.e., it is my own higher will such that I suffer no loss of freedom when I am required to act in accordance with it.

[41] The habits that concern me here are motives that function independently of perceived reasons for action, *not* habits (such as those encouraged by Aristotelian moral education) of attending and responding to certain types of reason. I explored this distinction in Chapter 1.

[42] As I note in Chapter 4, fostering a particular habit will often also arouse a taste for the action in question; therefore, fostering particular habits of compliance will often have the additional effect of generating particular *in se* prudential reasons for compliance.

This distinction between general and particular habits of compliance is important: habituating children to do whatever the law requires is very different from habituating them to perform (or refrain from) certain actions that the law presently requires (or prohibits). Given that laws can change, the latter strategy could only be wise for laws that fall into one of two categories: either we have a high degree of confidence in the *in se* reasons for compliance (e.g., the law against assault) or the principal reasons for compliance are *prohibitum* and the law is very unlikely to change (e.g., the laws requiring motorists to drive on the right in the United States).

A single example will illustrate both particular and general habits of compliance. Sally is an American philosophical anarchist on vacation in France. It is her first trip outside the United States. Sally is driving her rental car and is just about to enter an intersection when the traffic light goes red. She stamps on the brakes. This was, we may assume, an instinctive reaction, a habitual response rather than a reasoned decision. And it was clearly motivated by a *particular* habit of compliance: Sally certainly did not have time to recognize that it would be illegal to drive through the red light and thereby to activate any general habit of compliance with laws.

Having screeched to a halt, Sally looks around carefully and discerns that it would be safe for her to make a right turn while the light remains red. But, just as she is about to do so, she remembers that French law, unlike the various state laws in her home country, prohibits right turns on red. She removes her foot from the gas pedal and waits for the light to go green. Why? As a philosophical anarchist, Sally sees no moral reason not to proceed. She is confident that there are no police officers or traffic cameras watching her, so she sees no prudential reason not to proceed. And she has no particular habit of refraining from making a safe right turn on red: she could not have developed such a habit because (back in America) she routinely makes safe right turns on red. But she does have a general habit of complying with laws, and it is this general habit that motivates her to wait.

If we extend this same example a little we can illustrate another important feature of habitual motives for compliance. Sally waits at the red light for twenty seconds. Then, although the light is still red, and after checking that it is still safe to do so, she steps on the gas and turns right. Why? After a short period of reflection, the various reasons that Sally perceives for making the turn on red proved motivationally strong enough to outweigh her continuing instinctual reluctance to break the law. I am most interested in situations, like this one, in which a person has time to think and thereby arrive at reasons for action (whether or not those reasons prove to be motivationally efficacious when pitted against habitual motives). Compliance decisions will often be determined by a combination of habitual and rational motives. But we shall see that one possible advantage of a habit of compliance arises precisely when habit preempts reasoning: compliance in those cases imposes no decisional costs on the agent whereas all rational action involves some such costs, although these may be minimal when one acts on trust reasons.

Inculcating a general habit of compliance is different from cultivating trust reasons to comply. Habit is a nonrational motive; trust is a belief that reasons to comply are often unseen or underestimated. If one trusts that there are moral reasons to comply, there is no guarantee that one will have sufficient moral motivation to give these reasons appropriate weight, or even any weight. In addition, the motivational power of habit cannot in the short term be nullified by reasons (although it can be outweighed), but a trust reason for compliance can potentially be so nullified in particular cases. In this sense, a trust reason is like a rule of thumb and unlike a habit: the motivational force of a rule of thumb is nullified when one stops carefully to consider the decision and has a high degree of confidence in one's resulting judgment, whereas the motivational force of a habit persists after rational reflection. This persistence of habitual motives is both their beauty and their curse.

Having emphasized the distinction between habits and trust reasons, I should nonetheless acknowledge that someone who regularly acts on trust reasons is likely to develop a general habit of compliance (and therefore that teaching children to comply on trust will tend to produce such a habit in them). It may also happen that someone who trusts the law will *decide* to develop a habit of compliance or, perhaps more likely, to reflectively endorse and even strengthen the habit that she finds herself to have acquired. In such cases, the agent rationally affirms her own habit as a counterbalance to her self-acknowledged tendency to underestimate (and/or derive insufficient motivation from) the reasons for compliance when she makes decisions (especially but not only when there is insufficient time for reflection).

As we shall see in Chapter 3, reflective endorsement of a habit may confer intrinsic value on the motivation it provides. Note, however, that reflective endorsement does not mean that the habit is under the agent's control: she might well have continued to experience the habitual motives even if she had determined that the habit was an undesirable feature of her psychology. In colloquial English we talk of "quitting the habit" (of smoking) when we mean simply ceasing to perform the action for which one experienced *and may continue to experience* habitual motivation. One can "quit the habit" by finding other motivations that are strong and reliable enough to outweigh its urges. But *eliminating* a habit entails no longer feeling those urges.

Finally, it is important to see that habits can masquerade as reasons and therefore that educational methods that instill nonrational motives for compliance can be mistaken for or misrepresented as the cultivation of reasons. In this context we might recall the argument that identification with and/or affection for a polity can generate reasons for compliance with its laws. It is surely true that some instances of compliance are motivated by such reasons, but we must be careful not to attribute reasoning where none truly exists. Consider a person who is repeatedly told in school: "If you love your country, follow the law!" This educational strategy might appear to be an attempt to provide children with reasons for compliance. After all, a child who is successfully educated in this way will have a ready answer when asked why in some particular instance she acted in accordance with the demands of the law. "Because I love my country," she will say. But the fact that she gives this answer does not show that she acted on a reason, any more so than my saying "I blinked because you punched the air in front of my face" shows that my blinking was a rational action rather than an instinctual response.

Of course, her response suggests that she believes that she was acting on a reason, whereas mine does not. But this inference may be mistaken. And even if it is not, her belief may be false. Assuming that the citizen in question truly loves her country, the key question is whether two further conditions are satisfied. First, does she know and endorse (or at least trust in the existence and validity of) an argument that purports to deduce a reason to comply with the law from love of country? Second, did the agent's conscious invocation of that argument (or of a heuristic that she adopted because she endorses the argument) significantly motivate her compliance in this case?[43] If either of these conditions does not obtain, it is misleading to say that the agent's compliance was (directly) motivated by a reason grounded in her love of country. But, as I discussed a moment ago, it is possible that there is an indirect relationship: it could be that the agent acted from a habit that she reflectively endorses on account of her belief that her love of country yields a general reason to comply with its laws.

2.4. Conclusion

Aristotle (1984, Book 3, Chapter 4) tells us that citizenship is a matter both of ruling and of being ruled. How could we prepare children for the second component of that role? I have argued that the idea of educating children in ways that conduce to their compliance with the laws of their polity must be disaggregated into nine different motives for compliance (eight types of reason plus habit) that could be cultivated through education. And I have used this analysis to explore the four fundamental educational strategies for promoting compliance: instilling beliefs, including both *moral* beliefs and *non-moral* beliefs; shaping prudential values; inculcating trust (that the reasons to comply are often stronger and/or more numerous than the agent perceives); and fostering general and/or particular habits of compliance. In the next chapter I propose a framework for evaluating these four strategies in terms of their impact on recipients' future compliance decisions.

[43] We should not insist that the motivation provided by the argument was either necessary or sufficient to explain the action. Other perceived reasons for action may well have been necessary and/or (jointly) sufficient. And, importantly, an action qualifies as rational whenever the various perceived reasons provided sufficient motivation, even if there was also a sufficient nonrational motive.

CHAPTER 3

Evaluating education for compliance: a cost-benefit analysis

In Chapter 2, I identified and analyzed the four fundamental educational strategies for promoting compliance. Three of these strategies—shaping prudential values, inculcating trust, and habituation—are straightforwardly incompatible with the orthodox view of civic education because they compromise the goal of preparing children to be autonomous citizens. And this same goal places severe limits on the remaining strategy, instilling beliefs. My principal claim in this chapter is that the orthodoxy's highly restrictive view of permissible education for compliance is deeply misguided. My argument has two essential components. First, I argue that the orthodox view, were it ever actually to be implemented, would not come close to producing the very high rate of compliance with laws that is morally required in a reasonably just liberal democracy. And I explain how the various strategies I identify—especially those that the orthodox view rejects outright—would do a great deal better in this respect. This establishes a *prima facie* case for abandoning the orthodox view.

Second, I systematically identify the various costs associated with educational strategies that sacrifice autonomy for the sake of compliance. In Chapter 2 I noted that promoting compliance by instilling contestable beliefs can have highly undesirable *side-effects* if the beliefs are in fact false: even if these false beliefs improve the holder's compliance decisions, they may cause him to make poor decisions of many other types. In this chapter I acknowledge that the *direct* effects of education for compliance can also be undesirable. But these direct costs are often surprisingly difficult to locate and describe. The principal challenge is to identify the various ways in which compliance can be suboptimal despite being morally permissible. I focus especially on acts of compliance that are not morally required and that either fail to express the agent's own judgment or express a judgment that reflects inauthentic preferences or false beliefs.

Complementing the familiar concept of unjustified noncompliance (a "false negative") with a careful treatment of the other kind of error, suboptimal compliance (a "false positive"), my account thus explains precisely why it matters if we educate people to comply with laws even when they are not morally obligated to do so. In addition, I suggest that when compliance is morally required, it matters not only *whether* but also (to some degree) *why* people comply. In conclusion, I shall argue that the costs of education for compliance can be considerable and certainly place limits on the use of highly aggressive strategies but that they cannot plausibly be seen as outweighing the benefits of moderate deviations from autonomy-maximizing education. To emphasize an important point I made in Chapter 1, I am *not* claiming that there is at present, in the United States or elsewhere, a general deficiency of education for compliance. My point is rather that, *contra* the contemporary theoretical orthodoxy, we *should* educate children in various ways that encourage nonautonomous compliance (while being appropriately sensitive to the costs of doing so).

3.1. The limits of autonomous motivation

What would education for compliance look like if it was limited to strategies that do not detract from the development of children's autonomy? As we saw in Chapter 2, it would amount to no more than instilling those beliefs that it would be irrational and/or unreasonable to reject. Children would be taught certain plain facts about the expected consequences of compliance and noncompliance as well as the set of very basic universal values that are the prerequisites for sound moral reasoning. For most people, the autonomous and informed (albeit often imperfect) moral reasoning that would be facilitated by such an education would generate sufficient motives for compliance in a significant number of decision contexts. And, even without having been shaped for the purpose, most people's prudential values will often yield net reasons for compliance: at the very least, most people will be significantly averse to risk in general and to prison and monetary fines in particular. So I do not mean to suggest that the orthodox prescription for promoting compliance would lead to anarchy. But it is pure fantasy to suppose that it would generate anything close to the very high levels of compliance that are morally required in realistically favorable political conditions.

Because prudential values often favor a particular act of noncompliance over compliance even (and sometimes especially) when one is well informed about the expected consequences of both options, the orthodox view depends very heavily on both the quality of people's autonomous moral reasoning and the motivational force of the perceived reasons for compliance that emerge from that process of moral reflection. In short, the orthodox view expects ordinary people to be both geniuses and saints. It prescribes an education that aspires to teach us (no more than) the basic principles of morality plus as many uncontestable non-moral facts about particular acts of compliance and noncompliance as time and competing educational priorities will allow. Equipped only with what we managed to glean from such an education, we are expected to deduce both the particular moral reasons for compliance with a polity's many laws and the extent to which there are general, trust-based moral reasons for compliance with laws of various kinds. And, even less realistically, we are supposed to experience these moral reasons for compliance as so compelling that we very rarely succumb to the temptation to pursue our prudential values through morally impermissible acts of noncompliance.[1] Most people will fall far short of these lofty expectations.

Rates of unjustified law-breaking would doubtless be lower if we relaxed the orthodox view's restrictions on transmitting beliefs. If education for compliance included teaching children to believe various moral and non-moral propositions that, although not uncontestable, are well warranted, it would make fewer and

[1] Someone who is aware of this weakness in his moral motivation could autonomously decide to develop in himself various habits of compliance. But I shall argue later in this chapter that leaving individuals to make and act on their own autonomous judgments about the desirability of habits of compliance will systematically yield fewer and weaker habits than would be morally optimal.

more realistic demands on its recipients' capacity for moral reasoning. For example, as I noted in Chapter 2, a person whose education successfully instilled the belief that there is a *prima facie* duty to obey the law will always perceive this simple general moral *prohibitum* reason for compliance, whereas he will often fail to perceive (the full force of) all the particular expectation-based moral *prohibitum* reasons.[2] This is especially important in complex societies wherein many wrongful acts of noncompliance are not *mala in se*: the particular moral reasons to refrain from performing these acts can often only be appreciated via complex appeals to the hypothetical consequences of widespread noncompliance or to the harms potentially caused by frustrating the expectations of unseen and distant others. Furthermore, if we are willing to trade off autonomy against compliance, we can tailor a citizen's education for compliance to the established laws of her polity. Someone who was taught to believe in the merits of the jury system is more likely to perceive particular moral reasons to comply when called for jury duty than someone whose civic education scrupulously avoided all such bias.[3]

Relaxing the restriction on belief transmission would certainly constitute an improvement on the pure orthodox view, but it would still leave unresolved the more serious problem with that view, namely, its faith that perceived moral reasons will translate into robust motivation. Moral reasons, even when they are accurately perceived in their full force, are notoriously weak and unreliable motives. And we should be mindful of the human tendency to self-deception whereby a dearth of moral motivation leads us conveniently not to see (the full force of) moral reasons. Most people prefer not to believe that they are acting wrongly, and we are often remarkably adept at finding ways to satisfy that preference while performing acts for which we would readily condemn a stranger or an enemy.

Education could do more to reduce rates of unjustified law-breaking by shaping children's prudential values, inculcating trust reasons to comply, and forming habits. Let us see how this is so.

[2] He is also, as we shall shortly see, unlikely to be fully aware of these deficiencies in his particular judgments and therefore unable to fully compensate for them by acknowledging trust reasons for compliance.

[3] I explore these issues at greater length in Chapter 7.

3.2. Beyond belief

Shaping children's prudential values to favor compliance has the potential to compensate for the motivational inadequacy of moral reasons that are normatively sufficient: in other words, this educational strategy may be justified if it gets people more often to do the right thing (albeit not for the right reasons, as we shall discuss later in the chapter). But, of course, even if a person's prudential values have been extensively manipulated to encourage compliance, her prudential reasoning will still realistically favor noncompliance in a significant number of cases, especially those in which she calculates that noncompliance is very unlikely to be detected and punished. In most of these cases, presumably, noncompliance would be morally wrong.[4] So educators would have special cause for caution if the cultivation of prudential reasons for compliance tended to diminish the strength of moral motives for compliance, much as the introduction of material incentives for prosocial behavior may "crowd out" intrinsic motives for that same behavior (Frey and Jegen, 2001). This is an important empirical question: if there is no such trade-off, cultivating prudential reasons for compliance may not lead to any instances of unjustified noncompliance. There is obviously no conceptual incompatibility between prudential and moral reasons to comply. But in pedagogical practice, cultivating the former may tend to detract from cultivating the latter. And, as a practical matter of human psychology and moral development, cultivating prudential reasons to comply with the law may encourage children to place more weight on their self-interest in general, including in cases when self-interest is best served by noncompliance, and less on moral reasons in general, whether those moral reasons count in favor of compliance or noncompliance.

But notice that the goal of educators in cultivating self-interested reasons to comply with the laws is presumably *not* to make children more selfish in the sense of rendering their prudential reasons more motivationally efficacious. Rather, it is to (re)direct children's selfish motivations, which are presumed to be strong enough already. The

[4] We should also note, and I shall shortly discuss, the potential for prudential motives to lead to the opposite type of moral error, namely, failure to act on a moral obligation to *break* the law.

educational strategy is twofold: first, shape children's conceptions of their self-interest in ways that favor compliance, and second, as we shall shortly see, bring them to *trust* that compliance serves their self-interest. By contrast, when educators try to cultivate moral reasons for compliance, they presumably do try to strengthen children's motivational commitment to morality more generally.[5] In this sense, educators are trying to make children *less* selfish, even if they also try to cultivate prudential reasons for compliance.

The primary justification for shaping children's prudential values to favor compliance must be that it promises to reduce rates of impermissible noncompliance. But we should also consider whether shaping children's prudential values to be easier and less costly to realize, given the particular laws of their polity, is a justified form of paternalism. Little Bobby likes the taste of marijuana, and he enjoys taking his clothes off in public. I may think that these are perfectly innocuous pleasures, that they ought to be legal, and that there are no weighty moral *prohibitum* reasons to refrain from indulging in them. But I recognize that Bobby will get into trouble with the law if he smokes marijuana or exposes himself and that he will be miserable if he does not realize his desires, so it would be better for him if I manipulated his tastes such that he has *in se* prudential reasons for compliance with the laws in question.[6] Admittedly, his resulting preferences may be inauthentic, but he will find it easier to satisfy them.[7]

[5] But see my forthcoming discussion of the ways in which supererogatory compliance can be suboptimal, even when morally motivated.

[6] This argument is analogous to Bruce Ackerman's (1980, p. 148) claim that one may be justified in instilling self-control in a child, at some cost to her present freedom, because doing so will "increase the youth's capacity to remain free of the special restrictions imposed on aggressive adults by the criminal law." It sometimes appears that Ackerman regards this paternalistic rationale as the *only* justification for instilling self-control in children. His principle of neutrality entails that "authority over children is not justified by adult pretensions to moral superiority" (p. 148); apparently this means that when children do not share their parents' belief that violence is presumptively wrong, the parents cannot appeal to the wrongness of violence to justify teaching their children not to be violent. This strikes me as absurd. As I have already emphasized, I regard paternalism as at most an auxiliary justification for shaping children's prudential values to favor compliance: the primary justification of such educational practices must be that they reduce rates of morally impermissible noncompliance.

[7] I shall address the normative questions raised by inauthentic preferences later in the chapter.

Let us now turn to inculcation of trust. In the absence of trust reasons to comply, and leaving aside for a moment the potential force of habits, people will act in some noncompliant way whenever they privately judge that they have most reason to do so. There are two questions we must ask about the consequences of introducing trust reasons for compliance. First, will such reasons be motivationally efficacious? And second, if they do make a difference to people's actions, will the change be for the better? Let us address each question in turn.

Recall that trust can generate both *in se* and *prohibitum* reasons for compliance. One might be especially dubious about the motivational efficacy of *in se* trust reasons. We can illustrate this concern by revisiting Rousseau's classic characterization of trust in democratic decisions. "When . . . the opinion contrary to mine prevails, this proves merely that I was in error." Rousseau's claim is *not* that a democratic decision can and should prompt me to reexamine the issue and discover the substantive error underlying my opposition to the decision. Rather, Rousseau asserts that (under appropriate conditions) my trust in the democratic process should override my *continuing* judgment that the decision was wrong. How likely is it that someone who remains (in his private judgment) convinced of the *in se* permissibility of Y will be significantly motivated to refrain from Y by his general belief that he often fails to perceive and/or underestimates the *in se* moral reasons for compliance with laws?[8] Perhaps this is why Rousseau does not even consider the *motivational* power of trust, focusing instead on the need to *force* dissenting citizens to be free.

On the other hand, we should recognize that trust reasons can function by preempting rather than overriding private judgment: when trust reasons for compliance are not competing with private judgments, there is every reason to think that they can be motivationally efficacious. And, even when an agent has formed a private judgment that noncompliance is both permissible and prudent, it is not hard to imagine that judgment's being outweighed motivationally by the agent's trust that her judgment neglected or underestimated some *prohibitum* reasons to comply. As we saw in Chapter 2,

[8] We could also ask the parallel question about prudential reasons for action.

expectation-based *prohibitum* reasons are often numerous and complex, and it is perfectly realistic to expect that people will act on their belief that they are unlikely to have fully grasped all of these considerations favoring compliance.

Assuming, then, that trust reasons can motivate people to comply even when their private judgments (would) favor noncompliance, we must still ask whether the resulting increased compliance can be expected to constitute an improvement. The answer is likely to depend on the *degree* of trust. In a real-world contemporary representative democracy, which differs in so many important respects from Rousseau's ideal direct democracy and wherein very few laws enjoy anything approaching unanimous support among citizens or their elected representatives, Rousseau's arguments hardly recommend blind faith in the laws. But we may nonetheless think that the typical citizen has grounds for defeasibly trusting the judgment of her peers as it emerges from the democratic system (including the *prima facie* undemocratic institutions that are ultimately regulated by and accountable to citizens and their representatives). To the extent that the system operates in majoritarian fashion, we might, for example, be moved by some variant on Condorcet's jury theorem, his famous mathematical observation that if each citizen is more than 50 percent likely to vote correctly then a large electorate's majority decision is overwhelmingly likely to be correct.[9]

Admittedly, for some small number of persons whose private judgment is particularly poor and who are unable to identify a more reliable authority than the laws, a simple policy of absolute compliance with those laws might be the best strategy for acting in accordance with the balance of reasons that would ideally guide one's judgment in each decision about compliance.[10] But I suspect that the problems associated with accurately identifying the set of such persons are acute enough that we should adopt the same educational approach for all children. And that approach will fall well short of inculcating blind trust in the laws. In other words, civic education should never foreclose the possibility that a person will

[9] There has recently been a resurgence of interest in Condorcet's jury theorem among political theorists. See, for example, List and Goodin (2001).

[10] Here I am guided by Raz's (1988, pp. 53–57) idea of the "normal justification" of authority.

say to herself: "I've thought about this decision carefully and I cannot see any particular reasons to comply. I am therefore dismissing general reasons of trust, and I shall make my decision simply by weighing the particular reasons for noncompliance against the remaining general reasons for compliance: fear of punishment and (perhaps) the duty of obedience."

The delicate question for the educator is therefore how strongly and across what range of cases children should be taught to trust the laws or to believe that there are probably unseen or underappreciated *prohibitum* reasons to comply. How much confidence should children be encouraged to have in their own judgments (both while they remain children and once they become adults)? How do we identify the virtuous mean of *humility* between the opposite vices of hubris and excessive deference? The individual agent has the benefit of knowing the particular circumstances in which the compliance decision must be made: the law is a generalization, and these may be exceptional circumstances. The agent may be able reliably to recognize exceptional circumstances, and in such cases he should have a higher degree of confidence in his private judgment. But laws will generally be informed by much greater expertise and breadth of perspective than is an individual's private judgment. It is especially difficult for a private citizen to anticipate all the coordination costs resulting from her own (or widespread) noncompliance. Private judgments are always liable to be colored by one's self-interested biases, although the law may be distorted by different biases that are at least as morally important. And finally, as I shall shortly discuss, some people believe that there is intrinsic prudential value to acting on one's own (first-order) judgments rather than deferring to the judgments of others (as articulated through the law, in this case).

Of course, each person could be educated in ways that would empower and encourage her to make her own autonomous judgments about the extent to which, for each broad category of laws, the particular reasons for compliance are typically stronger and/or more numerous than she will perceive. This would be the orthodox view's preferred approach. But it strikes me as profoundly unwise, even reckless, to entrust these complex judgments to each individual's undirected reason rather than using education to shape children's beliefs in accordance with the collective and accumulated experience and wisdom in the polity.[11] If children are evenhandedly presented with evidence and arguments that, on balance, ought to persuade them that people tend to overlook and underestimate reasons for compliance, there is no guarantee that the children will actually be so persuaded.[12] And, in familiar psychological fashion, even those individuals who acknowledge the general tendency are likely to believe groundlessly that they themselves are exceptions to it and therefore to retain excessive confidence in their private judgment concerning compliance decisions.[13] Hence there is a strong *prima facie* case for using civic education to cultivate trust reasons for compliance rather than encouraging and equipping people to make autonomous and informed judgments about the existence and strength of such reasons.

Educators should cultivate trust in those domains where, and to the extent that, such cultivation yields an improvement in the expected profile of actions that citizens will perform over the course of their lives. I intend this to sound like a truism. But I shall add some content to it very soon, when I identify the various ways in which decisions about compliance can be suboptimal: as we shall see, trust reasons for compliance almost certainly avert more moral errors than they cause, but regrettably they also inhibit citizens from acting on their own particular judgments in cases when both compliance and noncompliance are morally permissible.

Before I turn to this analysis of suboptimal compliance decisions, I want to complete the *prima facie* case for deviating from the orthodox view of education for compliance by briefly explaining how some degree of habituation to comply with laws promises to improve the profile of a person's future compliance decisions. Given that cases in which noncompliance is permissible are very much the

[11] I argue at length for a closely related position in Chapter 7's defense of status quo biases in civic education. There I also argue that status quo educational biases should be retrospectively disclosed to avoid the problem of each generation's unknowingly ratcheting up the level of bias in the next generation's civic education. For parallel reasons, this kind of retrospective disclosure would also be appropriate with respect to the practice of preempting or bypassing children's rational capacities to instill the belief that reasons for compliance are often unseen or underestimated.

[12] In Chapter 7 I make a parallel observation about the teaching of evolution.

[13] This is simply one instance of the well-documented cognitive bias that psychologists call the "illusory superiority effect;" it is also a manifestation of the equally well-established "overconfidence effect."

exception rather than the rule, habits of compliance will clearly be valuable when there is insufficient time to reason. But, even when there is no such time constraint, a habit of compliance may correct for predictable shortfalls of moral motivation, the inadequacy of the motives of trust and fear of punishment, and agents' characteristic failure to see (the full force of) all the expectation-based reasons for compliance. Habituation is a blunt instrument, especially when we contemplate fostering *general* habits of compliance, but for some tasks one needs a hammer rather than a needle.

On this view, when faced with a series of decisions about whether to comply with particular laws in particular cases, people will tend to make better choices (in terms of fulfilling their moral duties, and perhaps even satisfying their preferences[14]) if they have to overcome psychological, even physiological, discomfort in order to break a law.[15] Many of us were raised such that we experience this kind of discomfort, for better and for worse. It keeps us on the straight and narrow at times when we might otherwise stray. But sometimes it gets in the way of justifiable acts that serve one's self-interest in some small way: jaywalking on a deserted street, for example. And, in more serious cases, it may prevent one from participating in an important campaign of civil disobedience. As we shall see in Section 3.3, the habit of compliance would ideally be strong enough always to motivate compliance that is morally required when rational motives fail, but it would also be weak enough that it can be overridden whenever noncompliance is morally required as well as in many cases when noncompliance is supererogatory or merely permissible. In practice, of course, no habit of compliance could meet this ideal standard: most habits will simultaneously be too strong for certain decision contexts and too weak for others.

Why should educators habituate children to comply rather than equipping those children to make and act upon their own judgments about the extent to which such habits are desirable? As I noted above in my discussion of trust, people routinely overestimate the quality of their own judgment; they will therefore tend to

[14] Again, recall Ackerman (1980, p. 148). Habituating children to some degree to comply with the law may be a justified form of paternalism.

[15] By psychological discomfort I mean a feeling of unease that one cannot shake; by physiological discomfort I refer to nervous shivers, sweaty palms, and the like.

underestimate their need for habits to correct systematic errors therein. Children, and especially teenagers, are especially prone to make this mistake. And, although adults will often see and try to correct the more egregious of these mistakes that they made in their youth, the delay in habituation efforts promises to be very costly both because habits are most effectively formed during childhood and because people are confronted with all manner of important compliance decisions before they reach adulthood.[16]

3.3. The costs of educating for compliance

So far in this chapter I have argued that the goal of reducing rates of impermissible noncompliance with laws is best served by rejecting the orthodox view's strict limits on education for compliance and instead utilizing a set of educational strategies that diverge from the path of maximizing children's future autonomy. But this evidently only tells a part (albeit, I shall argue, much more than half) of the story. What are the costs of more aggressive compliance-promotion strategies? We have already seen that one of these strategies has undesirable side-effects, by which I mean bad consequences that we will not see if we look only at the effects on compliance. I acknowledged in Chapter 2 that these side-effects can be sufficiently bad that we should reject the strategy that produces them even if it also improves the profile of recipients' compliance decisions. Specifically, I argued that instilling false beliefs has such broad and negative consequences, especially in a democratic society, that we should never teach children to believe propositions that are known (or even strongly suspected) to be false unless we are justifiably confident that these false beliefs will not persist beyond childhood. But I also argued that the prospect of improved compliance decisions can outweigh even a significant risk that we are unwittingly leading children into error when we teach them to believe propositions that we ourselves accept and are warranted in

[16] Even if (as seems to me most unlikely) a general habit of compliance is undesirable in adults, such a habit is surely strongly desirable in children, and it may well be impossible to eradicate once it exists. And, if all this were true, it is not implausible that the benefits during childhood would outweigh the costs during adulthood.

accepting. I suggested that "there is a general *prima facie* duty to comply with the law" may be an example of such a proposition.

But what would count as improving the profile of someone's compliance decisions? Reducing the incidence of impermissible noncompliance is certainly one important desideratum, but it is not the only one. We also rightly care about the decisions people make when noncompliance is permissible. And, I shall argue, even when compliance is morally required, not all acts of compliance are equal: we should attach some intrinsic value to moral motivation. Compliance promotion can have undesirable *side*-effects, to be sure, but some of its *direct* effects will also be undesirable. For some or conceivably even all educational strategies that generate nonautonomous motives for compliance, these direct costs could outweigh the benefits of reducing rates of impermissible law-breaking.

In this section, I therefore propose a comprehensive framework for evaluating educational policies and practices by their effects on the next generation's decisions regarding compliance.[17] An obvious place to start—but only to start—is with the observation that, *ceteris paribus*, we should prefer programs of education that lower their recipients' propensity to perform morally impermissible actions when they must decide whether to comply with a law, especially in important cases. Such moral errors come in two types. Most familiarly, there are acts of impermissible noncompliance: stealing without adequate justification, for example. These are the acts that have understandably preoccupied us so far in this chapter. But there are also errors of the opposite type, that is, acts of compliance when noncompliance is morally required.

Uncontroversial examples of impermissible compliance are hard to find in reasonably just states, but a likely candidate would be

[17] Although I previously invoked effects beyond compliance decisions to rule out teaching children to believe propositions that we know (or strongly suspect) to be false, henceforth I narrow my focus to education's effects on compliance decisions. I simply cannot systematically explore all the possible side-effects of every compliance-promotion strategy. But I certainly do not mean to deny the importance of such side-effects. As I discussed in Chapter 1, the educational tools we use to pursue worthy goals are always crude: they should not be deployed without attending to their unintended but predictable effects. So, for example, we should not promote compliance with laws by arousing general conformism and risk-aversity without first evaluating the broader implications of encouraging these character traits.

abiding by the speed limit en route to a hospital on an empty road while one's injured and unconscious passenger bleeds to death. More controversial examples might include journalists revealing the identity of their sources or doctors passing confidential medical records to the government as required by an unjust homeland security law.[18] Especially in reasonably just societies, there are few instances in which noncompliance is morally *required*. Even when a law is unjust, compliance is often permissible; I usually do no wrong by complying with an excessively demanding law. And in those exceptional circumstances where it is permissible not to comply with a just law, noncompliance is again rarely a duty. Although it will sometimes be permissible to break a law on the grounds that one believes it would be unconscionable to comply, such acts of conscientious objection are only obligatory when the agent's belief is objectively true. And the moral reasons to engage in civil disobedience, even when the cause is just, are very rarely strong enough to override not only the opposing moral reasons but also the agent's general moral permission not to perform an action that would be morally best—a permission that often exists even when there are no compelling prudential reasons for the agent not to act in the morally preferred way.[19]

Thus, in those cases in which compliance is suboptimal, the suboptimality will not typically consist in failure to do one's duty. We must look elsewhere to find the bulk of "false positives" that education for compliance is liable to produce. In particular, we must consider cases in which noncompliance is morally permitted but not required (although it may be supererogatory). Compliance in such cases may be suboptimal in one of two ways. In the first, the suboptimality lies in the fact that the act of compliance fails to express, and often contradicts, the agent's own judgment as to what there was most reason to do. Call this problem *failure of judgment*. (Either the agent fails to make her own judgment or her judgment fails to determine her action.) The second form of

[18] The controversy regarding whether these actions are morally impermissible remains even if we stipulate that the law is unjust because there may be *prohibitum* reasons (including aversion to punishment) that render compliance at least permissible.

[19] It is this general permission that makes conceptual space for supererogation and prevents morality's demands from intruding intolerably on each person's freedom to live as she chooses.

suboptimality arises when, although the act of compliance expresses the agent's judgment, that judgment is flawed because it is grounded in inauthentic preferences or false beliefs. Call this problem *defective judgment*. I shall examine each of these two *problems of judgment* in turn.

3.3.1. *Failure of judgment*

Failure of judgment occurs when an agent refrains from an act of permissible noncompliance for which her own assessment of the particular reasons for action would provide sufficient motivation, were it not for the force with which her habits and/or trust reasons incline her to compliance. Both habits and trust reasons can generate failures of judgment either by preempting or by outweighing the agent's own assessment of the particular reasons for action. As examples, consider a person who refrains from illegally smoking marijuana or performing a particular act of civil disobedience only because of her (ex hypothesis, misplaced) trust that there are strong reasons for compliance that she fails to perceive. Or, alternatively, she may have confidence in her judgment that the balance of reasons favors noncompliance, but those reasons are less motivationally efficacious than her habits of compliance.

The suboptimality of actions that constitute a failure of judgment relies on the normative premise that there is value in persons' acting on their own judgments when doing so is morally permissible. This value is often seen as *instrumental*. For example, John Stuart Mill (1859/1989, pp. 76–77) argued that each person is the best judge of his own interests and of actions intended to advance those interests. But even the best judge is not infallible. And there is certainly no guarantee that people's preferences and moral judgments will reliably impel them to supererogation. In short, the particular reasons that an agent perceives may sometimes call for noncompliance that, although permissible, is foolish and/or selfish.

Turning first to foolishness, noncompliance in a particular case may be permissible but deeply unwise. Consider, for example, a man who ignores the "Danger—No Entry!" sign and consequently plunges to his death—if only we had taught him to trust signs or obey them out of habit! Should we regret the dominance of habit and trust in cases when these motives lead to compliance that is morally permissible and clearly best serves the agent's interests?

Turning next to selfishness, we should consider cases in which compliance is supererogatory. For example, imagine particular circumstances in which there are moral reasons to comply with a European "Good Samaritan" law but compliance would be so demanding as to go beyond the call of duty. If I comply only because of the strength of my habitual or trust motives for compliance, is this a regrettable failure to live according to my own judgments?[20] Or consider the case in which my habits of compliance are so powerful that I adhere to the speed limit while driving to the hospital despite the fact that *I* am bleeding heavily. Or I abide by an unreasonably demanding curfew law simply because of my trust in the government. These are all, ex hypothesis, cases in which compliance is supererogatory and recipients of a robust education for compliance are likely to sacrifice their self-interest because of the strength of their habitual or trust motives.

What should be our normative assessment of cases in which motives of trust or habit preempt or outweigh a person's own judgment and lead her to perform a morally optional act of compliance that is either supererogatory or prudent? The answer will depend in part on the degree of *intrinsic* prudential value, if any, that we ascribe to acting on one's own judgments. This strikes me as a matter about which reasonable people can and do disagree. Some will accept Mill's (1859/1989, p. 59) claim that the good life consists importantly in making choices that exercise and develop the uniquely "human faculties of perception, judgment, discriminative feeling, mental activity, and even moral preference... It is possible that [a man] might be guided in some good path, and kept out of harm's way, without any of these things. But what will be his comparative worth as a human being?"

Mill's position, roughly speaking, is that there is intrinsic value in living *autonomously*.[21] One could subscribe to a weaker position that attributes intrinsic value to acting on one's own judgments whether or not those judgments derive from beliefs and values that

[20] I consider later the alternative case in which my action is morally required but nonetheless suboptimal because of its motive.

[21] Elsewhere (MacMullen, 2007, p. 89) I have explored the difference between autonomy and Mill's ideal of "individuality."

have been reflectively and critically endorsed.[22] I have argued elsewhere (MacMullen, 2007, pp. 92–93) that a liberal state has no business either endorsing or rejecting the position that autonomy has intrinsic prudential value, and I would say the same about the weaker position, too. More generally, I do not see any authoritative standpoint from which anyone could insist that a particular child's civic education be designed and delivered on the basis of a definite position in this debate about the nature of the good life. Each person should ultimately determine her own position, but children will not have done so at the point when decisions must be made about their civic education.

Although reasonable people can and do disagree about whether there is intrinsic prudential value in acting on one's own (autonomous) judgments, they will all agree that there is some value in a person's being able to live in accordance with her own view on the matter. Therefore, when we consider an adult who attaches intrinsic value to acting on her own (autonomous) judgments, the fact that the education she received makes it harder for her to do so whenever one of her options is legally pre- or proscribed is a mark against that education (even if it is, all things considered, a price worth paying). In other words, only in retrospect can we know for sure whether education that cultivates habits of and trust reasons for compliance is (at least on one dimension) an obstacle to that person's living well by her own lights. But, assuming that a child is more likely to develop into an adult who attaches intrinsic value to acting on her (autonomous) judgments if she is raised in an environment wherein that view is widely held,[23] we should give more weight to this concern about education for compliance when we are dealing with children in such environments.

3.3.2. Defective judgment

The problem of *defective judgment* arises when noncompliance is morally permissible and the agent complies with the law only

[22] Note, however, that the judgments of autonomous persons are less likely to be defective on account of an inauthentic preference. See MacMullen (2007, p. 98).

[23] This assumption has an ironic quality, to be sure, but I am convinced that it is true. Truly autonomous people do not *unreflectively* accept the values that are dominant in their environment, but reflection often fails to identify any compelling reason to abandon the values with which one was raised. See MacMullen (2007, pp. 78–80).

because of an error in her assessment of the particular reasons for and against compliance. There are various possible sources of such defective judgment, but I shall focus on the two that are especially likely to result from education for compliance: false beliefs and inauthentic preferences.

It is often easy to see the suboptimality in morally optional acts of compliance that are performed only because the agent holds some false belief. Consider, for example, a gay man who complies with a law against same-sex intercourse only because he falsely believes that gay sex is morally wrong and/or that it is bad for his health.[24] Alternatively, imagine a woman running a small business who complies with an unnecessary and hugely burdensome government regulation only because she falsely believes that there is a high probability that her business will be audited. Of course, I have already argued that we should not promote compliance by instilling beliefs that are both known (or strongly suspected) to be false and expected to persist beyond childhood. Are educational strategies that respect this principle nonetheless likely to generate false beliefs? Yes, they are, unless they are severely limited in the manner prescribed by the orthodox view.[25] As I argued earlier, promoting compliance by instilling beliefs has the potential to be much more effective precisely when one is willing to accept some risk that the beliefs are false. This was the point of the examples of teaching children to believe that there is a *prima facie* duty to obey the law or that the jury system is an excellent institution. One could find many other examples. Let me offer just one that is especially interesting.

The force of many expectation-based moral *prohibitum* reasons to comply is diminished, and at the limit eradicated, if the laws are unjust. This injustice could arise at the aggregate level even if each law by itself looks acceptable. For example, the laws collectively

[24] We should also recognize the alternative suboptimal outcome in which a false moral belief is insufficient to motivate compliance but sufficient to leave the agent with a morally inappropriate guilt. Imagine a gay man whose education in the supposed sins of homosexuality is insufficient to secure his compliance with a law against sodomy but does "succeed" in leaving him wracked with guilt.

[25] It is true, as I argue in Chapter 7, that autonomous reasoning is also liable (and perhaps even more likely) to generate false beliefs. But the false beliefs that arise from errors in autonomous reasoning will not systematically favor compliance with a polity's particular existing laws.

may deny equal concern and respect to a particular group of citizens by tending systematically to instantiate the social coordination scheme that, of the various options that justice would permit if each problem were viewed in isolation, is least favorable to that group. Suppose I believe that my polity's laws are not collectively unjust in this sense, and let us assume that my belief is warranted. If I instill this belief in children, they will perceive their moral *prohibitum* reasons for compliance to be undiminished. But the fact that my belief is warranted does not mean that it is true. It is entirely possible that I have overlooked some systematic legal discrimination against a particular group of citizens—perhaps even a collection of individuals whom I do not think of as a group. If this is so, I will have caused my children to overestimate the force of the moral *prohibitum* reasons for compliance with many laws: this, in turn, will predictably lead those children to act on defective judgments, complying when noncompliance is permissible and would have been chosen but for the false belief.

Compliance can also be suboptimal if it expresses an inauthentic preference (Taylor, 1979, pp. 175–93). A profoundly closeted gay man has an inauthentic preference not to have sex with men. Of course, he does no wrong by acting on this inauthentic preference—no one is morally required to contravene an unjust law against same-sex intercourse—but, even in a society that has and enforces such a law, a person's decision to comply with the law is suboptimal if it is due to inauthentic sexual preference. We might contrast this explanation for compliance with the case of a man whose (authentic) preference for same-sex intercourse is outweighed by his aversion to risking legal punishment and the social stigma of criminality. As much as we might regret the existence of the law that constrains both men's choices in this way, we should not regard the latter man's compliance as suboptimal unless we believe that the strength of his aversion to risking punishment and stigma is itself inauthentic, perhaps exaggerated by his education.

For some preferences the question of authenticity does not seem to arise. But each of us has quite a wide range of natural predispositions to enjoy certain activities. It is one thing to curb these predispositions in ways that reduce immoral behavior. But it is quite another to do so in ways that affect people's choices among morally permissible options. I would suggest, as examples, that the creative instincts of someone with an artistic temperament might properly be deemed authentic preferences, but that typically one would not regard flavors of ice cream as the objects of preferences that could be called authentic or inauthentic. Therefore, a society that unjustly criminalizes the consumption of vanilla ice cream would not generate defective judgment by teaching children to gag at the smell of vanilla. We should also recall the possibility that a particular manipulation of prudential values may be justified on the paternalistic ground that it leaves the person more readily able to satisfy her preferences. Preference-satisfaction can be more important than preference authenticity. In cases where the manipulation was so justified, a resulting act of compliance that is not morally required would *not* be suboptimal.

One might wonder whether the manipulation of preferences involved in education for compliance is just as likely to improve the fit between children's actual and authentic preferences as to widen the gap between the two. After all, we should not assume that in the absence of education for compliance, children's actual preferences would all be authentic and therefore that the manipulative effects of education for compliance can only be adverse. MTV is motivated by profit, not by the goal of promoting accurate introspection. But at least some of the significant formative influences in a child's life—not least the child's own independent causal contribution, however this is best conceptualized[26]—are favorable to the discovery of her authentic preferences, whereas it is no part of the goal of an education for compliance to assist the child in that quest. It is always possible that preference manipulation geared to increasing rates of compliance with laws will fortuitously counteract influences that detract from authenticity and therefore unintentionally contribute to solving the problem of inauthentic preferences, but it seems more likely to aggravate the problem.

The same question about supererogatory compliance that I raised in relation to failures of judgment recurs in the context of defective judgments. Imagine that I comply with the great demands of a "Good Samaritan" law on a particular occasion not out of habit nor because I trust the laws but rather because I falsely believe that it

[26] For an interesting discussion of this difficult issue, see Feinberg (1980, pp. 140–51).

is my moral obligation. It would not be wrong of me to pass by the injured person, but I believe it would be wrong. It may seem odd to call my act of compliance suboptimal. Alternatively, imagine a very different explanation for my compliance: I was raised to be extraordinarily averse to the sanctions that society imposes on law-breakers. Again, it may seem odd to treat my resulting act of supererogatory compliance as a mark against my education.

Readers may feel differently in cases wherein the moral reasons for compliance are less weighty than those that favor helping a severely injured person. Public decency laws provide such an example. There may be *in se* moral reasons for compliance with public decency laws, and there are certainly *prohibitum* reasons—some people only take their children to the park because the law leads them to expect that no one will expose herself there. But if, for the sake of argument, the combined force of these reasons renders compliance only supererogatory, not morally required, how should educators approach such laws? Should they aim to encourage compliance by heightening children's sense of embarrassment at being naked in public?[27]

More generally, as we think about supererogatory compliance, it is important to observe that there are often expectation-based *prohibitum* moral reasons for compliance with even the most unreasonably demanding laws. And, typically, when compliance with an unreasonably demanding law would not harm others, there are no moral reasons for noncompliance: therefore, the balance of moral reasons favors compliance. Given the strength of prudential reasons for noncompliance, these moral reasons for compliance are not sufficient to establish a moral obligation to comply—one is not required to commit an act of great self-sacrifice to avoid merely

[27] Given the limited motivational efficacy of moral beliefs, one might be tempted to argue that educators should deliberately misrepresent compliance with public decency laws as morally obligatory rather than merely supererogatory. When citizens contemplate breaking these laws, it would be better if their moral inhibitions were as strong as those they experience when they contemplate violating what they perceive to be a moral duty rather than the much weaker qualms they will feel if they see public nudity for what it truly is, namely, selfish but morally permissible behavior. But, as I argued in Chapter 2, we should not instill false beliefs even if doing so improves the holder's compliance decisions. It is important for citizens to know that noncompliance with a particular law is (usually) morally permissible because they ought to oppose such laws.

inconveniencing other persons by violating their expectations—but compliance in such cases is supererogatory, not merely permissible. This conceptual analysis shows that some instances of supererogatory compliance are clearly suboptimal. My giving up a lot so that you may have a little is usually supererogatory, but this net loss of human well-being will often strike a third party as undesirable.

For an example that illustrates the dilemmas raised by supererogatory compliance in relation to both failures of judgment and defective judgment, let us turn to Wellman's (2005, p. 84) discussion of the Australian law requiring citizens to vote. For the sake of argument, let us assume that Wellman is correct that the law is unjust and that there is no moral obligation to comply (and nor is there an obligation to be noncompliant in order to protest the unjust law). Imagine that election day falls during the best week of the fishing season and that, alas, there is no provision for absentee ballots, so one cannot both vote and spend that whole day fishing. We should distinguish three scenarios in which a wealthy citizen (for whom the fine levied on non-voters is trivially small) gives up her fishing trip to comply with the mandatory voting law. In the first scenario, she would prefer to go fishing and sees no strong moral reasons to vote instead, but she cannot overcome her (educationally induced) general habit of compliance with laws. This is a case of failure of judgment. In the second scenario, she would enjoy fishing but is more powerfully motivated by her inauthentic preference for participation in the democratic process; she was raised to feel that life is hollow without such participation.[28] This is a case of defective judgment. In the third scenario, the citizen's true moral belief (that voting is morally praiseworthy but not obligatory) is motivationally sufficient to outweigh her desire to fish.

How should we evaluate the act of compliance in each of these three scenarios? If the moral value of voting warrants passing up the opportunity to satisfy the (authentic) preference to fish, it might seem that none of the three scenarios actually constitutes an example of overcompliance. But, if the citizen attaches intrinsic prudential value to acting on her own (autonomous) judgments, the first (and second) scenarios might then constitute overcompliance: for this citizen, given

[28] As we saw in Chapter 1, this is the kind of civic education that Richard Flathman (1996, p. 23) deplores.

her conception of the good, the fact that her action did not express her own (autonomous) judgment would constitute a loss of prudential value (in addition to the loss involved in forgoing satisfaction of an authentic preference). This additional prudential cost could tip the balance of values in favor of noncompliance. Furthermore, as we shall now discuss, the first and second scenarios are surely suboptimal to some degree on account of the citizen's non-moral motive for acting in accordance with moral reasons.

3.3.3. The intrinsic value of moral motivation

It is time to revisit the issue of the intrinsic value of motivation. In our earlier discussion of failures of judgment I considered the position that it is inherently desirable for people to act on their own judgments even when this leads them to engage in foolish or selfish behavior that would have been avoided if they had instead been motivated by habits or trust reasons to comply with the law. I argued that this position is a proposition about the good life concerning which reasonable people can and will disagree and that it is therefore of severely limited significance for the justification of civic education. I also indicated that I take the same view of its stronger cousin, the claim that autonomous action is intrinsically valuable. This is why, in the subsequent discussion of defective judgment, I focused on the concern that education for compliance may tend to generate false beliefs and inauthentic preferences rather than on the position that it is intrinsically undesirable for human actions to be guided by beliefs and preferences that are not autonomously held (even if they are true and authentic, respectively). And I have not even considered the view that the intrinsic prudential value of people's acting on their own (autonomous) judgments might compete with the value of their acting only in morally permissible ways. We should not structure civic education to facilitate pursuit of a contestable prudential value (that the recipients themselves may well not endorse in adulthood) when the cost of doing so is higher rates of impermissible noncompliance.

But, whereas claims about the intrinsic prudential value of acting on one's own (autonomous) judgments should play at most a minimal role in guiding our civic educational policies and practices, the same cannot be said about the proposition that moral motivation has intrinsic value.[29] The primary moral consideration in evaluating compliance decisions is undoubtedly that people should not violate their duties to others, and a secondary consideration derives from the moral value of supererogatory conduct, but it is also independently valuable for people to act from moral motivations whenever there are significant moral reasons for action. In other words, what I owe to my fellow persons is mainly that I perform certain actions and refrain from others but also that I be moved by the moral reasons for these actions and omissions.[30] I do not fully live up to the demands of morality unless I both recognize the special value and status of personhood and act on that recognition.

In addition to moral errors and problems of judgment, there is therefore another way in which compliance decisions can be suboptimal: actions that are morally required (or supererogatory) may be suboptimal because of their motivation. The most obvious examples are acts of compliance that are morally required but motivated in a way that detracts from or eliminates the moral worth of the action: for example, a driver's abiding by the speed limit near an elementary school only because he does not want to pay a stiff fine. Altogether less common, presumably, are acts of noncompliance that are morally required but similarly ill-motivated: for example, a doctor's refusing to hand over her patient's medical records to the government simply because she dislikes the FBI agent who makes the legally binding but unjust request, or a driver's speeding on the way to the hospital with a severely injured passenger just because she enjoys driving fast.

Specifically, it is the *absence* of a sufficient moral motive (not the *presence* of habitual and/or prudential motives) for an act of morally requisite (or supererogatory) compliance that renders such an act

[29] We shall see in Chapter 7 that autonomous action can have intrinsic *moral* value and that this does have important implications for civic education. The autonomy of citizens' consent to their political institutions is one of the factors that legitimate the polity's use of coercion: as such, the preservation and development of children's capacity to give autonomous consent is a proper goal of civic education, albeit a goal that does not always outweigh competing priorities.

[30] I cannot here fully explore the issue of the moral evaluation of motives. But I should note that my position, although reminiscent of Kantian moral philosophy, diverges from Kant in one major respect: whereas Kant insists that moral motives are autonomous by definition, I maintain that nonautonomous moral motivation is both possible (indeed, common) and intrinsically valuable.

suboptimal from the moral point of view, albeit far preferable to impermissible (or permissible but selfish) noncompliance. This gives us grounds to be concerned about educational practices that foster habits of compliance because habits can preempt the reasoning that would be necessary to generate a sufficient moral motive. And the cultivation of prudential reasons for compliance might also be problematic if and to the extent that it detracts from the cultivation of moral reasons and/or the motivational efficacy of those reasons. I discussed earlier the worry that cultivating prudential reasons for compliance might perversely lead to more impermissible noncompliance. Now I make the companion observation that shaping prudential values to favor compliance may reduce the moral worth of some of the morally requisite (or supererogatory) compliance we observe.

In short, I think we must care not only *whether* but also (to some degree) *why* people do their duty. Other things being equal, that is, holding constant the number and severity of cases in which compliance is suboptimal on account of problems of judgment, we might prefer a world in which there are (a few) more instances of unjustified noncompliance but also (many) more compliant actions that have moral worth in the sense of being not only morally required but also sufficiently motivated by appropriate moral considerations.[31] So, in particular, there are two different grounds on which we might prefer an education that encourages its recipients to think for themselves about the morality of compliance decisions to one that would minimize violations of moral duty by strongly cultivating habitual motives for compliance. First, the latter strategy will have unwanted effects on the choices people make when compliance is not required (failure of judgment). Second, even when compliance is morally required, the compliant action lacks moral worth if it is motivated by habits that preempted the formation of a sufficient

[31] What should we say about morally requisite actions that are motivated by a false moral belief? For example, if the philosophical anarchists are correct and there is no general duty to obey the law, how should we evaluate cases in which a person's perceived moral reasons for compliance only constitute a sufficient motive because they include her false belief in the duty to obey? My view is that certain false beliefs can constitute motives with intrinsic moral value. If Jane (erroneously) derives her belief that she has a *prima facie* duty to obey the law from her intrinsically morally valuable attitude of respect for her fellow citizens, that belief can confer moral worth on actions that it motivates even if the belief is false.

moral motive. On the flipside, however, a complete analysis would have to take into account the decisional costs associated with forming one's own judgment: these costs can be avoided if habit does not outweigh but rather preempts judgment. And we should ascribe the honorary status of "moral reasons for action" to habitual motives that the agent has reflectively endorsed on moral grounds: such motives inherit the moral value of the reasons for which they were endorsed, even if (as I discussed in Chapter 2) the agent would have been unable to eliminate the habit had she wished to do so.

3.4. Conclusion: striking the balance

Let us assume that decisions to be made regarding compliance with laws are drawn randomly throughout one's life from a particular distribution.[32] The distribution has two dimensions. One of these has discrete categories: morally, compliance can be required; permissible and supererogatory; merely permissible; permissible but such that noncompliance would be supererogatory; or prohibited. The other dimension is a continuous variable, namely, the importance of the decision to be made.[33] For a given distribution, each combination of educational strategies will generate its own pattern of expected incidence of the various types of suboptimal action (moral errors, problems of judgment, and motivations that lack moral worth) at various levels of importance. My analysis has throughout recognized the blunt nature of our educational tools: we must make trade-offs among the various suboptimalities that will unavoidably result from any approach to education for compliance. It

[32] I assume for present purposes that the distribution is not affected by educational efforts to promote compliance. This assumption is false: given that the cultivation of *in se* reasons for compliance often generates support for (or at least weakens opposition to) the law in question, decisions about whether, when, and to what extent to cultivate such reasons in children will have long-run effects on which laws are repealed and therefore on the future shape of the distribution that I discuss. But I postpone to Chapters 6 and 7 consideration of the ways in which education may generate support for existing laws.

[33] This importance variable is hard to define and measure precisely, but it is a reasonably intuitive notion. Deciding whether to dodge the draft is more important than deciding whether to smoke pot, which is more important than deciding whether to drop one's chewing gum wrapper as litter.

is hard, as I argued in Chapter 1, to believe that there could be an algorithm for making these trade-offs, and I certainly do not propose one. My primary goal is rather to frame the decision problem for educators (and more generally for the adult citizens of a democracy) by identifying the various different ways in which education could promote compliance with laws and highlighting the distinctive costs and benefits associated with each of those ways given the multiple competing values that are at stake.

One's preferences over educational strategies in a particular society will obviously be guided by one's beliefs about the distribution from which compliance decisions are drawn in that society. If one believes that noncompliance is permissible very rarely and typically only in cases of little importance, one will tend to favor strategies that more aggressively cultivate motives for compliance (especially if one is not too concerned about the intrinsic value of moral motivation). If, by contrast, one believes that noncompliance is more frequently permissible, including in a significant number of cases of considerable importance, one will be much more cautious about cultivating motives for compliance.

The fact that we disagree about the distribution helps to explain why we must ultimately turn our attention to the question of educational authority: "*who* should decide how children are educated?"[34] However, even if we stipulate the distribution and therefore know the expected costs and benefits associated with each strategy, choosing a strategy demands difficult normative judgments. As I have just discussed, one such judgment concerns the extent to which motivation matters when we consider actions that are morally required. In addition, one must decide the relative importance of moral errors, on the one hand, and problems of judgment when choosing among permissible options, on the other, since "conservative" educational strategies will reduce the expected incidence of impermissible noncompliance at the expense of increasing the number of cases of compliance that was not morally required and that reflects either failure of judgment or defective judgment. Within these cases, how do we weigh failures against defects: are we more troubled by overcompliance that arises from habits and trust

[34] As explained in Chapter 1, my book does not address this question.

reasons or from inauthentic preferences and false beliefs? And how do we evaluate supererogatory or prudent actions that result from problems of judgment? Finally, we must determine the rate at which to trade off important suboptimal actions against less significant ones.

Having just said that I will not propose an algorithmic solution to this highly complex and multi-dimensional optimization problem, I shall nonetheless suggest that it is wildly implausible that the best approach to education for compliance is the extreme one recommended by the orthodox view: abstain entirely from shaping prudential values, inculcating trust, and habituation; and instill moral and non-moral beliefs only when this can be done without detracting from the development of children's autonomy. We have seen that this approach will predictably lead to a great deal of impermissible noncompliance that could have been prevented by the use of educational strategies that do not rigidly prioritize autonomy over all competing values. The problems of judgment, inferior motivations, and occasional moral errors that will result from these more aggressive compliance-promotion strategies constitute significant costs, to be sure. But they cannot plausibly be viewed as being so severe that they rule out even moderate and judicious use of such strategies: on the contrary, we should accept that these costs will often be a price worth paying for the considerable benefit of enabling a reasonably just liberal democracy to draw closer to the very high levels of compliance that are morally required of its citizens. Nonautonomous motives for compliance will be especially desirable in childhood, while and to the extent that moral and cognitive development are incomplete. But to some significant degree these motives will also be desirable in adults.

PART II

FOSTERING CIVIC MOTIVATION

CHAPTER 4

Sources of civic motivation

The public discourse of contemporary democratic societies is laced with lamentations about citizens' low levels of engagement in civic and political life. The complaints take many forms. One common theme is inadequate participation in the electoral process, especially at the local level and when the offices and issues at stake have a relatively low profile: turnout is low; most voters have not devoted much if any time to informing themselves about and debating the choices to be made; most well-qualified citizens show no interest in running for office; and campaign activity is minimal, even among those citizens who have clear and strong opinions about what the election's outcome should be. But concerns about levels of civic engagement are certainly not limited to the electoral process. When the votes have been counted, the vast majority of citizens disengage from politics altogether: only a few will found, lead, or join social movements, lobby their elected representatives, or even pay significant attention to activities in the corridors of power.

And there is a similar dearth of motivation to contribute in less ideologically charged ways to the polity's efforts to provide vitally important public goods. Jury service is shirked whenever possible. Crimes go unreported by witnesses who were not also victims. Local government surveys requesting feedback from residents are widely ignored unless participation is mandated or compensated. Fines for antisocial and illegal conduct are improperly treated as fees (that, with luck, one may never be forced to pay). And, perhaps most importantly, citizens routinely prefer private sector employment to those occupations that directly serve the polity: military and other uniformed service, public school teaching, the civil service, etc. These complaints and others like them are a familiar part of the soundtrack of life in a mass democracy.

In this chapter and its successor, I ask what role(s) education could and should play in addressing the perceived problem of insufficient civic and political engagement. As noted in Chapter 1, I take for granted the vital importance of education that equips (future) citizens with the skills and knowledge to participate effectively if they choose to do so. My focus here is on motivation. How could education enhance citizens' motives for particular civically valuable actions as well as their more general motives to contribute to the polity by participating in its decision-making processes and helping to discharge its various functions? Answering this conceptual question is my primary task in the present chapter. It clears the ground for the normative questions of Chapter 5. Are there (always) strong moral reasons for people to contribute to the particular polities of which they are citizens? Does education for civic motivation pose a threat to justice at the global (or even at the domestic) level? What are the costs of different educational strategies for increasing civic motivation, and how should we weigh those costs against the benefits of a more engaged citizenry? In particular, should we follow the orthodox view of civic character formation by rejecting all strategies that detract from citizens' capacity to make critical and autonomous judgments about their polity and its actions?

In the present chapter, I shall argue that there are several distinct ways in which education could foster civic motivation: teaching children to perceive moral reasons for civic action, cultivating particular habits and/or tastes, arousing patriotic love, and encouraging civic identification. Section 4.1 reviews some of the putative moral reasons for civic action that children could be taught to perceive; in partial concurrence with the orthodox view, I argue that many of these reasons are sufficiently contestable that we cannot teach them to children without incurring an unacceptable risk that we are instilling false beliefs. Section 4.2 explores the nature and origins of habits of and tastes for civic action, laying the foundation for my argument in Chapter 5 that cultivating these motives is an important part of the best educational response to concerns about low levels of civic engagement. Sections 4.3, 4.4, and 4.5 analyze the two remaining sources of civic motivation—patriotic love and civic identification—and argue that they are not only conceptually distinct but also realistically capable of existing without one another. Identification with one's polity is usually treated as if it were inseparable from love of that polity. But this is a mistake born of an excessive focus on the concept of patriotism.[1] It can be argued that patriotism requires not only love of a polity to which one (objectively) belongs but also (subjective) identification with that polity.[2] But one can certainly love a polity without identifying with it. And, more importantly for my purposes in Chapter 5, one can identify with a polity without loving it. Section 4.6 sketches an approach to civic education that promises to foster civic identification without unduly arousing patriotic love.

4.1. Perceived moral reasons for civic action

One obvious way in which education could arouse civic motivation is by teaching children to perceive moral reasons for civic action. As we saw in Chapter 1, the orthodox view of civic education embraces this strategy provided that it does not involve instilling contestable beliefs and thereby detracting from the development of children's autonomy. And happily enough, as I shall argue in Chapter 5, there are strong moral reasons for civic action that are grounded only in the basic moral values of liberal democracy and the distinctive opportunities that people undeniably have by dint of their citizenship and/or residency in a particular polity. At a minimum,

[1] Twenty years ago, Stephen Nathanson (1989, 1993) performed a great and long-overdue service to political philosophy by pointing out that we routinely use the term patriotism to refer not to a simple object but rather to a complex of personal characteristics. But he simultaneously did us a disservice by continuing to frame the normative debate about those characteristics as a debate about their virtues when taken as an indivisible set. This approach excludes (or at least ignores) the possibility that some but not all of the characteristics of patriotism are morally desirable.

[2] See, for example, Nathanson (1993, pp. 34–35) and Primoratz (2008, p. 18). For an opposing view, see Keller (2008, pp. 65–67). Interestingly, at least one writer denies that love is a necessary condition for patriotism: "Patriotism in my view means accepting and fulfilling a duty to promote and protect just institutions and relationships in a polity—generally the polity in which one is a citizen. Love of country or special affection for fellow citizens are not essential attributes of such a patriot" (Thompson 2008, p. 158). I take no position on any semantic questions about the necessary or sufficient conditions for a person to qualify as a patriot.

therefore, education should foster civic motivation by teaching children to see the force of these moral reasons.

But should educators seek to bolster children's civic motivation by teaching them to perceive *other* moral reasons to contribute to their particular polity, i.e., reasons that are grounded *not* in distinctive opportunities to advance core liberal democratic values but rather in a putative special moral relationship that exists either between compatriots or between an individual citizen and his polity? For example, should children be taught that they have so-called associative duties to their compatriots and/or obligations to reciprocate benefits they have received from the actions of those fellow citizens?[3] Should children be taught that they are morally bound by any promises they have made to serve their polity (and, if so, should they be encouraged or even required to make such promises)?

The orthodox view of civic education rejects teaching children to perceive contestable reasons such as these on the grounds that doing so interferes with the autonomy of moral belief formation and thereby runs the risk of generating false beliefs.[4] I argued in Chapter 2 that we should indeed refrain from instilling beliefs for their motivational value when we know or strongly suspect those beliefs to be false (unless we can be confident that the beliefs will not persist beyond childhood). This principle surely rules out teaching children that their schoolroom pledges of allegiance constitute moral reasons for action: even when a child is not formally required to recite such a pledge, the act of recitation cannot plausibly be

[3] There is a voluminous literature exploring these issues. For a recent contribution that helpfully and concisely summarizes the main arguments and positions, see Lazar (2010).

[4] Is it ever *intrinsically* valuable for people to decide autonomously whether or not to be civically engaged? For example, if I decide to vote based on my true belief that I have strong moral reasons to do so, does it matter whether I hold that belief autonomously? As with compliance decisions (discussed in Chapter 3), some people may see intrinsic *prudential* value in autonomous motives for decisions about civic engagement. But is there any intrinsic *moral* value here? This strikes me as a borderline case. I shall argue in Chapter 7 that autonomous consent is one of the conditions that legitimates state coercion. My consent to a law is straightforwardly nonautonomous if my belief in the merits of that law is not autonomously held. But is my consent nonautonomous in the morally relevant sense if, although that belief is autonomously held, my decision to *express* it is motivated by a nonautonomously held (albeit true) belief in the moral reasons to do so? I am not sure what to say about cases such as this.

regarded as sufficiently voluntary to generate a genuine promissory obligation. I think that concerns about instilling false beliefs also rule out teaching children to believe that they have obligations of reciprocal benefit to their compatriots: as I noted in Chapter 2, Robert Nozick (1974) and A. John Simmons (1979) have argued compellingly that mere receipt of benefits is insufficient to generate reciprocal obligations and that citizens are unable to "accept" the benefits provided by their polity in the special sense that would incur reciprocal obligations.

But I am not so sure what to say about associative duties. We do not *know* that there are no such duties among compatriots. But we certainly do have grounds to doubt their existence. Wellman (2000) makes a strong case that there is a "reductionist" explanation that fully accounts for the strength of one's moral reasons to contribute to the polities of which one is a citizen. There is no "magic in the pronoun 'my'," he argues, no intrinsic and irreducible moral importance to one's membership either in a polity or in a nation.[5] But I argued in Chapter 2, *contra* the orthodox view, that the motivational value of a belief can justify instilling that belief even when there are unresolved doubts about its truth. I suggested that we might thereby be justified in teaching children to believe in a general duty to obey the law. And the same can be said of teaching children to believe in associative duties to fellow citizens.

The belief that I have a special moral relationship to my compatriots may well be more motivationally efficacious than the belief that I have distinctive opportunities to benefit my compatriots in morally important ways,[6] just as the belief in a general duty of obedience promises to be a more reliable motive than many of the moral reasons for compliance that are compatible with philosophical anarchism. But, as we saw in Chapter 3 and will explore further in Chapter 5, there is only so much motivation that can be generated by shaping children's perceptions of the moral reasons for action.

[5] In Samuel Scheffler's (2001, pp. 114–19) terminology, Wellman is an "extreme cosmopolitan"—*contra* Scheffler himself, Yael Tamir (1993), David Miller (1995), and Ronald Dworkin (1986).

[6] Note, however, that the distinctive opportunities afforded by citizenship in a particular polity can also be used to benefit *other* polities and their members, and there are especially strong moral reasons for citizens of rich countries to use their opportunities in this manner. I explore this important point in Chapter 5.

Additional perceived moral reasons (beyond those grounded in distinctive opportunities) may somewhat bolster citizens' civic motivation—for example, by leading citizens to regard certain civic actions as not only morally *valuable* but also morally *obligatory*[7]—but the bottom line is that moral motivation often fares poorly when it is unsupported in its contest with prudential motivation.

Later in this chapter we shall have occasion to consider (and reject) two other alleged sources of special moral reasons for civic action. I shall devote more time to responding to these moral claims because they are bound up so closely with two of our central concerns, namely, the promotion of patriotic love and civic identification. Once we have reviewed the possibility of fostering civic motivation by teaching children to love their polity, I shall consider the argument that citizens who feel such affection thereby have stronger moral reasons for civic action. And, while delineating the concept of civic identification, we shall encounter the view that citizens bear partial responsibility for their polity's actions as distinct from and in addition to being responsible for their own role (or lack thereof) in the decision process that led to those actions. I do not think that either of these arguments succeeds. And, because of the aforementioned limited scope for increasing civic motivation by causing people to perceive additional moral reasons for civic action, it is unlikely that our doubts about the veracity of these contestable moral claims will be outweighed by the marginal motivational value of citizens' believing them.

4.2. Habits and tastes

Teaching a child to perceive moral reasons for civic action typically fosters *general* civic motivation in that child. By this I mean simply that a perceived moral reason to contribute to one's polity constitutes a motive for *any* action that helps to realize the moral value(s) underpinning the perceived reason. We shall shortly explore two

[7] The extra motivation that results from regarding a morally valuable action as morally obligatory will typically be desirable, even if the action in question is not in fact obligatory. (I discuss in Chapter 5 the concern that increased civic motivation could be undesirable if it leads people to perform fewer actions that are of greater moral value than contributing to their polity.)

other sources of *general* civic motivation that can be induced by education: a citizen who loves and/or identifies with her polity thereby has a motive to perform a wide range of civic actions. But first I want to acknowledge the important educational option of fostering *particular* motives for civic action. There are two such motives that we need to consider: habits and tastes.

First, let us consider *habits* of engaging in particular civic activities. A citizen's habits may motivate her to contribute to her polity in various ways quite independently of any perceived moral reasons or other motives she may have for such actions. She may have habits of showing up to vote at her local polling place (which is not to say that she habitually votes for the same party), listening to a news program in the morning (and thereby equipping herself to be an informed participant in the life of her polity), discussing current affairs over dinner, attending town-hall meetings, assisting with voter-registration drives, and so on.

Since habits are formed by repetition of a particular action, educators can instill many civically valuable habits simply by arranging (via some combination of carrot and stick, where necessary) for children to perform the action frequently. For example, Niemi (2012, pp. 33–34) emphasizes the habit-forming value of requiring children routinely to engage in debates about controversial political issues, and Levine (2012, p. 51) and Kahne and Sporte (2008) argue that service learning and community service should be mandated or strongly incentivized as components of civic education in part because they can form valuable habits. Levinson (2012, Chapter 6) urges that children be encouraged to engage in overtly political action, not merely in apolitical forms of community service.

But some civic habits cannot straightforwardly be formed during childhood because the actions in question cannot (legally) be performed by children: voting in the polity's elections is an obvious example.[8] Of course, to the extent that mock elections in schools

[8] Parents lack the legitimate (and often also the effective) authority to force their *adult* children to behave in ways that would be habit-forming. And the state does not attempt to do so when the action is not legally required. But we can readily imagine the polity or another agent (perhaps a civically-minded grandparent or a voluntary association whose mission is to promote good citizenship) providing incentives for young adults (and newly naturalized adult citizens of all ages) to perform such civic actions, e.g., a small cash payment if you vote in the municipal election the first time you are eligible to do so.

simulate the experience of casting a real vote, the appropriate habit could be developed even before one is permitted to perform the real action.[9] It might even be appropriate to *require* students to vote in mock elections (much as one might require them to take civics classes, participate in community service, and listen to stump speeches by fellow students representing the real candidates): this would ensure that the voting habit is developed while always leaving students the option of abstaining actively by spoiling their ballot (both in the mock elections and subsequently in real elections).[10]

Next, we should acknowledge the potential role of *tastes* in motivating engagement in particular civic activities. In some instances, taste may even constitute a sufficient motive, as will be clear when it is the only motive. A US citizen may closely follow American politics simply because she finds find it interesting, even entertaining. There are moral reasons for her to act in this way, and she may indeed perceive those reasons, but they play no role in motivating her (as she will acknowledge if she is candid). After all, this citizen also knows that there are strong moral reasons for her to serve on a jury when summoned, but she regularly lies to avoid jury service because she finds it mildly inconvenient. Her recognition of the moral reasons for civic action is shockingly impotent motivationally: it is, at least from her perspective, simply a coincidence that her taste for consuming domestic political journalism motivates an action that she has moral reasons to perform. She could equally well have been fascinated by the politics of Australia (or by Italian soccer), in which case she would have paid no attention to current affairs in her own country. Indeed, her motives for following American politics are essentially no different from those of an Australian

[9] Student government elections could be designed to serve the same purpose. Crittenden (2002, p. 192) argues more generally that democratic procedures *within* schools should closely resemble those *outside* in the polity. His concern is that the *skills* learned in schools should be readily transferable. This is indeed an important concern, but I would also emphasize that the habits (and/or tastes) children acquire by participating in school activities will have most civic value if those activities are closely modeled on the activities we want adult citizens to perform for their polity. See also Flanagan (2013, pp. 18, 118) on schools as "mini-polities" within which civic habits are formed.

[10] Fuhrman and Lazerson (2005, p. xxxi) argue that professional educators should "teach in ways that enable students to think of themselves as involved citizens even as they attend school."

citizen who finds the whole spectacle of American political theater vastly amusing.

Although taste can be a citizen's sole and/or sufficient motive for a particular civic action, it will usually function in combination with other motives. A college graduate who turns down a lucrative job in finance to join the US Marine Corps may do so partly from a sense of civic duty (and some affection and/or identification with the country, as discussed below) but also because he expects to enjoy military life and is especially attracted by the image and traditions of the Marines. Or, even if he does not anticipate positive enjoyment of his life in uniform, his tastes are likely to be such that he is not actively averse to the prospect: civic motives have a mountain to climb if they must overcome such aversion.

To take another example, someone who volunteers to supervise her local polling station on election day may well have several motives for doing so, but it is likely that she would not make this sizeable time commitment unless she expected to enjoy the activity to a significant degree. One might be tempted to think that the pleasure she takes in volunteering at the polls must be an expression of her love for her polity. But this need not be so. Having a taste for particular actions that contribute to one's polity need not be associated with feeling any affection for that polity. In just the same way, having a taste for Big Macs need not be an expression of affection for McDonald's Corporation. Indeed, someone who *loathes* McDonald's Corporation might nonetheless have a strong taste for Big Macs, perhaps even strong enough to motivate regular purchases notwithstanding a genuine aversion to improving the hated corporation's bottom line.

Education (in which, the reader will recall, I include upbringing) can shape tastes with lifelong effect. Tim acquired a taste for campaigning in Chicago's local elections through happy childhood experiences of accompanying his mother as she went from door to door in her quest for a seat on the school board. And Tim's parents made listening to the USA's National Public Radio appealing to a small child by devising all kinds of games: guess how many times they'll say "President" in the next five minutes, listen for your favorite newsreader, etc. Tim the adult is quick to point out that he does not play these games any longer, but the happy childhood associations persist: the theme music to "Morning Edition" still brings a smile to his face. Tim's parents also found ways to give their son a taste for certain civic activities before he was old enough to be allowed to engage in them. Just as they successfully cultivated in the young Tim a desire to wash the dishes by pretending to enjoy the activity themselves—cooing with delight as they made the clean plates squeak, enthusing about how good the warm soapy water feels, and thereby arousing his jealousy that he was not allowed to take a turn at the sink—they made voting and jury service sound like forbidden fruits by waxing lyrical about how much they had enjoyed their time at the polling station or the courthouse. Reinforcing this parental message, Tim's school presented voting in its mock elections and competing on its mock trial team as fun activities.

Habits and tastes are often mutually reinforcing. Tastes motivate frequent performance of a particular action, and a habit results. A citizen gradually comes to find enjoyment in an activity that her parents mandated during her childhood and that she engaged in during her early adulthood mostly because of the habit she acquired as a child. But tastes will not breed habits when there are too few opportunities to perform the action in question: however much I enjoy participating in mass protests, I will not develop a habit of doing so if such events are very rarely organized anywhere near my home. And habits can sustain practices in which the person takes no pleasure: I may repeatedly act on my habit of voting without developing any fondness for the experience.[11]

Motives of habit and taste are neither moral nor instrumentally rational, so they cannot be expected to apply to another action that "feels" different even if that other action is morally equivalent and serves the same purpose. If I vote mostly out of habit and for the ritualistic pleasure of chatting with my old friends while waiting in line, I am unlikely to continue voting when I am (but my friends are not) reassigned to a different polling station (even if it is no less conveniently located for me), and I almost certainly will not bother voting when the process is moved online. Analogously, chewing

[11] If I start to find voting significantly unpleasant my aversion is likely to be more motivationally powerful than my habit. If I lack other motives to vote I will cease doing so and, over time, my habit will erode. If I continue to vote, this must be because other motives combine with my habit to outweigh my aversion to the experience.

gum after meals may be good for dental health, but if I routinely chew cinnamon gum after meals only because of some combination of habit and taste, when cinnamon gum is unavailable I may not be sufficiently motivated to chew peppermint gum instead, and there is certainly no reason to expect me to take the time to brush my teeth after eating (unless cinnamon-flavored toothpaste is available!).

In different polities with different political institutions and a different political culture, civic actions with the same import are likely to feel very different. So, most habits of and tastes for performing civic actions constitute special motives for contributing to a particular polity rather than general motives for acting in ways that would benefit any polity in which one happened to live and hold citizenship.[12] If education for civic character includes cultivating habits of and tastes for civic action, it must therefore be tailored to the particular polity in which children are being prepared for citizenship. This is a departure from the orthodox view, but—as we shall see in Chapter 5—it need not detract significantly from citizens' capacity to express critical and autonomous judgments through their civic actions.

The fact that habits and tastes are neither moral nor instrumentally rational motives could be misinterpreted in a way that makes them sound like deeply dangerous motives for civic action. We do not want citizens to engage in civic life without a moral compass and with a reckless disregard for the consequences of their actions! But this concern is misplaced, as the following example will illustrate. Let us stipulate that Jane's primary motive for voting is habit and that she reports for jury duty (rather than inventing some excuse) mainly because she enjoys the experience. This does not mean that when Jane votes or serves on a jury she is indifferent to the outcome of the election or the trial. She has non-moral motives for showing up at the polling station and the courthouse, but the candidates for whom she votes and her conduct as a juror are (largely) determined by her

[12] General motives of this kind will typically be moral motives, but they could also be grounded in an Aristotelian or Arendtian conception of the good according to which political participation is a necessary component of the best human life. One could arouse civic motivation by cultivating in citizens the view that political participation is partially constitutive of the good life (see my discussion in Chapter 1), but doing so would compromise individual autonomy much more severely than does the practice of shaping particular tastes and habits.

moral motives. It is perfectly common for moral considerations to be motivationally salient enough to guide someone *within* her chosen activity but not to motivate her choice of activity. To say that a surgeon's behavior as a surgeon is guided by the moral importance of promoting patients' welfare is not to say that this same moral consideration would have been sufficient to motivate her to become a surgeon rather than an advertising executive. Presumably many surgeons chose their career in large part because they found that they enjoyed the work, but when they make decisions in the operating room they routinely prioritize moral considerations over personal enjoyment. Even when they are confident that they would not be punished for using the surgical technique they most enjoy instead of the one that is most likely to promote the patient's health, most surgeons opt for the latter.

4.3. Patriotic affection

One source of civic motivation that education has traditionally sought to instill is patriotic love, a special affection for one's polity.[13] To have affection for a polity is to care about its well-being and therefore to experience some motivation to act to promote that well-being, just as loving one's mother is a motive to promote her well-being.[14] Patriotic love therefore constitutes a certain kind of self-interested motive for civic action. Any plausible conception of self-interest must recognize that the concept includes not only interests *in* the self but also interests *of* the self (Gauthier, 1986); if we understand a person's self-interest in terms of the satisfaction of her preferences, some of those preferences are other-regarding as

[13] I use the terms "love" and "affection" interchangeably. In Chapter 5 I entertain and reject the view that love can manifest itself as special concern for an object's well-being without any special affection for that object.

[14] There are forms of affection that do not include special concern for the object's well-being, but these are not my subject here. Following Keller (2005, p. 567, n. 14), "I am not going to talk about cases in which you can love something (like a pop star or a teacher or a piece of art) without showing it loyalty." Callan (2006, p. 528) makes the same point by observing that patriotic love, unlike Callan's love of the music of Beethoven, must involve "some general willingness to incur significant cost for the sake of the beloved." I return to this theme in Chapter 5.

opposed to self-regarding. Even people that we would describe as narrowly self-interested typically have some interests *of* the self in the well-being of close family and friends. By including the good of the polity among the interests of the self, the introduction of patriotic love expands the range of actions for which citizens will experience self-interested instrumental motivation. In the words of Eamonn Callan (2006, p. 543), "love of country blurs the distinction between self-interest and the interests of compatriots in a way that makes action to support the creation of just institutions less costly." A citizen's affection for her polity can also underpin *expressive* reasons for civic action, just as my love for my son constitutes an expressive reason for me to fold his clothes neatly even when my doing so does not benefit him in any way.[15]

Although patriotic love is a prudential rather than moral motive for contributing to civic life, this does not mean that the substance of citizens' resulting contributions—their conduct as public officials, the electoral candidates for whom they opt to campaign, etc.—cannot be determined (or at least constrained) by moral considerations. This point applies generally to non-moral motives for civic action: I have already discussed it in the context of habits and tastes, and we shall encounter it again in Chapter 5 when we consider the prospect of channeling narrow self-interest by offering rewards for civic action and/or imposing penalties for inaction. Activities that are non-morally motivated may nonetheless be effectively guided and constrained by moral considerations that appear salient to the actor. People who love their polity have a non-moral desire to see it flourish, but this does not entail that they will want their polity to act immorally in pursuit of its material interests. Some people's conception of a flourishing polity will prominently feature the morality of that polity's acts, omissions, and institutions.[16] And even those people whose conception of a polity's well-being

[15] I noted in Chapter 2 that one can also have such expressive reasons for compliance with one's polity's laws.

[16] Primoratz (2008, p. 32) describes such conceptions as being focused on a "country's distinctively moral well-being, its moral identity and integrity." For someone whose conception of a flourishing polity is moralized in this way, loving a particular polity is a motive to oppose its immoral actions even when those actions further the polity's material interests. But, as we shall shortly see, such actions will not arouse shame unless the person also identifies with the polity.

is largely or wholly non-moral may be effectively motivated by moral considerations to oppose immoral means of pursuing that well-being.

Despite the fact that loving one's polity is not itself a moral motive for promoting that polity's well-being (however conceived), one might think that it ought to change one's moral calculus, that someone who loves his country has special moral reasons to play an active part in contributing to it. Does affection for a polity create new moral reasons to perform actions that would benefit that polity? Yael Tamir has argued that it does. She proposes that we have moral reasons to prefer those for whom we feel affection: according to the "morality of community" that she defends, "the 'others' whose welfare we ought [especially] to consider are those we care about" (Tamir, 1993, p. 121).[17] If Tamir is right, teaching children to love their polity will, if successful, generate additional moral reasons for those children to engage in civically valuable actions. And it would presumably be appropriate for educators to teach children to believe in the existence of these hypothetical moral reasons for action: if you love your country, then you have a(n additional) *prima facie* duty to promote its well-being.

I shall argue in Chapter 5 that we do have strong moral reasons to contribute to our polities, but Tamir is wrong to believe that these reasons ever derive from and therefore depend on our affections.[18] Rather, they derive exclusively from the special opportunities we have to contribute to our own polities and thereby to the realization of the important moral goods that are best pursued through a democratic polity. A citizen who lacks affection for his polity still has these opportunities and the corresponding moral reasons for action; if he subsequently acquires affection for the polity, his moral reasons for civic action are unchanged (although his motivation to act in accordance with these reasons increases, assuming that his conception of a flourishing polity coincides with the goods that he has moral reasons to promote).

[17] I insert "[especially]" because Tamir believes that we have other moral reasons to consider the welfare of those about whom we do not care.

[18] Indeed, if Chapter 2's basic account of moral reasons is correct, it is incoherent to say that a moral reason exists only for people who possess certain sentiments or desires.

As a general matter, Tamir's position entails that people whose affections are few or weak have correspondingly few or weak moral reasons for action, but it is hard to see why morality should demand any less of these people. And Tamir's principle has highly counter-intuitive implications in particular cases: if a citizen and resident of Nigeria previously had no special moral reason to promote the good of France, his waking up this morning with an inexplicable Francophilia surely does not change his moral situation. Tamir (1993, p. 99) tries to support her position by appealing to our ordinary moral judgment that it is morally worse to neglect one's friends or children than to neglect a stranger, but these analogies do not succeed in establishing the moral salience of affection. The special moral reasons to aid friends and children derive from the expectations aroused by one's history of interactions with those persons and by social conventions and legal rules that distribute responsibilities for meeting human needs. A biological parent's moral reasons to provide for her child do not diminish when her love for the child diminishes unless and until that moral responsibility is clearly transferred to some other agent, such as an adoptive parent or the state. And, once that transfer is completed and assuming that it is not reversed, the biological parent's moral reasons to provide for the child do not increase if her love returns. Affection can be a potent motive to promote someone's well-being, but it is not a moral reason to do so.

4.4. Civic identification

Civic identification, although often found together with patriotic love, is conceptually distinct from and, I shall argue, can exist without any such positive affect.[19] To identify with a polity is to feel a special connection to that polity's agency. Nathanson (1993, p. 35) describes identification as "a sense of 'my-ness' that gives rise to feelings of pride when the country acts well or shame when it acts poorly." Nathanson is right to focus on susceptibility to feelings of

[19] In a rare example of political science scholarship that appreciates this possibility, Zachary Elkins and John Sides (2007, p. 696) "conceive of attachment [to a state] as involving two dimensions: self-categorization as a member of that state and a positive affect for the state."

pride and shame as the principal hallmark of identification. And we should add that a person who identifies with her polity will have these feelings about the polity's significant omissions as well as its positive actions.

Pride and shame are triggered by one's evaluations of a particular polity's actions if and only if one identifies with that polity. But it is worth noting that identification with a polity manifests not only as pride and shame, understood as emotional responses to *one's own* evaluations of the polity's actions, but also as distinctive emotional responses to *other people's* expressed evaluations of those actions. To a person who identifies with a particular polity, and especially one who also feels some responsibility for that polity's actions (as I shall shortly discuss), judgments of that polity feel (to some degree) like judgments of oneself. Hearing someone else express a positive judgment about the polity elicits the distinctive positive emotions associated with receiving personal praise. Conversely, hearing a negative judgment about the polity feels like receiving personal criticism. And, in each case, the emotions that are triggered by hearing the judgment do not depend upon the hearer's concurring with it. If she already believes that the judgment of her polity's actions is correct, hearing it expressed by others may well intensify her feeling of pride or shame, but the experience will also arouse the distinct emotions associated with reputational gain or loss.[20] And if she does not concur in the judgment, even after hearing it expressed, that experience cannot induce pride or shame, but it will nonetheless trigger an emotional response. We are emotionally invested in the reputation of objects with which we identify in much the same way as (albeit usually to a lesser degree than) we are emotionally invested in our own individual reputations.

As we have seen, the sense of "my-ness" that constitutes civic identification discloses itself through distinctive emotional reactions

[20] My feelings of pride and shame are typically *magnified* by my belief (or mere suspicion) that other people concur with the judgment that underlies my feelings, especially when those people express that judgment publicly and/or directly to me. But these feelings can and will *exist* without any such belief. I can feel ashamed of my (father's) action even if I am sure that no one else knows what I (or he) did. Similarly, I can feel ashamed of an action that everyone else judges favorably. And, conversely, I can feel proud of an action that no one else approves of (perhaps because no one else knows of its existence).

to both one's own and other people's evaluations of the polity's actions. But the mere fact that a person refers to a particular country as "my country" does not show that she identifies with it in any meaningful sense, let alone in the sense that concerns us here. If, when discussing what she regards as some terrible misdeed by the US government, an American citizen says that "my country did it," she is not necessarily thereby expressing shame. A listener will sometimes be able to judge based on emphasis: "*my* country did it" is usually an expression of shame, whereas "my *country* did it" often expresses a sense of detachment from one's country's actions that constitutes precisely the absence of civic identification. When the words are spoken with the latter emphasis, the use of "my" typically signals only that the speaker is a citizen of that country and perhaps also a belief that her audience regards her citizenship as a significant element of her *ascriptive* identity.[21]

If a willingness to speak of "my country" is a necessary but insufficient condition for civic identification, willingness to speak in the language of "we" when describing the country's actions is sufficient but not necessary. A citizen who uses the first-person plural in this way will not only be susceptible to pride and shame (Gilbert, 2009, p. 344) but will typically also feel a degree of ownership of the polity's actions in the sense of feeling some responsibility for them even when she did not support them and may indeed have vigorously opposed them (Gilbert, 1997). When she judges her polity's actions to have been bad, this sense of responsibility goes by the name of guilt, and it is importantly distinct from shame. We can see the conceptual distinction most clearly in a different context: I can feel ashamed of my cousin's misdeed without feeling at all guilty about it. Oddly, the English language lacks a word that uniquely names the feeling of responsibility for an action one perceives to have been good, the feeling that relates to pride as guilt does to shame. For present purposes I will use the word "praiseworthiness" for this feeling, and it is importantly distinct from pride:

[21] The phenomenon that concerns us here is emphatically *not* ascriptive identity: the point is *not* that my membership in the polity partially defines me in the eyes of others. Perhaps other people see me in this way and, if so, the identity they ascribe to me may have helped to shape my own sense of identity, but neither of these conditions need obtain.

I can feel proud of my wife's achievement without feeling at all "praiseworthy" about it. Feeling some responsibility for one's polity's actions may well be an attractive source of civic motivation, and I periodically include it in my subsequent analysis for that reason, but, unlike susceptibility to pride and shame, it is not a necessary concomitant of civic identification.

Even when a person's susceptibility to pride and shame at a polity's actions is accompanied by a sense of responsibility for those actions, he may not hold the corresponding *belief* that he bears any responsibility for those actions (as distinct from the straightforwardly true belief that he is responsible for the role he personally played—or failed to play—in the process whereby those actions were determined). There is a difference between *feeling* (partially) responsible and *believing* that one is (partially) responsible; in particular, the former can arise without the latter. A young German citizen today may *feel* responsible for Germany's actions both during the Nazi era and in the contemporary European financial crisis but not *believe* that he is in any way responsible for either; he was not born until long after the Second World War, and, let us assume, he went to great lengths to oppose Germany's imposition of austerity on other European countries.

The feeling of guilt is neither identical to nor inseparable from its corresponding belief. I can feel guilt about my child's or my great-grandfather's wicked actions without believing that I am in any way morally responsible for those actions. The feeling may persist no matter how often and how forcefully my friends remind me that I am not responsible. Ex hypothesis, it is not that my friends fail to persuade me; in fact, they are preaching to the choir because I already believe what they are telling me, and I continue to believe it. My feelings of responsibility extend beyond my beliefs about responsibility.

I want to suggest that it is *good* for people's feelings of responsibility for their polity's actions to extend beyond their beliefs about responsibility. Susceptibility to feelings of guilt (and "praiseworthiness") about one's polity's actions is a valuable source of civic motivation (Gilbert, 1997, p. 83), but the corresponding belief that one is (partially) responsible for those actions would be false. One can be responsible only for one's own actions (including, of course, the actions one performs—and fails to perform—in the process that determines a polity's actions).[22]

The position I have just stated is surprisingly controversial. Igor Primoratz argues to the contrary that "I ought to be concerned about immoral practices of my society, immoral laws and policies of my polity, since they tend to impose collective moral responsibility I, too, have to shoulder, or to taint the moral record of many members or citizens, including myself." By concerning myself with my polity in this way, Primoratz concludes, "I will also be concerned for an important aspect of my own moral identity and integrity" (2008, p. 34). Nathanson makes the same argument: "Citizens have special reasons for wanting their country to behave well. Their own integrity is at stake in the behavior of their country" (1993, p. 47). According to Primoratz and Nathanson, the link between my polity's actions and my integrity exists as an objective moral reality that I cannot overcome by my actions (except, presumably, by the action of renouncing my citizenship): I share in the moral responsibility for my polity's actions no matter how I have behaved as a citizen. Hence "we are all to some extent guilty whenever our government commits injustices against our fellow citizens (or against the citizens of other states), or permits injustices to go unpunished or unrelieved (either at home or abroad)" (Scorza, 2007, p. 89).

Primoratz, Nathanson, and Scorza are all wrong about this. No matter what a citizen *feels* when he knows that his polity has acted wrongly, his moral integrity is unaffected by that action. Of course, to reiterate, his moral integrity may be very much affected by the role he himself played (or failed to play) in the democratic process that led to the action.[23] And I shall argue that it is morally desirable

[22] For a brief review of the philosophical literature in support of this position, see Margaret Gilbert (1997, p. 66).

[23] In the language of Iris Young (2004), citizens are morally *liable*—responsible in the backward-looking sense—only for their own actions but they have a forward-looking *political responsibility* to contribute to the determination of the polity's future actions. This political responsibility, grounded in the special opportunities that citizens have to influence their polity, is just another name for the moral reasons I briefly referenced earlier and will explore in greater depth in Chapter 5. Notice that someone who vigorously opposed his polity's unjust actions (and therefore does not share in the moral liability for them) nonetheless has strong moral reasons—a political responsibility, in Young's terms—to press his polity to act in ways that would make amends for those previous injustices.

for him to *feel* responsible for the polity's actions, but this is not because he *is* actually responsible. He is not. To help see this, notice that if it were true that one bears partial responsibility for one's polity's actions even when one went to reasonable (or even extraordinary) lengths to oppose them, this would have to be true regardless of the moral status of those actions. Just as citizens who vigorously opposed some *morally prohibited* action of their polity would nonetheless be partially responsible for the wrongdoing, so other citizens who strenuously opposed a *morally obligatory* action of their polity would properly be deemed to share in the responsibility for that rightful action. This would be absurd—morally outrageous, even. The only way to avoid the absurdity and remain consistent is to reject altogether the notion that citizens are responsible for their polity's actions.[24]

If I am right about this, a person whose feelings of responsibility do not extend beyond her beliefs about responsibility must either lack a valuable source of civic motivation or hold a false belief. There is no need to accept either of these costs. Although the feeling that one is partially responsible for one's polity's actions cannot be justified by appealing to the facts about individual moral responsibility, the feeling can nonetheless be sufficiently justified by appeal to its utility in providing much-needed motivation for morally important actions.[25] Analogously, I would argue that it is morally desirable for parents to *feel* responsible for their child's actions, as opposed to feeling responsible only for their own behavior as parents, despite the fact that they *are not* directly and independently responsible for the child's actions; the extra sense of responsibility increases parents' motivation to raise good children. But, although it

[24] It is a further question whether and when citizens who are not morally responsible for their polity's misdeeds may nonetheless be morally obligated to pay some of the costs of rectifying those misdeeds on some principle of collective liability. See, for example, David Miller (2007, p. 119) and Stilz (2011).

[25] In a related context, Hand (2011, p. 334) distinguishes these two different ways of justifying emotions: "We can ask of our emotional responses not only whether there is evidence to support them, but also whether it is helpful or harmful, beneficial or burdensome, for us to have them." Gilbert (1997, pp. 83, 84) argues that, irrespective of utility considerations, it can be rationally appropriate for a morally innocent "member of a *plural subject* that bears guilt" to feel the guilt "in which [she] shares—but does not own."

is valuable for parents to have this feeling, it is undesirable for them to have the corresponding belief because that belief would be false.[26]

Because feeling responsible for one's polity's actions is a concept entirely distinct from feeling responsible for one's own contributions to the process of determining those actions, the presence and intensity of the former feeling need bear no relation to the extent of one's (potential) influence on the latter process. Absence of influence is compatible with feelings of responsibility; someone who lives under a dictatorship may be powerless to affect the polity's actions and yet feel not only ashamed but also guilty when the polity behaves badly. The same is true for a dis- or un-enfranchised person in a democratic polity: consider, for example, a felon who long since lost the right to vote or a 17-year-old who has yet to attain it. Conversely, someone who possesses a great deal of political power and acutely feels the personal responsibility attending that power may feel no direct and independent responsibility for her polity's actions. To illustrate this possibility via an extreme case: if I am one of only three people whose votes determine my polity's actions, and even assuming that I take this responsibility very seriously, when the other two voters override my vigorous opposition and my polity therefore acts in a way that I regard as terribly wrong, I may feel no guilt (for all that I may feel deeply ashamed).

I now want to address two important concerns about the effects of feeling responsible for, and especially guilty about, one's polity's actions. First, are the civic motivational effects as reliable and positive as I suggest? Specifically, guilt can be paralyzing rather than galvanizing. Feeling guilty about my polity's bad behavior can cause me to push that behavior to the back of my mind as too painful even to think about, let alone to address through civic action geared to making amends. On other occasions, guilt can have the opposite effect, causing me to focus obsessively on trying to rectify and atone for my polity's past misdeeds: these efforts may be futile and/or they

[26] I assume, both in the case of children's actions and in the analogous case of the polity's actions, that we should not encourage the false *belief* about responsibility even if that is the most effective way to arouse and sustain a morally desirable *feeling* of responsibility. I proposed in Chapter 2 that the costs of false beliefs routinely outweigh their motivational benefits, and I believe that this proposition remains true even when our analysis (appropriately) recognizes the additional motivational value of feelings that are supported by false beliefs.

may lead me to unduly neglect other political issues that are equally or more morally important.

These concerns are legitimate. Human psychology is complex and varied, and guilt surely will not always yield the motivational benefits I have attributed to it. This is especially true when guilt feelings are very intense. But, when we consider people's feelings about *their own* actions, the aforementioned concerns do not normally lead us to deny that, for most people and in most cases, there is motivational value in being susceptible to moderate feelings of guilt when one believes oneself to have done something wrong. Although guilt will sometimes have a net demotivating effect when it is actually experienced, we are always at least somewhat motivated by the desire to avoid feeling guilt in the future. And the obsessive motivation that can result from very strong feelings of guilt is usually understood as proof of the dictum that one can have too much of a good thing. As I shall argue in Chapter 5 in a somewhat different context, having a conscience does generate some bad effects, but it is nonetheless presumptively a virtue from the consequentialist perspective. I think we can and should say the same about feeling directly responsible for one's polity's actions. The important thing is to keep those feelings of responsibility within reasonable limits. I see no reason to doubt that civic education could be roughly callibrated to render most people susceptible to guilt at levels that are salutary on balance.

Second, it is important to acknowledge the potential psychological costs of feeling guilty specifically for actions for which one (rightly) believes that one is not responsible. Cognitive dissonance of this kind can be painful and upsetting in itself and could even, in extreme cases, lead to self-destructive behavior. Could the costs of such cognitive dissonance outweigh the motivational benefits of feeling responsible for one's polity's actions?

They could. But, again, I think the solution is to avoid arousing excessively strong feelings of guilt. Cognitive dissonance of low-to-moderate intensity is an extremely common psychological phenomenon and does not significantly threaten our well-being. For example, parents are not usually torn apart by moderate feelings of responsibility for their children's actions that extend beyond their beliefs about such responsibility. And, I would suggest, many of us already live quite happily with the equivalent combination of feelings and beliefs vis-à-vis the actions of some or all of the polities to which we belong. That is not to deny that, other things being equal, we would be better off eliminating cognitive dissonance altogether. But if, as I have argued, feelings of responsibility for one's polity's actions are motivationally valuable and the corresponding false beliefs about responsibility are undesirable, other things are not equal in this case.

As I noted in Chapter 1, whenever we translate a worthy educational goal into a set of concrete practices for realizing that goal in the population at large, we will generate some unintended and undesirable effects. If adult citizens share the goal of inculcating in all children moderate feelings of responsibility for their polity's actions, they will in practice generate excessively strong feelings in some children and little or no sense of responsibility in certain others.[27] And, given the inevitability of such errors, we may need to adjust our goal in light of our judgments about the relative importance of errors in each direction. It may be considerably worse to render citizens excessively susceptible to feeling guilty about their polity's actions than to fall short of the optimum. If this is so, and if errors can be expected to distribute symmetrically around our target, we shall need to aim lower than the optimal degree of felt responsibility. But this fact, although important, neither diminishes the value of knowing what the true optimum is nor warrants abandoning the goal of educating children to feel responsible for their polity's actions.

As a final note on the topic of guilt, I should remind the reader that susceptibility to guilt, unlike susceptibility to pride and shame, is not a necessary part of civic identification. So, if it turns out that guilt (including anticipated guilt) does not have the net effect of enhancing civic motivation (which strikes me as very unlikely) or that the psychological costs (cognitive dissonance) of experiencing moderate feelings of guilt without possessing the corresponding belief outweigh the civic motivational benefits (possible, but still unlikely,

[27] One might also worry that the educational tools used to induce feelings of responsibility for the polity's actions will (unintentionally) increase people's *general* susceptibility to feelings of responsibility that do not track their beliefs about responsibility. Such cognitive dissonance does not always have the redeeming virtues that it has in the special case of civic identification. I thank Harry Brighouse for pressing me on this point.

I suspect), I can and happily will drop my claim that education should render citizens susceptible to feeling directly responsible for their polity's actions. Dropping this claim would not in any way compromise my argument for cultivating civic identification.

4.5. Identification without affection

Although identification and affection are conceptually distinct, are they psychologically separable? In one respect the answer is obviously yes: it is perfectly common to feel special affection for a particular country of which one is not a citizen and with which one certainly does not identify in any sense. But, when the object of a person's affection is a polity of which she is a citizen, can this affection realistically arise and persist without the kind of subjective identification I have described? I believe that it can, but I shall not belabor the point because, as Chapter 5 makes clear, I see no reason to try to promote affection without identification. People feel pride and shame in response to the actions of some but not all of the agents for whom they feel affection, and education is a major determinant of the members of that subset. Some children learn to regard their cousins simply as dear friends with whom they happen to have a familial relationship; others learn also to identify with them.[28] Attitudes to polities are presumably malleable in much the same way.

But what about the inverse possibility: can there be civic identification without patriotic love? I shall shortly offer a hypothetical example to suggest that this is not such an outlandish idea. And I shall argue in Chapter 5 that it is an appropriate goal for civic education. But it is important to note that the force and practical significance of that argument do not depend on the possibility of achieving a society in which many or even most citizens exhibit civic identification without a shred of patriotic affection. Neither identification nor affection is a simple binary matter; both are feelings that exist by degree. Someone who identifies strongly with his polity will experience intense shame when he perceives that polity to have acted badly; someone else whose civic identification is much weaker

[28] As we shall shortly see, still other children learn to identify with their cousins without developing any special affection for them.

will have a correspondingly weaker emotional reaction to the same action, even assuming that her evaluation of that action does not differ from the first person's. A citizen who ardently loves her country will be much more strongly motivated to serve that country than a second citizen who is identical to the first in all relevant respects except that his affection for the country they both love is much less intense. If, as I shall argue in Chapter 5, civic identification is preferable to patriotic love as a source of civic motivation, this constitutes an important reason to promote civic identification without, as far as possible, simultaneously arousing patriotic love. Even if it proves impractical to educate and socialize most citizens so that they exhibit strong civic identification without any patriotic love, it should be possible to design social institutions that will induce rather more identification than love. I shall return to this point at the end of the present chapter.

To demonstrate the psychological, as opposed to the merely conceptual, possibility of civic identification without patriotic love, one would ideally point to actual examples of people who feel no special affection for a particular polity (and therefore no special concern for its well-being) but who nonetheless see themselves as specially connected to that polity as evidenced by the fact that they feel pride and shame at—and perhaps also some responsibility for—its actions (independently of their own role in determining those actions). But any such purported "existence proof" in this domain is bound to be contestable because feelings cannot be directly observed. Real people's feelings have to be imputed from their actions, including their self-reports of feelings and motives, and this imputation is notoriously difficult to perform accurately.[29] For this reason, I shall offer instead a hypothetical example. My goal in doing so is to show that civic identification without patriotic love is neither psychologically implausible nor pathological (although it is sure to be rare in societies whose major institutions routinely treat these two attitudes as inseparable and may also promote them both).

For the sake of simplicity, my example will be of a person who has no affect whatsoever towards his polity. But it is important to note that the absence of patriotic love does not require the absence of all

[29] Self-reports of feelings and motives are unreliable both because sincerity cannot be assumed and because of deeper concerns about the accuracy of introspection.

affect towards one's polity, merely that there be *no net positive* affect. Readers who find it hard to imagine (or to identify apparent cases of) civic identification entirely without affect towards the polity may have rather less difficulty imagining (or identifying apparent cases of) civic identification that is bound up with a complex bundle of emotions, some positive and some negative, with no net positive valence. I shall limit myself to describing an instance of the simple psychological phenomenon, but I am open to the possibility that the complex phenomenon is more commonly observed and/or easier to generate through civic education.

Isaac, a citizen and lifelong resident of the United States, was raised to feel that his membership in the American polity is a central part of his identity. Guided by the examples set by his parents and other persons with a formative influence in his early life, Isaac learned to feel proud when his country acts well and ashamed when it acts poorly. He even developed a sense of responsibility for America's actions that is independent of Isaac's sense of responsibility for his own actions: Isaac feels guilty when America acts badly (in Isaac's judgment) regardless of the role, if any, that he played in producing or supporting the offending action.

Why does Isaac identify with America in this sense? The explanation is *neither* that Isaac sees himself as especially similar to other American citizens *nor* that he sees his own character traits distinctively expressed in America's civic and political institutions. Isaac's identification with America transcends such issues of resemblance just as his identification with his family (including those far-flung relatives that he has never met) does not depend on Isaac's believing that he possesses any particular traits in common with other family members.[30] In fact, there are no beliefs underlying Isaac's civic identification. Isaac identifies with America simply because he was, throughout his formative years, inducted into various social practices of expressing pride, shame, and feelings of responsibility about that country's actions. Much as he learned to feel sorry for his misdeeds by participating in the social practice of apologizing, he learned to feel proud or ashamed of his country by routinely

[30] I acknowledge in Chapter 5 that civic identification is *more likely* to develop, persist, and manifest strongly for a citizen who does perceive some such resemblance between herself and the polity and/or her fellow citizens.

observing and engaging in the forms of communication that are used to express such feelings.

When Isaac reflects on the individual character traits and institutional qualities that he regards as typically and distinctively American, he finds much to admire: his evaluative beliefs about the objective merits of his polity and its people are generally quite positive.[31] But that assessment is neither influenced by nor generative of any love for the country. Isaac feels no special affection for America despite the twin facts that he identifies with the country and regards it as admirable in many respects. He was raised both to *feel* that America is *his* country and to *believe* that it is a *good* country, but those lessons did not, even in conjunction, lead Isaac to feel any fondness for America. In just the same way, he was raised to feel pride and shame at the actions of his cousin, Mary, and to believe that she is a good person, but he never developed any special affection for her. Isaac does periodically experience positive emotions—feelings of pride and even "praiseworthiness"—in response to the *actions* of his country and of his cousin. But what is strikingly absent from his relationships to these two objects—America and Mary—is a positive emotional attitude to the object itself.[32] In the absence of any such positive affect, Isaac feels no special concern for the well-being of either object, for all that he is susceptible to pride, shame, and feelings of responsibility with respect to their actions.

To understand why Isaac never developed a positive emotional attitude to America, we must examine the ways in which the country was presented to him during his formative years. Isaac was introduced to America's civic and political institutions, including what he was taught to regard as their merits, in sober and literal terms. He was not encouraged to see America as especially beautiful or its history as especially interesting or exciting. More generally, Isaac was never exposed to the kinds of traditional patriotic rituals, rhetorical exercises, and affecting displays that serve to associate

[31] I specify that these beliefs are positive to avoid any impression that what I shall describe as Isaac's lack of affection for America is really a set of predominantly negative judgments about a country that he nonetheless loves.

[32] Absence of affection for one's immediate family members arguably poses a significant threat to one's prospects for a flourishing human life, but the same cannot plausibly be said about not loving one's cousin or one's polity.

positive emotions with symbols of the country and thereby with the country itself (as distinct from that country's particular actions, some of which Isaac was indeed encouraged to view with pride in the course of cultivating his civic identification). By contrast, Isaac's early encounters with France—its people, institutions, language, culture, geography, and history—were routinely and systematically framed in ways that made that country appear intriguing, attractive, and emotionally compelling. As a result, although Isaac does not regard France as objectively superior to America,[33] he feels a special affection for France that is absent from his relationship to America.

A well-intentioned friend once suggested to Isaac that he should emigrate to France and seek French citizenship in order to reside in and contribute to the civic life of the country he loves. Isaac's response was simple and powerful: "I may *love* France, but I *am* American." Isaac wants to see France flourish, but he feels no special connection to the actions and omissions of the French state. He does not experience pride or shame, let alone a sense of responsibility, when France acts well or badly. Furthermore, if a pill existed that would redirect Isaac's civic identification from America to France, Isaac would not take it; he feels no fondness for America, but he nonetheless regards his membership in the polity as constitutive, an important part of his self-concept, not as a disease to be cured. In particular, Isaac's identification, his sense of belonging, strikes him as a more fundamental aspect of his non-moral psychology than are his sentiments and affections.

Just as Isaac's relationship to America resembles his relationship to his cousin, Mary, Isaac's relationship to France can helpfully be analogized to his relationship to his friend, Ruth. Isaac feels great affection for Ruth, and he has a correspondingly strong concern for her well-being, but Isaac does not identify with Ruth. In other words, Isaac does not feel the special connection to Ruth's agency that he does to Mary's. As a result, if Isaac sees Mary and Ruth both preparing to attack an innocent person and he can restrain only one of them, he will restrain Mary. Isaac's motive for doing so is to avoid the shame (and perhaps also guilt) he would feel if his own cousin were to engage in unjustified violence. And, to be clear, Isaac's

[33] Again, I emphasize that Isaac's affections do not simply track his evaluative beliefs to avoid any impression that I am conflating the two.

prioritization decision is driven only by the psychology of identification, not by any perceived moral considerations. Isaac does not believe that the familial nature of his relationship with Mary generates any special moral reason for him to try to prevent her from acting wrongly. As we saw earlier, even when one *feels* responsible for an agent's actions one may not *believe* that one bears responsibility. Therefore, even if Isaac's motive for restraining Mary rather than Ruth is a desire to avoid the guilt he would feel in response to Mary's violence (but not in response to Ruth's), it does not follow that he perceives any moral grounds for prioritizing in this fashion.[34] Indeed, Isaac might well choose to restrain Mary even if he knows that there are stronger moral reasons to avert Ruth's intended attack (because, for example, Ruth's violence would be more severe than Mary's).[35]

Identification with one's polity enhances civic motivation to the extent that one believes that one has the potential to positively influence the actions of that polity and thereby increase one's chances of feeling pride rather than shame (and perhaps also "praiseworthiness" rather than guilt). Civic identification can also yield non-instrumental, expressive motivation: I may engage in civic action in part to express the constitutive significance of my membership in the polity.[36] In both these ways civic identification is similar to patriotic love. But, I shall argue in Chapter 5, civic identification has the great advantage over patriotic love that it poses much less of a threat to people's capacity to critically evaluate their polity and its actions.

[34] One could try to argue that the psychological fact of identifying with a polity changes one's moral situation. I would respond to such an argument much as I did (earlier in this chapter) to Yael Tamir's argument that affection generates moral reasons and (in Chapter 2) to Joseph Raz's proposition that civic identification can give rise to an obligation to obey the law. One fundamentally mistakes the nature of morality by suggesting that its demands are conditional on our attitudes.

[35] If I know that a person will have the opportunity to perform one or other but not both of two morally valuable actions (X and Y), would not the fact that X is of greater moral value than Y mean that I should abstain from increasing the person's motivation to perform Y? Not if the expected consequence of my abstention is that the person performs *neither* X nor Y. If this person suffers from a general weakness of motives to perform morally valuable actions—as most people do—I should seek to strengthen *all* such motives in him. I explore this theme in Chapter 5.

[36] I noted in Chapter 2 that one can also have such expressive reasons for compliance with one's polity's laws.

4.6. Conclusion: educating for identification without affection

I have argued at length that it is both conceptually coherent and, more controversially, realistically possible for civic identification to exist entirely without patriotic love. But I certainly do not deny that many approaches to fostering the former will also tend to arouse the latter. Since I shall argue (in Chapter 5) that civic identification is superior to patriotic love as a source of civic motivation, it is therefore important to ask how education could promote civic identification without simultaneously fostering affection for the polity to much the same degree. This is obviously a complex empirical question that lies beyond the scope of my study (and my expertise), but the preceding analysis sheds some light on the matter.

If I am right that people, and especially children, learn to *feel* pride and shame at their polity's actions in large part by being exposed to and participating in various social practices of *expressing* precisely such feelings, then civic identification will best be promoted by fostering this kind of expression in multiple venues: schools, families, museums, the arts, voluntary associations, the media (in its many forms), and a polity's civil discourse and public sphere more generally.[37] But, since it is reasonable to suppose that people who are exposed almost exclusively to expressions of pride in the polity, rarely encountering and scarcely ever participating in expressions of shame, are likely to acquire a measure of affection for the polity with which they are coming to identify, it is important that expressions of pride should not dominate a citizen's experience, at least during her most formative years. And, given that (as I discuss at length in Chapter 5) we all prefer to feel (and therefore also to sincerely express) pride rather than shame, there is a standing danger that citizens' development of civic identification will be dramatically skewed in this fashion.

For example, a country's history is all too often presented to its citizens with a heavy emphasis on great achievements and episodes

[37] To what extent, in which venues, and in what ways it is prudent and legitimate for the polity itself to encourage expressions of civic pride, shame, and responsibility (and whether it is realistic to expect a polity sufficiently to foster expressions of shame and guilt vis-à-vis its own actions) are further questions: I cannot explore them here. As I noted in Chapter 1, I do not engage with questions about the proper allocation of educational authority.

of virtue, about which citizens can feel proud, and scant attention to the debacles and sins, which would prompt unpleasant feelings of shame. One challenge for a society that takes seriously the goal of fostering civic identification without unduly encouraging affection for the polity will therefore always be to ensure that its members, and especially its children, are sufficiently exposed to expressions of shame (and perhaps also guilt) in the course of inculcating and reinforcing their identification with the polity. In part this challenge can be met by emphasizing the polity's missteps (both moral and non-moral) in the distant past, but exclusive reliance on this strategy risks conveying to today's citizens that the polity was once somewhat ugly but is now thoroughly lovely. Children should learn and adult citizens should regularly be reminded that there is plenty to be ashamed of in the polity's very recent past. I do not mean to suggest that citizens must be exposed *equally* to expressions of shame and pride in their polity, let alone that expressions of shame should predominate. But if negative emotions do not figure significantly in the experiences through which citizens come to identify with their polity, affection for that polity is likely to be a byproduct of the process.

In short, if one is serious about avoiding the cultivation of patriotic love, the positive emotions (of pride) that are aroused for the purpose of promoting civic identification should be significantly offset by negative emotions (of shame), whose arousal conveniently serves the same purpose. And societies should strive to avoid all practices that associate positive emotions with the polity if those practices are not necessary to promote identification. In general, this means eliminating the use of stirring images, music, and rhetoric whose function is to cultivate positive sentiments towards the polity itself (as distinct from arousing feelings of pride at some of the polity's specific actions, which will be justified as a component of the best strategy for promoting civic identification).

CHAPTER 5

Doing without love

People's motives to contribute to the democratic polities of which they are citizens (and/or residents[1]) are often weaker than the moral reasons for them to do so. Call this the civic motivation problem.[2] In the first half of this chapter, I examine the sources of this problem. In Section 5.1, I argue that the distinctive opportunities afforded by citizenship generate strong moral reasons for action. Democratic polities have the potential to be our best instruments for the pursuit of many morally important goods, but that potential in a particular polity is only realized when most of its citizens contribute conscientiously to the functioning of its institutions. Each citizen has strong moral reasons to play her part in this important moral project rather than free-riding on the efforts of others. Furthermore, I argue that the existence of strong moral reasons for citizens to contribute to their polity does not depend upon the moral merits of that polity's recent actions or existing institutions.

In Section 5.2, I argue that, especially in the case of purely voluntary contributions but also when there are positive incentives or legal sanctions in play, citizens' motivation to contribute to their polities is rarely commensurate with the strength of their moral

[1] As I shall shortly explore, citizenship and residency are independently important in terms of the distinctive opportunities they afford. And this is a deeply significant fact given the large numbers of people around the world who are not citizens of the country in which they reside. But, in order to streamline the presentation of my arguments, I will often speak simply of citizens and citizenship. It should be evident that many of my remarks are also applicable to non-citizen residents of a polity (albeit for somewhat different reasons, which I will soon discuss).

[2] For a recent statement and brief history of this general problem, see Berger: "Justifying and motivating reasons may coincide but often do not" (2011, p. 123).

reasons to do so.[3] In particular, the combination of narrowly self-interested and disinterestedly moral motives does not by itself lead most people to contribute to their polities at anything like the levels we would desire. Free-riding problems loom large in mass democracies, and moral motives are notoriously unreliable. Habits of and tastes for engaging in particular civically valuable activities have important (and often neglected) roles to play, and they pose only a very limited threat to the capacity for critical civic judgment, but they seem unlikely by themselves to make up the motivational shortfall.

In Section 5.3, I evaluate the traditional (proposed) solution to the civic motivation problem: patriotic love, that is, special affection for one's polity.[4] Patriotic love promises to solve the civic motivation problem, but advocates of the orthodox view worry that the cure may be worse than the disease. Patriotic love is commonly associated with a diminished ability to perceive one's polity's faults, both because "love is blind"—it inhibits critical thinking about its object—and because patriotic love is often aroused by a form of civic education that offers an exaggeratedly rosy view of the polity, its history and its current institutions. I argue that this critique of patriotic love is powerful but that it may not succeed in showing that the cure is truly worse than the disease. If patriotic love were the only way to solve the civic motivation problem, we might be best advised to accept the accompanying impairment of citizens' critical judgment as a necessary evil, a(n admittedly high) price worth paying for increased levels of civic contribution.

But, as we saw in Chapter 4, there is an alternative: civic identification can be a potent source of civic motivation and can exist independently of patriotic love. Indeed, I shall argue in Section 5.4

[3] Strictly speaking, my analysis and argument do not depend upon the truth of this claim. As I noted in Chapters 1 and 3, I certainly do not make the empirical claim that any existing polities are trying to subsist on the meager motivational resources that the orthodox view of civic education would allow adult citizens to cultivate in the rising generation. Some polities may even have implemented a full solution to the civic motivation problem: their citizens may exhibit *no* shortfall of such motivation. But it would remain to ask whether such polities have found the *best* solution. My goal in this chapter is to critique one very common (proposed) solution—patriotic love—and argue for the superiority of an alternative—civic identification.

[4] As noted in Chapter 4, I use "love" and "affection" interchangeably. I shall defend this practice in the course of my critique of patriotic love.

that this formula—identification without affection—is an attractive solution to the civic motivation problem. Identification with one's polity does not impair civic judgment as severely as patriotic love does. And, once we liberate ourselves from the orthodox view's dogged refusal to compromise on its ideal of critical citizenship, this lower degree of impairment looks like a very fair price for enhanced civic motivation. In the remainder of the chapter I defend civic identification from two objections. In Section 5.5, I argue that, although getting large numbers of citizens to identify strongly enough with their polity realistically requires the promotion of a shared civic identity with some culturally specific content, claims that this identity must be highly exclusive and ethnocentric are greatly exaggerated. And finally, in Section 5.6, I defend identification (as well as habits of and tastes for civic action) from the claim that all non-moral motives to participate in the civic life of one's polity constitute psychological barriers to morally appropriate reconfigurations of political space.

5.1. Moral reasons for civic action

As we discovered in Chapter 4, there is no shortage of arguments intended to show that (certain) individuals have strong moral reasons to contribute to the polities of which they are citizens. We also saw in Chapter 4 that many of these arguments are eminently contestable and therefore presumptively unsuitable to be advocated to children in an effort to instill civic motivation. More fundamentally, of course, if all attempts to establish the existence of strong moral reasons to contribute to one's polity were inconclusive, this would severely undermine the case for using education to instill civic motivation of any kind. But there is, I believe, a conclusive argument that people have strong moral reasons to make appropriate use of the distinctive opportunities afforded by their citizenship and polity of residence.[5] Unlike the various other arguments we have seen, this argument's normative premises extend no farther than the basic

[5] My argument from distinctive opportunities owes much to the work of Deigh (1988), Goodin (1988), and Stilz (2009, especially pp. 195–204), but my position is distinct from each of theirs.

moral values of liberal democracy. When its conclusions are properly understood, the argument is not vulnerable to a standard objection grounded in concerns about global justice. And the argument does not presuppose that the polity in which one holds citizenship (and/or resides) is even minimally just. Let me try to substantiate these claims.

Democratic polities whose citizens and residents all contribute conscientiously to the functioning of their various institutions are the best instruments we can have for the pursuit of a set of vitally important moral goods: justice, security, social coordination, and the legitimation of coercion. Citizenship of a particular polity affords certain distinctive opportunities to contribute to that polity's success in pursuing these goods (by, for example, casting an informed and considered vote, serving conscientiously on a jury, or standing for and performing well in public office). And residence in a polity (by which I mean merely the *fact* of living within its borders, regardless of legal status) affords other distinctive opportunities: a polity's residents are the only people who are routinely in a position to enable that polity to realize morally important goods by complying with its laws (or, when necessary, engaging in civil disobedience), supporting its agents (unless they abuse their authority), and indeed serving responsibly as one of those agents to execute some of the polity's many functions. Although the marginal impact of any one person's civic contribution is sometimes negligible or even zero, a polity's prospects for realizing the moral goods that justify its existence are greater when more of its citizens and residents make appropriate use of these opportunities. And those prospects are decidedly poor when most citizens and residents are disengaged from their polity's institutions.[6] Given the great importance of the moral goods at stake and the weighty moral objections to free-riding on other people's efforts to produce them, each individual therefore has strong moral reasons to contribute conscientiously to the polities of which she is a citizen and/or a resident.

[6] Admittedly, relatively low levels of participation can be sufficient to sustain very roughly liberal democratic institutions, and this state of affairs is far preferable to the complete demise of liberal democracy, but we should not mistake survival for flourishing. Without widespread and vigorous popular participation in directing, supporting, and (where necessary) constraining the power of the state, a society will never come close to realizing the liberal democratic ideals of individual freedom and equality.

To be clear, the moral objection to free-riding does not apply at the level of each particular civically valuable activity. A "division of civic labor" (Scorza, 2007, p. 72) is perfectly appropriate; indeed, it is often necessary. "Many different kinds of political work need to be done" (Scorza, 2007, p. 6) in a democracy, and it is neither realistic nor requisite for each citizen to contribute in all these many ways. But there are strong moral reasons for each person to do her fair share in creating or sustaining a flourishing liberal democracy, to perform at least some of the civically valuable actions that her citizenship and residence make possible.

Of course, all people (and especially those with significant wealth and/or disposable income) have lots of other opportunities to promote important moral goods besides contributing to the polities of which they are (at present) citizens and/or residents. For example, one can promote important moral goods by being a good parent, friend, or neighbor; supporting charities that directly help needy people at home and/or abroad; supporting organizations that are promoting liberal democracy in polities to which one does not belong; and, most radically, moving to another polity, acquiring citizenship if possible, and availing oneself of the resulting opportunities to contribute to that polity.

The moral reasons to act on these other opportunities are often more powerful than the moral reasons to contribute to the polities to which one belongs. Note, however, that sometimes the best way to try to help needy people both within and beyond the borders of one's polity is to try to harness and redirect the resources of that polity.[7] Indeed, it is realistically only through the actions of polities

[7] Interestingly, there are also two important ways in which my participation in the politics of my country may contribute to the realization of moral goods at the global level even if I do not aim to do so. If so-called democratic peace theorists are correct, citizens who help to sustain and improve their country's democratic credentials thereby reduce the likelihood that the country will engage in unjust aggression against other countries. [For a review of this vast literature, see Kinsella (2005).] And, as critics of the so-called democratic deficit in supra-national governance institutions are quick to point out, the legitimacy of international laws typically depends upon their being endorsed by democratically legitimate national governments rather than being imposed by a supra-national bureaucracy that cannot realistically be held accountable by the people it is supposed to serve. In both these ways, contributions to one's democratic polity can function as unintended contributions to the pursuit of international moral goods.

that major progress can be made towards realizing distributive justice, both domestically and globally.[8] The steps that polities must take, and for which their citizens can and should agitate, are not simply to increase domestic transfer payments and (in the case of rich countries) budgets for international humanitarian aid. More fundamentally, justice requires dismantling policies and institutions that systematically frustrate disadvantaged people's efforts to help themselves and the creation of new political arrangements that facilitate and support those efforts.

We should also note that, because the moral reasons to contribute to one's polity are grounded in the moral goods that one is thereby helping to realize, not all civic actions that would benefit one's polity are morally recommended or even permissible. In particular, one often does not have moral reasons to support measures that would promote the well-being of one's own polity at the expense of other polities and their members, even when doing so would be morally permissible. Supporting one's polity's efforts to compete with other polities for scarce resources is morally recommended only if those efforts push in the direction of greater global distributive justice. By contrast, promoting good governance in the municipality or country wherein one resides does not disadvantage people who reside elsewhere. But, of course, there is an opportunity cost to every action, and this leads me to the true crux of the issue.

Notwithstanding both the moral importance of the various *domestic* goods that are best pursued through a democratic polity and the potential to promote *global* justice by harnessing the power of one's polity, it is manifestly the case that the moral reasons to contribute to one's polities are rarely, if ever, the strongest of all the various moral reasons for action that apply to an individual.

[8] Focusing on the issue of global justice, Amy Gutmann (1996, p. 69) argues that "it is primarily (not exclusively) through our empowerment as democratic citizens that we can further the cause of justice around the world." In much the same spirit, Richard Vernon (2010, pp. 5, 6) points out that "in the world as it is, the prospects for global justice can be achieved only if (actual) citizenship is valued even more than it currently is." The various "actions that would have to be taken to promote justice globally...can occur only if citizens accept such things as legitimate and necessary objectives of their states." In particular, the distinctive opportunities afforded by citizenship in a rich polity will often generate strong moral reasons to press for that polity to act in ways that benefit poorer polities and their citizens.

Therefore, it could be objectionable to foster civic motivation in children if doing so leads them to neglect even more pressing moral concerns. But how *likely* is this possible effect? And can a program of character education realistically be designed and delivered in ways that successfully mitigate or eliminate the risk?

I assume that, whether or not it fosters civic motivation, education should encourage many other activities that have considerable moral worth. I am certainly not proposing that cultivation of civic motivation should *replace* cultivation of motives for other morally valuable actions, as might be the prescription of civic republicanism when taken to an absurd extreme. Children should not be taught to believe (or to act as if they believed) that all other interests and concerns are subordinate to the flourishing of their polity.[9] Given an appropriately balanced approach to character education, it seems very unlikely that educationally-induced acts of good citizenship will come at the expense of good parenting, friendship, neighborliness, etc. Granted, some of the time that a parent spends campaigning for elected office could have been spent with her children, but it is farfetched to oppose the inclusion of arousal of civic motivation as one element of a balanced character education on the grounds that it will generate citizens who are so immersed in civic life that they neglect their children.

Many of our opportunities to promote important moral goods involve using our personal financial resources: to a great extent we can act on these opportunities without reducing our capacity to contribute to our polities because the civic actions upon which a flourishing democracy depends demand primarily our time rather than our money. Admittedly, however, it will often be the case that time spent performing civic actions (such as campaigning for municipal office in Milwaukee) could have been better spent earning (or raising) money that would then be used to promote other moral goods (such as the alleviation of river blindness in Africa). And in some instances we could directly use our time in more morally valuable ways, especially

[9] The classic account of a citizen who has been "successfully" educated in this extreme manner is found in Rousseau's *Emile* (1762/1979, p. 40), where Rousseau describes a Spartan mother who regards the death in battle of all five of her sons as utterly inconsequential when compared to the fact that the battle in question was won by her polity.

if we are willing to relocate to a polity whose needs are more pressing than those of the polity in which we currently live.

For this reason, contributing to the polities of which one is (presently) a citizen and/or resident is usually not morally obligatory. It is typically permissible, and often even supererogatory, to redirect whatever time one would have devoted to civic action to certain other morally valuable activities, especially when one is justifiably confident that the polity's institutions will be sufficiently well supported by the contributions of many of its citizens and residents. In such cases, the moral reasons not to free-ride on other people's efforts to generate a set of important moral goods are counterbalanced or even outweighed by the great good that one will do with the time liberated by one's free-riding. But, of course, although there is often no single (civic or non-civic) project that I am morally obligated to pursue, I am not at liberty to pass up *all* of my opportunities to promote important moral goods. I am entitled to pick my battles, but I must fight the good fight in some way or another.[10]

But here is the critical point. It does not seem likely that omitting cultivation of civic motivation from people's education would lead many of those people (whether by emigrating or by less drastic means) to dedicate more time to causes that are of greater moral value than contributing to the polities in which they were educated (and will typically continue to reside). It seems far more likely that declining to foster civic motivation will simply lead most people to devote more of their time to narrowly self-interested activities.[11] I acknowledge that this is ultimately an empirical question. It is conceivable that optimal character education will entirely omit the cultivation of civic motivation because there is no way to include this element without unduly reducing the expected rate at which the recipient will perform actions that are of even greater moral value than acts of good citizenship. But it would be very surprising if this turned out to be true.

I have argued that one has strong moral reasons to contribute to the polities of which one is a citizen and/or resident because of the

[10] I cannot here explore the complex and controversial issue of morality's *demandingness*, i.e., the extent to which one is obligated to dedicate oneself to morally valuable projects.

[11] For arguments of this type in defense of patriotism, see Nathanson (1993, p. 21), Barber (1996, pp. 30–7), and McConnell (1996, pp. 78–84).

important moral goods that one can thereby help to realize. But it might seem that these reasons exist only when the polities in question are above some threshold of justice or moral decency. Do I really have moral reasons to engage in the civic life of a polity that systematically perpetrates grave injustices both domestically and overseas? Do I not thereby become complicit in serious wrongdoing? Several participants in the scholarly debate over patriotism have approached this question by asking whether it is always desirable for citizens to be motivated to contribute to their polity. Stephen Nathanson and Simon Keller (2005, p. 574) both conduct the analysis in terms of loyalty,[12] and they reach the same conclusion: in Nathanson's (1993, pp. 118–19) words, "loyalty to one's country is appropriate only when it has qualities that make it worthy of its citizens' devotion." Janna Thompson (2008, p. 159) stakes out essentially the same position: "love of country, if it is to have a defense, must have as its rationale the goodness of a polity's institutions, relationships, political projects or political culture." These claims all strike me as profoundly mistaken.

The fact that a polity is very unjust does not undermine and may well actually bolster the claim that the distinctive opportunities afforded by citizenship in that polity generate strong moral reasons for action. As Ross Poole (2008, p. 138) observes, "the responsibilities of citizenship differ from those of political obligation... and do not cease when states cease to be even approximately just." Indeed, the moral importance of contributing to one's polity is presumably even greater when that polity is very unjust. The prospects for radical political reform are decidedly poor if citizens are disengaged from public life and focused exclusively on their personal affairs. If the moral reasons for civic action are not sufficient motives, the additional motivation that flows from loyalty and/or love will be desirable.[13] Why would motives for civic action be deemed morally inappropriate precisely when such action is most needed to combat profound injustice?

[12] Keller (2005, p. 567, n. 14) uses the concept of loyalty to refer to love that includes a special concern for its object's well-being. Nathanson (1993, pp. 34–5) uses the term to reference the "complex of attitudes" that constitutes patriotism on his account.

[13] This is true even if, as I shall shortly argue, it is preferable to derive civic motivation from sources that are less prone to distort civic judgment.

The answer to this question, presumably, is that Keller, Nathanson, and Thompson all presuppose that loyalty to and/or love for one's polity will be expressed by compliance with and support for its existing laws and institutions. But there is no good reason for this presupposition. As I discussed in Chapter 4, when people are non-morally motivated (by habits, tastes, patriotic love, or civic identification) to perform civic actions, the *substance* of those actions can nonetheless be determined (or at least constrained) by moral considerations, including a moralized conception of a polity's flourishing. Loyalty to one's polity can and should be morally infused. A patriot can be severely critical of her country in both thought and action. Citizens of good conscience who are strongly motivated to contribute to their polity may even be moved to use the extraordinary means of civil disobedience to oppose that polity's rotten institutions. Neither the moral reasons to use the distinctive opportunities afforded by citizenship nor the value of non-moral motives to engage in such civic action is called into question by the fact that a polity falls below some threshold of moral merit.

5.2. The civic motivation problem

One might imagine that there will be no shortage of civic motivation in a polity as long as the moral reasons for civic action are widely recognized among that polity's citizens. Just teach children to perceive the strong (opportunity-based) moral reasons for civic action and the educator's job is done. This is the prescription of the orthodox view, strictly applied, and it is naïve in the extreme. As we saw in Chapter 3, very few people are powerfully and reliably motivated by disinterested moral considerations, even those that they reflectively endorse. Human nature being what it is, perceived moral reasons for civic action are often motivationally insufficient. Even when a person knows that her civic action would produce an outcome of significant moral value, this knowledge often will not provide her with enough motivation to act at some cost to herself. And, of course, it is often the case that my individual contribution is either redundant (because the good outcome would have occurred without it) or insufficient (because the good outcome does not occur despite it). There are many contexts in which the marginal effect of one person's civic action is very likely to be zero: when decisions are made democratically in a large polity, it is rarely the case that any one individual's contribution to the process is pivotal, and it is almost never the case that one *private citizen*'s contribution is pivotal. Voting is only the simplest and most familiar example of this general phenomenon. There are important moral reasons to do one's fair share rather than free-ride on the civic contributions of others (Wellman, 2005; Lefkowitz, 2007, pp. 210–11), but these reasons generally have even less motivational force than the moral reasons to act in ways that will have morally good consequences.

Given that moral reasons are insufficiently strong and reliable motives for civic action, we need non-moral motives to support them. Can we rely on the instrumentally rational pursuit of self-interest for this supplementary motivation? Almost every citizen benefits from the survival and flourishing of her polity, after all. But it is immediately apparent that a citizen's narrow self-interest—understood to comprise both interests *in* her self and interests *of* her self in the well-being of her family and friends[14]—will rarely provide any net motivation for purely voluntary civic contributions, i.e., civic actions that are neither coerced nor compensated. The collective action problem I just discussed with reference to moral motives arises with even greater force in the context of self-interested motives: the narrowly self-interested rational strategy in a mass democracy is almost always to free-ride.[15] Even when the marginal effect of one's civic contribution would be significant and positive, the benefits would typically be dispersed widely and would

[14] I again follow Gauthier (1986) in distinguishing between these two forms of self-interest.

[15] Tocqueville (1850/2006, pp. 525–8) seems not to recognize this free-riding problem. His influential doctrine of "self-interest properly understood" presupposes that citizens will be motivated to contribute to the administration of public affairs when they appreciate the many ways in which they benefit from (good) administration. But, in partial defense of Tocqueville, I should note that he is principally concerned with administration at the local level: free-riding problems are less severe when democracy operates close to the ground both because one's input to decision processes is much more likely to be pivotal and because the benefits of one's contributions to the polity are dispersed to many fewer people whose well-being does not figure in one's narrow self-interest.

therefore accrue mainly to other citizens whose well-being does not figure in one's narrow self-interest.[16]

But the preceding analysis does not show that civic contributions cannot be motivated by narrow self-interest. It might seem to suggest rather that we cannot rely on purely *voluntary* civic contributions and that we should turn instead to coercion and/or compensation.[17] With a carefully designed institutional regime of incentives, the desire to avoid punishments or secure rewards that have been attached to particular actions might provide the appropriate level of motivation for narrowly self-interested citizens to contribute to their polities.[18]

Coercion certainly has a role to play in overcoming the free-rider problem, but there are often principled and/or practical reasons for the polity not to try to force people to contribute to civic life. Polities exceed their legitimate authority if they coerce their citizens to perform actions that are not morally obligatory. And my analysis earlier in this chapter suggests that very few positive civic actions are strictly obligatory (because it is so often morally permissible to use the time that would be required for the civic action to promote some other important moral good). Furthermore, the legitimacy of the polity's coercing a citizen to do X is not entailed by X's being morally obligatory. Marital fidelity and the keeping of

[16] This concern about free-riding shows the inadequacy of Melissa Williams' (2003) suggestion that educators should promote a sense of citizenship as "shared fate," making each citizen vividly aware that his interests, like those of all his compatriots, are greatly dependent on the health of the polity of which they are all members. To a narrowly self-interested person, the realization that one's fate is bound up with that of millions of one's compatriots is an open invitation to free-riding.

[17] As discussed in Chapter 3, there is some *intrinsic* value to moral motivation, so we would ideally try to avoid "crowding out" moral motives through the introduction of incentives and, more generally, through the cultivation of non-moral motives for civic action. But it is so much more difficult to motivate voluntary civic actions (as compared to compliance with laws) that, I fear, we simply cannot afford to worry about the intrinsic value of motives in this domain.

[18] In the paragraphs that follow I focus on incentives provided by the polity. Admittedly, civic associations and public opinion more generally can also play a role in incentivizing civic action (Gerber, Green, and Larimer, 2008). But it is hard to imagine a society whose culture strongly encourages civic action despite the fact that most citizens feel no special connection to their polity. So I suspect that social norms and other non-governmental incentives for civic action are parasitic on widespread patriotic love and/or civic identification.

non-contractual promises are common examples of moral obligations that we ordinarily believe it would be illegitimate for the government to enforce, and arguably there are civic contributions that belong in this category: one plausible example would be the action of reporting a serious crime that one has witnessed.

In practical terms, some civic obligations are not realistically enforceable: assuming that there is a moral obligation to pay at least some minimal attention to public affairs, it is hard to imagine how the blunt instrument of coercion could ensure that citizens discharge such an obligation. More generally, enforcing laws is always costly: detecting and prosecuting offenders consumes valuable resources, especially when the polity is careful to respect citizens' procedural rights and to avoid punishing the innocent. And even when it is appropriate, all things considered, for civic contributions to be legally required, it is usually unwise to rely exclusively on fear of punishment to motivate compliance. It is, as we discussed in Chapter 2, often very costly and sometimes impossible for the polity to secure the desired level of compliance only by wielding a big stick.

Sometimes polities can and should use a carrot instead of a stick: citizens are typically paid to work as civil servants or to serve in some (but not all) elected offices. But polities benefit greatly if citizens' motives for wanting a government job are not exclusively financial. Some highly qualified citizens with more lucrative employment options in the private sector will choose to work in the public sector if they have non-financial motives to do so. And when public officials see their positions simply as means to a paycheck, we should not be surprised to see large numbers of them shirking their official responsibilities or actively abusing their positions for personal gain when they are sufficiently confident that their misbehavior will not be detected.[19]

In general, financial compensation and other incentives for civic action have a role to play, but such strategies for harnessing citizens'

[19] These concerns about abuse of public office are mitigated by the fact that moral considerations can be motivationally salient enough to guide someone *within* his chosen activity even if they did not motivate his choice of activity. I developed this point in Chapter 4's discussion of habits and tastes. Expanding on the example I offered there, it is not hopelessly naïve to believe that surgeons who chose their profession largely for its financial rewards nonetheless often prioritize their patients' well-being over their personal income!

narrow self-interest may increase the quantity of civic action at grave cost to its quality. Moreover, since a polity that provides financial rewards for civic action must pay these rewards out of tax revenues that are coercively extracted, paying citizens to perform common civic actions (such as voting) is vulnerable to the same principled arguments against threatening them with fines for non-performance. Payments and fines have different distributive implications, to be sure: using general tax revenues to fund a flat-rate monetary incentive to vote would be mildly redistributive, given that the fraction of the polity's general tax revenues paid by the rich is much higher than the fraction of voters who are rich. But when election day rolls around, any tax-paying citizen faces the same basic choice no matter whether his polity has taxed him to support payments for voters or threatens to fine him if he does not vote: in either case, if he does not vote he will be financially worse off than he would have been in the absence of any scheme of rewards or fines. The polity always gives with one hand and takes with the other.

If I am right so far, we cannot expect a satisfactory solution to the civic motivation problem as long as citizens' motives to contribute to their polities are limited to narrow self-interest and recognition of the disinterested moral reasons to do so. In other words, strict application of the orthodox view's limits on permissible character formation will predictably lead to woefully low levels of civic engagement. It is both complacent and naïve to argue, with Crittenden (2002, p. 84), that citizens should be left to "decide autonomously when to participate. They will no doubt decide to participate when the issue is judged to be important to their identities or ways of life. When citizens are able to help make actual decisions on political issues, participation may also be presupposed." Presuppositions of this kind do not take the civic motivation problem seriously because they ignore both the weakness of moral motivation and the instrumental rationality of free-riding. As Callan (1997, p. 11) notes in delightfully understated language: "autonomous reflection does not necessarily lead everyone to a way of life in which civic engagement has an impressively prominent place."

One important response to this conclusion is to assert the vital roles of habits and tastes in motivating civic action (Berger, 2011, pp. 148–57). We saw earlier that the civic motivation problem is hardest to solve in cases, such as voting in a mass democracy, where the marginal effect of a citizen's civic contribution is almost always zero. Habits of and tastes for engaging in particular civic activities are the surest bets to make up the motivational shortfall in cases of this kind because they are motives that do not depend upon any (moral or self-interested) consequentialist calculus of instrumental rationality and therefore are immune to the excruciating logic of free-riding. If I am not moved to vote solely by my recognition of the moral objections to free-riding on the efforts of my fellow citizens, no amount of cost-benefit analysis will get me to the polling station, but a habit of and/or taste for voting may do the trick. Similarly, my habit of listening to NPR News on my morning commute and my taste for watching *The Daily Show* on Comedy Central may suffice to motivate these actions even if I know that the resulting increases in my political understanding do not render me, as one adult citizen among many millions, significantly more likely to have a positive influence on political outcomes in the USA.

Habits can provide vital motivation to perform low-cost civic actions such as voting. Tastes can do this, too, and they can also motivate civically valuable actions that would appear very costly to a person without the taste in question. I may volunteer to spend many hours supervising my local polling station, campaigning for an electoral candidate, or serving as an unpaid public official in large part because I expect to enjoy the activity in question.[20] But the motivational importance of tastes is not limited to civic actions that are voluntary. Even when holding public office is compensated, few people are willing to serve unless they have at least some taste for performing the activities attached to that office.[21] And, of those

[20] Purely and disinterestedly moral motivations are most unlikely to suffice in cases such as these. But, as we shall see, the addition of tastes will rarely be enough to tip the balance. Most people who devote long hours to civic action would not do so if they did not feel some special connection to the polity: affection or identification.

[21] In part this is because the compensation for holding public offices is often low (relative to the employment alternatives for those people who are qualified to hold the office). More people with no taste for the activities attached to a public office would be willing to serve if financial compensation was higher. But those higher salaries would have to be paid from tax revenues—as previously discussed, the polity always gives with one hand and takes with the other—so there is an important sense in which all tax-payers benefit from the prevalence of tastes for holding public office.

people who would be willing to serve in a particular compensated public office, many would probably not be willing to commit time and other resources to an uncompensated campaign for election to that office, knowing that their bid might well be unsuccessful, unless they took some pleasure in the activity of political campaigning.

Supporters of the orthodox view of civic education can embrace cultivation of tastes for and habits of civic action without deviating significantly from their concern for critical citizenship. It is true that these educational strategies do, by definition, detract from the autonomy of people's decisions to perform civic actions.[22] But, as I noted in Chapter 4 (building on the arguments of Chapter 3), there is little or no intrinsic value in citizens' making such decisions autonomously. And autonomous reasoning leads to a dearth of civic motivation.

Habits and tastes would be much more troubling for the orthodox view if they detracted from the autonomy of the judgments that citizens express through their civic actions. But in most cases habits and tastes can provide valuable civic motivation without significantly impairing (or impeding expression of) civic judgment in this way. Admittedly, some habits of performing particular civic actions would constitute severe impediments to (expressing) critical civic judgment. For example, the habit of voting for a particular political party would obviously impede a citizen's capacity to make and express critical judgments about the rival merits of the candidates and party platforms before her. But this observation merely illustrates that the truly valuable habit for citizens to have is the habit of turning out to vote *simpliciter*, not of casting one's vote for a particular party.

The analysis is a little different when we consider tastes for civic action, which typically do threaten to impair citizens' judgment but only in very specific contexts. The taste for voting need not be and typically is not a taste for voting for a particular party: in this important way, tastes and habits are equivalent. But because the taste for voting is always at least partially a taste for casting one's vote via some particular mechanism, e.g., by showing up in person

[22] As I noted in Chapter 4, shaping particular tastes and habits compromises individual autonomy much less than instilling a conception of the good life in which political participation is a central component.

to mark a single X with a pen on a ballot paper, any such taste may be an impediment to endorsing proposed reforms of the system for casting votes. A citizen who enjoys the pen-on-paper experience of marking that single X has a motive to oppose the introduction of voting machines, or online voting, or Single Transferable Vote systems that require voters to rank candidates, etc. Similarly, although a taste for serving as a US Marine would not impede one's ability to think critically about a proposed or actual deployment of the Marines, it would incline some young citizens to oppose abolishing or downsizing the Marine Corps or significantly changing its traditions.

To summarize my evaluation, habits and tastes can be extremely valuable sources of civic motivation, especially in contexts where free-riding problems loom large. And there need not be any great cost to the *quality* of civic actions: suitably formed habits of civic action can be fully acquitted of interfering with citizens' capacity to make critical judgments about their polity, and tastes for civic action are vulnerable to this charge only in very specific contexts. This informal cost-benefit analysis manifestly favors the judicious use of education to boost civic motivation by forming habits and tastes. But, although there is doubtless always some scope for more effectively cultivating civic habits and tastes in the young (and rendering civic participation more appealing to citizens generally), it is hard to imagine that a combination of habits, tastes, disinterested moral motivation, and narrow self-interest could suffice to solve the civic motivation problem. What is strikingly absent from this list of motives is any sense of special connection to one's polity. The rest of this chapter examines the arguments for and against fostering the two distinct feelings of special connection that I described in Chapter 4: patriotic love and civic identification.

5.3. Patriotic love and distorted judgment

Patriotic love expands the range of voluntary civic actions for which citizens will experience some prudential motivation. I may have no taste for a particular civic action, and its expected effects may not serve my self-interest when narrowly conceived, but if the action will benefit the polity I love, it thereby furthers an interest of my self. Of course, the prudential costs (including the *opportunity* costs) of performing this action may outweigh the prudential satisfaction I would derive from benefiting the polity. But the introduction of patriotic love may nonetheless succeed in reducing the net prudential costs of civic action to a level that can be overcome by moral (and sometimes also habitual) motives to contribute to the polity. And this is especially likely if we relax the stipulation that I have no taste for the action in question.

For example, although I am very unlikely to volunteer as an election supervisor merely because I see moral reasons to do so and expect to derive some enjoyment from the experience, the addition of patriotic love has the potential to make up the motivational shortfall. Imagine that the United Kingdom is preparing for its general election and is looking for volunteers to staff a polling station in New York City (for UK citizens living in the United States). The British ambassador writes to the several thousand New Yorkers who staffed polling stations at the most recent American general election. After all, the ambassador reasons, these people presumably have both a taste for such volunteer work and strong moral motivation to help facilitate an important democratic process. He receives precious few positive responses. For the great majority of these people, unsurprisingly, a special feeling of connection to the polity whose election is being conducted is a necessary condition for their being willing to volunteer at the polls. That feeling could be and often is patriotic love.

A similar analysis applies to many civic actions that are not purely voluntary. Consider first actions that are compensated. Although material incentives, purely moral considerations, and (in some cases) a taste for military life may be jointly sufficient to motivate a few citizens to join the military in wartime, many others will not sign up unless they also feel a special connection to the polity. And patriotic love is the traditional candidate for that special feeling.

It is also worth considering actions that are legally required, building on the arguments of Chapter 2. Filing an accurate tax return is not in my narrow self-interest if the expected punishment for failing to disclose some income is sufficiently small (presumably because of the very low risk of an audit combined with the high probability that the tax authorities would accept my claim that

I made an honest mistake, at least the first time that I am caught). Again, purely moral motives for full disclosure are unlikely to be reliable. A habit would help, but one can only develop the habit of honestly declaring one's income by repeatedly doing so: what will motivate young adults to establish such a history and thereby acquire a habit of virtuous behavior? If we are left to rely on a taste for paying taxes, the situation is truly hopeless! But a citizen who loves her country may pay all the taxes she owes partially for the same non-moral reason that she pays for her father's retirement home, namely, that she wants to increase the well-being of an object of her affection.

The preceding paragraphs explain how patriotic love could straightforwardly resolve the civic motivation problem in cases wherein the marginal benefits of a citizen's civic contribution would be significant for the polity but insignificant or even nonexistent from the perspective of that citizen's narrow self-interest. But what about cases in which the marginal effect of the citizen's civic contribution on her polity is actually zero, e.g., voting in an election wherein she is not pivotal, which is to say essentially *any* election in a mass democracy? It is not immediately obvious how patriotic love provides any motivation to act in a way that will *not* in fact benefit the polity one loves. I have already argued that habits and tastes are the most promising solutions to the civic motivation problem in cases, such as voting, where instrumental rationality fails us. But we should not give up too quickly on the thought that citizens who love their polity may be more likely to vote. As I noted in Chapter 4, a citizen's affection for her polity can underpin *expressive* reasons for civic action; such a citizen's motive for participating in an election need not be to benefit the polity by influencing the outcome but rather to express her affection for the polity.

Patriotic love is the traditional solution to the civic motivation problem, but it invites a very important objection, namely, that such love is associated with a diminished capacity to think critically about one's polity. In its most straightforward and potent form, this objection consists in the claim that "love of country impedes the civic and political judgment of citizens [because] loving something *does* entail an inclination to view it in a favorable light" (Hand, 2011, pp. 341, 343, emphasis in original; see also Keller, 2005, p. 580).

Love may not be blind, but its vision is systematically distorted.[23] A related worry is that patriotic love is most readily and effectively *cultivated* through forms of civic education that present an exaggeratedly rosy view of the polity, its institutions and its history (Galston, 1989, pp. 90–91). Whether biases in civic judgment are caused directly by the presence of patriotic love or by the processes that arouse such love (or both), the link between patriotic love and impaired civic judgment takes the luster off the former as a potential solution to the civic motivation problem.

How might one respond to this objection? One possible response is simply to accept the force of the objection but to argue, *contra* the orthodox view, that impaired civic judgment is the price we must pay for a solution to the civic motivation problem. If, like Alexis de Tocqueville (1850/2006), we believe that the highest priority for a democratic polity is always to combat the ever-present tendency of citizens to disengage from public life, patriotic love's unfortunate side-effect may have to be viewed as a necessary evil. This seems to be Callan's (2006, p. 543) response,[24] which Michael Hand (2011, pp. 342–43) rightly regards as weak. It is not clear why we should follow Tocqueville and Callan in regarding the impaired civic judgment associated with patriotic love as less of an evil than low civic motivation. And, more fundamentally, if we concede the force of the objection to patriotic love, we should not endorse such love as the lesser of two evils unless and until we have exhausted the effort to find a third option, a less costly solution to the civic motivation problem.

[23] It is sometimes said that love (of one's child, for example, or a sports team) can render one *hypercritical* of its object. I suspect that "hypercritical" here typically refers not to negatively biased judgment of the loved object but rather to a very strong (perhaps excessive, sometimes even obsessive) *motivation* to engage in critical evaluation of the object and to act on any perceived possibility for improvement. But even if love's bias does occasionally turn out to be negative rather than positive, the general concern remains: love interferes with our ability to make accurate judgments about its objects.

[24] As we saw in Chapter 1, Callan now accepts that fostering patriotism for the sake of civic motivation both requires and warrants some deviation from the orthodox view's ideal of critically autonomous citizenship, but he believes that this deviation need only be slight if we attend carefully both to the kind of patriotism that we aim to arouse and to the particular tools that we use for this purpose.

But must we concede the force of the "love impairs judgment" objection to patriotic love? My view is that the objection, although less potent than it might initially seem, cannot be dismissed. To see why, we must briefly consider two possible defenses of patriotic love that are rather more robust than Callan's "lesser of two evils" response.

One robust defense of patriotic love flatly denies the empirical claim that love distorts judgment. Although many citizens who love their polity struggle to think critically about its laws and actions, this *correlation* does not show that love is the *cause* of impaired critical judgment. Citizens who love their polity are more likely to have been educated in ways that are biased in favor of existing laws and/or to have been taught to believe in the merits of the institutions through which the polity makes decisions and therefore to trust that the decisions themselves are good. And, although this kind of education may precisely be the source of many citizens' patriotic love, there are alternative ways to arouse patriotic love that do not involve exaggerating the polity's merits. So we should not draw any hasty conclusions from the correlation between patriotic love and distorted judgment.

Stephen Nathanson (1993, pp. 90–91) argues that the claim that love distorts judgment "relies on an exaggerated, highly romanticized account of love," insisting that "to think that this condition of blind passion is typical of love is to caricature love and to overlook its complexity... Admittedly, it may be painful to become aware of negative facts about those we love... Nonetheless, we are capable of seeing what the problems are, and our love is revealed in what we do with this knowledge, not in our inability to face up to it." This is a heroic attempt to vindicate patriotic love, but on examination it succeeds only in justifying the modest propositions that love is rarely fully blind and that less passionate forms of love typically enjoy better vision. Nathanson's protestations do nothing to undermine the similarly modest proposition that love often biases our perception and judgment in ways that systematically favor the object of our love. That proposition is a commonplace among academic psychologists (Murray, Holmes, and Griffin, 1996; Leising, Erbs, and Fritz, 2010). Indeed, Nathanson (1993, p. 61) himself seems unable consistently to sustain his heroic defense of patriotic love; his reference to humans' "deep and admirable need to believe in the goodness of the groups to which we are attached" leaves little doubt that affective attachments compromise the rationality of our processes of belief formation, retention, and rejection.[25]

The claim that love distorts judgment must not be overstated, but nor can it plausibly be denied; although loving one's polity is obviously not incompatible with finding fault with it, love does dispose one to be less critical. Even love's defenders typically acknowledge this fact. Callan (2006, p. 542) concedes that "one familiar frailty of love is our susceptibility to lose truthful perception of the beloved when its value has been severely compromised." And, for Troy Jollimore (2011, p. 52), "love does, by its nature, involve epistemic partiality."[26]

To claim that one's patriotic love has no effect on one's civic judgment is not unlike claiming that one is immune to the non-rational effects of advertising. The former claim should be treated with the same high degree of skepticism that is customarily and rightly applied to the latter. In both cases introspection is unreliable; one is often unaware of the non-rational ways in which one is influenced by advertising, and the same is surely true for the biases in civic judgment that result from patriotic love. This is certainly not to deny that people who love their polity differ greatly in the extent to which their civic judgment is thereby biased. There may even be a few people whose patriotic love truly has no significant effect on

[25] Note that Nathanson regards this need as not only "deep"—a descriptive claim—but also "admirable"—a normative claim. As Nathanson implicitly observes, there are two ways in which our "need to believe in the goodness of the groups to which we are attached" might express itself. One, which we are discussing and which Nathanson rightly regards as troubling, is that we (unconsciously) adjust our beliefs to suit our attachments. The other is that we adjust our attachments in light of our beliefs. Nathanson regards this latter phenomenon as morally desirable—indeed, sufficiently desirable to outweigh the concern about impaired critical judgment and therefore vindicate the on-balance conclusion that our "need to believe in the goodness of the groups to which we are attached" is admirable. I think this is a mistake: as I argued earlier in this chapter, it is not morally desirable, and it is often positively undesirable, for the strength of citizens' motives for civic action to depend upon their beliefs about the moral merits of their polity. Deeply unjust polities are especially in need of highly motivated citizens to combat the injustices.

[26] Jollimore (2011, pp. xi–xii) is avowedly concerned exclusively with love for persons, and he warns against assuming that all forms of love are alike, but it seems reasonable to believe that the epistemic partiality he diagnoses in love of persons would also occur in love of polities.

their civic judgment. But these super-citizens probably represent only a tiny fraction of the many people who claim to achieve this psychological feat. And any assessment of patriotic love as a potential solution to the civic motivation problem in a democratic society will have to reckon with its implications for all citizens, not just super-citizens.

If, as I have argued, affection distorts judgment, one might think that the best solution to the civic motivation problem is a form of patriotic love that involves no such positive affect. I have been using the terms "love" and "affection" interchangeably, but perhaps this unduly constrains our understanding of the ways in which love can manifest itself. In particular, one might think that there is a form of love that consists wholly in feeling special concern for the well-being of its object, without any special affection for that object. If patriotic love could take this form, it would generate civic motivation without distorting civic judgment. But, I shall argue, love of this kind is a mirage. There is no love without affection, no special feeling of concern for an object's well-being that is not grounded in positive affect.

It is certainly true, as Callan (2006, p. 528) has noted, that one can love an object without having any special motivation to promote that object's well-being. This is the sense in which some non-Londoners love London. They would not lift a finger to help the city, but they genuinely love it. To be clear, the people I have in mind do not merely believe that London is objectively a great city, although many do indeed believe this. They (also) have a positive and enduring emotional attitude towards London: they feel for the city a special affection that is typically the legacy of strongly positive sentiments that suffused their early perceptions of and encounters with it. But the fact that affection can exist without special concern does not show that the inverse is also true. Indeed, I maintain that special concern cannot exist without affection.

This claim may seem vulnerable to certain obvious counterexamples. But these putative counterexamples all turn out to conflate other psychological phenomena with either special concern or affection. For example, we can readily imagine, and many of us know, people who exhibit special motivation to contribute voluntarily to a particular polity for which they feel no affection. Are such people manifesting a feeling of special concern for the polity's well-being?

They are not. In some cases, they are simply dutiful: they are motivated by their belief that there are strong moral reasons to contribute to a polity of which one is a citizen. In other cases (as I discussed in Chapter 4), civic motivation derives from identification with the polity. Such identification is often accompanied by special concern for the polity's well-being, but it need not be. When special concern is carefully distinguished from other civic motivations, it should be clear that it is essentially an expression of affection and cannot be separated therefrom.

Of course, it is perfectly possible to feel special concern for an object about which one holds strongly negative evaluative beliefs. I may judge that my polity is incompetent and morally rotten while nonetheless feeling a deep concern for its well-being. But cases of this kind do not demonstrate that special concern can exist without affection. They merely make vivid the distinction between affection for an object and favorable judgments about that object.[27] Emotional attitudes can be positive despite cognitive assessments that are negative, and vice versa. And it is important to note that the existence of people who both love their polity and hold predominantly negative evaluative beliefs about it does not contradict my earlier conclusion that affection positively biases judgment. Such people would evaluate the polity even less favorably if they did not love it. And their love will positively bias their judgments about any efforts the polity makes to improve itself.

So much for attempts to deny that love biases judgment. An alternative and equally robust defense of patriotic love might be termed the conservative response: if (the cultivation of) patriotic love does indeed render one less likely to find fault with one's polity, this effect may be more desirable than undesirable.[28] In the absence of positive sentimental relationships to our polities, we would often be too quick to find fault with them. Under certain conditions that

[27] Love of one's polity need not be accompanied by any beliefs in the objective merits of that polity. Simon Keller (2005, pp. 574–6) and Stephen Nathanson (1993, p. 30) have argued that patriotism conceptually requires some such beliefs. As previously noted, I do not wish to get embroiled in semantic debates about the meaning of patriotism.

[28] This is conservatism in the literal sense of *conserving* the status quo, regardless of where existing political arrangements lie on the traditional left-right ideological spectrum or other continuums of political value. See my discussion in Chapter 6.

warrant confidence in the merits of existing political institutions, status quo biases in citizens' judgment improve the accuracy of their judgments.[29] I advance this argument at length in Chapter 7. Patriotic love may thereby usefully discourage each generation from unwisely dismantling established institutions that are of considerable substantive merit. And if the government's decision procedures are superior to the individual's private judgment and the individual would be insufficiently trusting of government decisions in the absence of patriotic love, the biases associated with patriotic love again may improve the accuracy of citizens' judgments. In short, if citizens who love their country see it through rose-tinted spectacles, that filter may usefully correct for our hubristic tendency to trust our own individual judgment over time-proven political formulas and the outcomes of reliable decision procedures.[30]

Furthermore, as we shall see in Chapter 7, a disposition to approve of status quo political arrangements may be desirable to some extent for three reasons that are independent of the substantive merits of those arrangements. First, citizens are more likely to comply with laws and executive orders that they support, so a widespread inclination to view these demands favorably conduces to political order and social coordination, which are valuable even if the government's demands are far from ideal. Second, the biases associated with patriotic love may serve as valuable counterweights to our instinct for costly and risky political experimentation; there is some value in political stability and continuity even when the arrangements that are preserved are decidedly suboptimal. And third, people are typically happier living under political institutions that they support.

The conservative defense of patriotic love succeeds in taking some of the sting out of the "love impairs judgment" objection, but it is

[29] More generally, there is now an extensive literature in social psychology on the relationship between bias and accuracy in judgment. For a classic early discussion, see Funder (1987).

[30] Jollimore (2011, pp. 52–73) defends a related but different proposition. He argues that loving an object may increase the accuracy of one's judgments of it because one attends more carefully and charitably to objects that one loves. Love's "friendly eye" lingers on its object in search of positive qualities that might elude the hasty judgment of the casual and unsympathetic observer. But I would propose that identification can provide these same epistemic benefits without the higher degree of epistemic partiality that accompanies love.

not wholly successful. In particular, although there usually are some status quo political arrangements that citizens would ideally see through rose-tinted spectacles, patriotic love is indiscriminate: it inclines citizens to approve of *all* features of their polity, including features whose merits ought to be the subject of lively and unbiased debate and which could safely be reformed without incurring serious costs in terms of compliance and stability. As we shall see, status quo biases have their place in civic education, but we should typically preserve the option of choosing when and where they are appropriate. The blanket status quo bias introduced by patriotic love is not desirable.[31]

5.4. Civic identification and self-deception

I argued above that although the "love impairs judgment" objection is somewhat weakened by the two robust responses I considered, it ultimately survives those responses. Should we therefore fall back on the aforementioned less robust response of Callan and Tocqueville, endorsing patriotic love as the lesser of two evils? We certainly should not do so if there is a less costly way to solve the civic motivation problem. And, I shall argue, *identification* with one's polity is this better solution because it is less of an impediment to the critical thinking that people should practice in their role as citizens of a democracy. Unlike love, identification has no positive valence to it; we saw this point illustrated in Chapter 4 by the example of Isaac and his relationship to America (and, indeed, to his cousin, Mary).

Despite the fact that civic identification does not involve seeing the polity through the proverbial rose-tinted spectacles of love, one might worry that efforts to think critically about a polity with which one identifies will be hampered by all the same problems that attend people's efforts to be self-critical. Most people are not

[31] As I discuss in Chapter 6, there are similar reasons to be concerned about the practice of teaching children to trust in the merits of established political arrangements. But trust of this kind is somewhat more discriminating than the status quo biases introduced by patriotic love because it favors institutions that have been democratically retained for longer periods of time.

good at self-criticism; indeed, many of us more readily find fault with those we love than with ourselves. But notice that the set of people that we love often includes ourselves! Moreover, much of the difficulty of being self-critical derives not from the fact that it would be painful to fault oneself but rather from the fact that the self which must do the criticizing is literally identical with (albeit a later manifestation of) the self that made the judgment or performed the action that is now to be critically assessed. This problem does not occur for someone who identifies with his polity; his individual faculties of judgment are not identical with the collective faculties possessed by the polity. Indeed, in many instances the individual citizen who identifies with his polity will have played no role whatsoever in making the judgment or choosing the action that he is now called upon to critically assess. So he is not being asked to find fault retrospectively with his own decision, to admit his own mistake. It was not his decision, for all that he identifies with the collective agent whose action it was and is therefore susceptible to feelings of pride and shame (and perhaps also "praiseworthiness" and guilt) with respect to that decision.

So it is easier to find fault with a polity with which one identifies than it is to find fault with oneself. But this is not to deny that the desire to feel proud rather than ashamed of one's polity can systematically color one's judgments of its institutions and actions. As Tocqueville (1850/2006, p. 237) wryly observed in describing the "irritable patriotism of the Americans," an American is quick to defend his country from criticism "for it is not only his country that is being attacked but himself."[32] More recently, drawing on social identity theories developed by Henri Tajfel and John Turner in the 1970s and '80s, social psychologists often explain positive biases in a person's evaluative judgment of her "in-group" by appealing to the notion that self-esteem depends in part on one's evaluative beliefs about groups with which one identifies.[33]

[32] People may also seek to *avoid hearing* criticism of a polity with which they identify both because they do not want to be persuaded that their polity acted badly and because, as I noted in Chapter 4, such criticism is painful to hear even if one rejects it.

[33] Regrettably, the experimental literature does not explore how these biases resulting from *identification with* a group compare in magnitude to biases resulting from *affection for* a group.

The principal worry with which we must contend is that civic identification distorts a person's moral judgment of her polity's actions (and inaction), where moral judgment is understood to include not only the evaluation of purported moral principles and values but also the assessment of morally relevant non-moral facts. For example, when I judge whether my country acted immorally by killing a non-uniformed citizen of a country with which we are at war, I must not only evaluate the purported moral prohibition on targeting of civilians but also assess whether the person who died was truly a civilian and whether she was in fact targeted.

We can more precisely analyze the distortions of moral judgment that accompany civic identification if we distinguish between moral and non-moral forms of pride and shame.[34] When a polity with which I identify treats other polities (or a vulnerable minority within its own citizenry) in a manner that I believe justice demands despite powerful incentives to do otherwise, I feel morally proud. When the polity fails this test, I feel morally ashamed. By contrast, when the United States put a man on the moon, many US citizens felt a non-moral form of pride. If NASA had botched the operation, those same people would have felt embarrassment and a non-moral form of shame. It is important to notice that moral judgment is liable to be distorted not only by the desire to feel moral pride and avoid moral shame but also by the desire to feel non-moral pride. Indeed, these two desires will often interact in a familiar fashion: the distortions of moral judgment caused by an aversion to feeling moral shame are heightened when there is simultaneously a desire to feel non-moral pride in the relevant action. If, shortly after Neil Armstrong first set foot on the moon, evidence had emerged suggesting that NASA had tested the effects of prolonged exposure to zero-gravity on various citizens of developing-world nations as a condition of their receiving US food aid, it seems likely that the desire of some US citizens to feel non-moral pride at their country's achievement would, when combined with their aversion to shame, have created a strong tendency to unreasonably discount this evidence or refuse to accept that such tests would be immoral.

[34] A parallel analysis could be performed with moral and non-moral forms of "praiseworthiness" and guilt.

So there is no doubt that civic identification distorts judgment. Does it do so as severely as patriotic love? Even if it does not, is the degree of distortion still too high a price to pay for a solution to the civic motivation problem? A revealing analogy strongly suggests that the answers to these two questions are both no. We normally think that susceptibility to feelings of pride and shame about *one's own* actions is a net virtue for an imperfect moral agent despite the fact that this susceptibility will introduce systematic bias and self-deception into the agent's self-evaluation. Having a conscience is not a wholly good thing, but it is a good thing! Susceptibility to pride and shame (and also feelings of responsibility, as discussed in Chapter 4) about one's own actions is a liability when it comes to accurately morally evaluating those actions in retrospect, but far more important is the fact that it dramatically increases one's motivation to behave morally in the future (including in cases when one ought to make amends for some previous misdeed). I see no reason why we should not render the same on-balance verdict about susceptibility to pride and shame about one's polity's actions.[35] By contrast, feeling special affection for oneself (and an associated special concern for one's own well-being) is not usually regarded as a net virtue for a moral agent.[36]

It may seem odd that my defense of civic identification appeals to the same "lesser evil" argument that I branded weak as a defense of patriotic love. But my analogy with attitudes to oneself suggests both that identification with one's polity generates less "evil" (impaired critical judgment) than does love of one's polity and that this lower degree of impairment truly is a lesser evil when compared with low civic motivation.

Even if identification suffices to solve the civic motivation problem in many contexts, might the passion of patriotic love still be needed to motivate certain "extreme" civic actions? In particular, if citizens do not love their polity, will enough of them be willing to fight for it when necessary, to kill and risk death? I cannot dismiss

[35] The "need to avoid shame and believe in our own rectitude as a people is a powerful obstacle to recognizing when our leaders are corrupt, or incompetent, or a menace, but it is also a powerful wellspring of reform when we do come to recognize such things" (Curren and Golmohamad, 2007, p. 122).

[36] It is also possible to care too little about one's own well-being. But few people err in this direction.

this worry altogether. But we should not underestimate the motivational work that could be done by a person's robust civic identification in combination with his moral reasoning, his desire for the material goods provided to incentivize military service, and (for some people) a taste for military life. Furthermore, if love does turn out to play a vital role in motivating people to kill and risk death for their polity, the love in question may not be love of one's polity. Most empirical research suggests that a soldier's willingness to kill and risk death in modern war depends much more on his love for the other members of his "primary group," the combat unit or so-called band of brothers, than on any love for the polity.[37] If this is true, and if some combination of the other motives I have discussed is sufficient to get enough people voluntarily to *join* the military (or if conscription is used), then patriotic love will not be needed even in this domain.

One might still worry that, like patriotic love, identification with one's polity is most readily cultivated in ways that paint an exaggeratedly rosy picture of that polity. There is a kernel of truth in this concern, I think. People are more likely to identify with a polity, and to do so strongly and robustly, if they think somewhat well of that polity. But, as I argued in Chapter 4, one powerful way to cultivate civic identification is to teach young children to feel ashamed of (some of) their polity's actions. Because identification, unlike love, has no positive valence, we should not assume that celebrations of one's polity are always the best ways to promote it. And I shall argue in Chapter 7 that the positive evaluative beliefs that do help to establish and sustain civic identification will often arise from status quo educational biases that can be justified in many ways other than by appealing to the value of civic identification.

5.5. Civic identity and ethno-cultural exclusivity

It is worth taking a moment to consider the view that a polity needs to have an exclusive ethno-cultural identity in order to be the object

[37] The classic study of this phenomenon is by Edward Shils and Morris Janowitz (1948). For more recent confirmation, see Holmes (1986), pp. 291–307, and Kellett (1982), pp. 97–112, 167–74.

of robust civic identification. If this is true, then identification with one's polity is not a good solution to the civic motivation problem in multiethnic or multicultural polities. If such a polity were to adopt (or retain) the full-blown ethnic or cultural identity of one portion of its population (presumably the dominant group[38]), it would alienate many of its citizens as the price of boosting the civic motivation of those in the favored group. This is hardly an attractive prospect. And, given that most contemporary polities are (becoming) culturally and ethnically diverse, this objection threatens to show that identification with one's polity is not a trait that we should promote in today's world, especially as we increasingly strive to create supra-national polities (such as the European Union) to more effectively address problems that cross the boundaries of nation states.

Must we concede the empirical claim that a citizen's sense of civic identity is always an expression of her ethnic or cultural identity, such that a citizen will identify with a polity only if that polity is itself identified with an ethnic or cultural group with which the citizen identifies? This claim strikes me as obviously exaggerated and therefore false if it is taken to mean that a person can only identify with a polity that fully and strongly expresses the norms and values of the ethnic or cultural group that provides her primary non-civic identity. And I believe that it is possible to identify with a polity in a way that transcends ethno-cultural factors, such that one would (continue to) identify with the polity even if it entirely failed (or ceased) to express one's ethno-cultural values. The example of Isaac in Chapter 4 illustrates this possibility: Isaac came to identify with America simply by being inducted into a social practice of articulating pride and shame in response to the country's actions, not by noting any resemblance between himself and his fellow citizens or American institutions. But most people are much more likely to form and then to maintain a strong sense of identification with a polity that has at least some distinctive cultural features with

[38] Melissa Williams (2003, p. 217) notes "a strong tendency... to read the identity of dominant social groups into the content of citizen identity." When, as is usually the case, a polity has a *staatsvolk*—"a national or ethnic people, who are demographically and electorally dominant" (O'Leary, 2001, pp. 284–5)—it strikes me as inevitable that the polity's identity will largely be dictated by the identity of its staatsvolk. But, as I shall shortly argue, the polity's identity can and should be a much "thinner" and thereby less exclusive version of the identity of its staatsvolk.

which they identify.[39] These aspects of a person's cultural identity need not precede the formation of her civic identity: social institutions (such as schools) that aim to cultivate civic identification may simultaneously promote the relevant cultural norms, values, and self-understandings in people who do not already possess them.[40]

The underlying premise here is that the identity of the polity with which one tries to promote identification must realistically be given to some extent by description rather than by mere reference: names and flags must ultimately be associated with something more substantive if identification is to be robust and a powerful source of civic motivation for most people. The distinctive identity of a polity will always have some particular ethno-cultural content (Kymlicka, 1995), but this content can and should be 'thin' "rather than a 'thick' ethno-culture that is characterized by (say) shared religious beliefs, family customs, and personal lifestyles" (Tan, 2002, p. 90). And, adapting Jurgen Habermas's proposal for so-called constitutional patriotism, concerns about exclusivity are further mitigated if the polity's identity is understood to consist in the ethno-culturally-inflected manner in which the polity expresses certain universal political values.[41] "Each national culture develops a distinctive interpretation of those constitutional principles that are equally embodied in other republican constitutions—such as popular sovereignty and human rights—in light of its own national history" (Habermas,

[39] Kok-Chor Tan (2002, p. 180) argues that "a national culture provides the sense of membership that undergirds a common citizenship or membership in a state." More generally, I would argue that it is a polity's cultural particularity that realistically enables it to be the object of widespread and powerful civic identification. But this cultural particularity need not take the form of a *national* culture, so it is possible for identification to play an important part in solving the civic motivation problem for multi-, sub-, and supra-national polities.

[40] "It is an inescapable and legitimate fact that states must engage in the practice of promoting, fostering, and protecting a particular national identity" (Tan, 2002, p. 110). I would argue more generally that *any democratic polity* will benefit greatly from cultivating a particular cultural identity through which citizens identify with the polity and thereby experience increased motivation to contribute to it.

[41] I say "adapting" Habermas both because I am advocating civic identification rather than patriotic love and because I reject his position that a polity's unique identity can be defined in purely political terms, thereby avoiding all ethno-cultural particularity: it seems to me that all particular interpretations of universal political values are necessarily inflected by a particular (but not necessarily thick) ethno-cultural tradition.

2000, p. 118).[42] A citizen's identification with her polity is secured via her commitment to universal liberal democratic values in the particular, historically and culturally influenced (and, as I discuss in the next paragraph, always imperfect) form in which these have come to be expressed by her polity's institutions.[43] The hope is that this particularity of expression is sufficient to translate commitment to universal values into identification with a particular polity but not so great as to exclude citizens whose primary culture would have expressed those universal political values in different ways.[44]

We should be wary of identifying the polity too closely with its existing laws and institutions: we do not want citizens' identification with their polity to weaken when that polity enacts (what may be much needed) political reforms, and we may also be concerned that citizens' identification with imperfect, perhaps even unjust or undemocratic, political arrangements will preempt or impede efforts to reform those arrangements.[45] But Habermas and his followers argue persuasively that these problems can be avoided, at least in polities whose institutions are roughly liberal and democratic. Although any actual institutionalized expression of liberal democratic values will presumably always be imperfect, it will contain within itself the potential for contestation, reinterpretation, and thereby improvement. One can identify with any tradition while accepting the need for that tradition to evolve, and all liberal

[42] Habermas (2001, 1992) also has a vision of a supra-national European identity of this kind.

[43] In the terminology of Jan-Werner Muller (2007, p. 59), the "object of attachment" is a "constitutional culture" that fulfills the "specificity requirement" because it is "necessarily related to particular national and historical contexts." Or, in Ross Poole's (2008, p. 143) words, "the universal principles which constitute the ideal are compatible with a range of different institutional embodiments. The choice [among these] is not just a matter of the fine tuning of democratic theory, but has to do with more local matters, that is, of a country's history, traditions, forms of cultural diversity, and the like. On this account, the particularity of national cultures is not superseded, but continues to play a role, not merely alongside, but implicated in the way in which universal principles are interpreted." Following Habermas, I see no reason to believe that these arguments cannot also apply to *supra*-national (or *sub*-national) polities and their institutions.

[44] For a review of the debates about how thin or thick civic identity can and should be, see Hayward (2007).

[45] However, as I argue in Chapter 7, status quo biases in civic judgment are not always a bad thing.

democratic traditions provide the very tools through which change can be instigated.[46] Hence, fostering civic identification by inducting citizens into a particular liberal democratic tradition is only minimally conservative.[47]

5.6. Reinforcing boundaries

Before concluding my defense of civic identification, I shall need to revisit the concerns about global justice that we encountered early in this chapter. There I argued that the imperatives of global justice are compatible with strong moral reasons to contribute to one's polity in part because those reasons will often call on citizens of a rich polity to help direct their polity's power and resources in ways that benefit poor polities and their citizens. But even if strong moral reasons for civic action can be reconciled with the equal moral importance of all human lives, one might still worry that nonmoral motives to act on those reasons pose a long-run threat to global justice. Specifically, the objection would be that, although there are strong moral reasons to engage in the civic and political life of the particular polities of which one is a citizen, cultivating nonmoral motives (habits, tastes, identification) for such engagement has the unwanted side-effect of creating psychological obstacles to the reconfiguration of political space. People who identify with their polity and possess habits of and tastes for acting within its particular civic-political culture will tend to resist efforts to change

[46] "Citizens see their constitutional culture as always open and incomplete—a project, in short, in which we can recognize those in the past as having been engaged and in which we would want our descendants to invest" (Muller, 2007, p. 61). See also, more generally, Alasdair MacIntyre (1981, p. 222): "Traditions, when vital, embody continuities of conflict... about the goods which constitute that tradition."

[47] One worry is that this minimally exclusive and conservative version of civic identity will be correspondingly minimal in the degree of civic motivation that it provides. On this pessimistic view, there is always a tragic trade-off: thicker versions of civic identity yield stronger civic motivations at the price of greater exclusivity and conservatism. [Wingo (2003, p. 129) expresses this view about motivation and exclusivity but neglects conservatism.] Perhaps the pessimists are right, but it seems worth experimenting with an ethno-culturally thin object of attachment before accepting the inescapability of the trade-off (Hayward, 2007, p. 189).

or even destroy that polity (and its culture) by acceding to a secessionist movement, merging with a neighboring polity, or revising boundaries in some other way.

The right response to this critique is to concede the descriptive claim—non-moral motives for civic action surely do have these effects—while contesting its moral significance. Why might we want to avoid psychologically reinforcing the status quo boundaries between polities? One concern could be that those boundaries are serving as barriers to the transfers required by principles of global distributive justice. Citizens of a polity that is affluent—because its territory is rich in natural resources or because of its history—may use political boundaries as an excuse not to honor their obligations to citizens of poorer polities.[48] But the solution to this problem is to stop using boundaries as an excuse for injustice, not to (periodically) redraw boundaries with the chimerical aspiration of thereby eliminating the problem of unjust inequalities between polities. We should not assume that "national boundaries . . . fix once and for all the outermost limits of people's moral concern" (Tan, 2002, p. 105). Global distributive justice is fundamentally not a matter of getting the boundaries right: it requires rather that 1) each polity is just when viewed as a closed society *and*, crucially, 2) there are fair terms of cooperation and coexistence among the polities that are defined by whatever boundaries exist. In this sense, it would not be a bad thing if the strength and ubiquity of civic habits, tastes, and identification meant that we spent less time squabbling about boundaries and more time working for justice within and between the polities that we have.

A more radical objection to civic education's inadvertently reinforcing the existing political configuration rests on the claim that all boundaries ought ultimately to be abolished in favor of a single world government. But this is not a claim we should accept. The cosmopolitan moral principle that all persons are of equal worth should not be confused with the institutional claim that a single

[48] This phenomenon is perfectly analogous to the domestic case in which a person who is affluent—because she has many natural talents or because of the advantages transmitted to her by her parents—may resist the demands of egalitarian justice to establish institutions that compensate her less fortunate fellow citizens for their undeserved disadvantages.

world government is the only political arrangement that could adequately respect the moral equality of persons (Tan, 2002, pp. 80–81, 94–95). We should endorse the moral principle while rejecting the institutional claim. Political philosophers have argued persuasively at least since Kant that we need multiple sub-global polities: as K. Anthony Appiah (1996, p. 29) succinctly puts the point, "humans live best on a smaller scale." One important advantage of a world of multiple polities—of which some are sovereign states and others sub- or super-state entities with more limited rights of self-government—is that it affords many national (and other ethno-cultural) groups the opportunity to be self-determining, that is, to "secure a public sphere and the relevant set of public institutions that best reflect and sustain their particular cultural identities" (Tan, 2002, p. 11; see also Tamir, 1993).[49]

While we should not be concerned that non-moral motives for civic action reinforce existing political boundaries, we would rightly be concerned if those motives impeded cooperation among polities, efforts to build new federations and supra-national institutions, and attempts to devolve power to (new) regional and local polities. We might call this the *jealous sovereignty* concern, and there is no doubt that such jealousy would be an obstacle to the pursuit of global justice.[50] But there is no particular reason to think that civic habits, tastes, and identification lead people to jealously guard the *sovereignty* of their polity when its continued *existence* is not in doubt. Pooling and/or dispersing sovereignty to some degree need not disrupt the rhythms and patterns of civic life with which citizens are familiar and that they have learned to enjoy. And civic identification should lead people to feel proud when their polity relinquishes some of its sovereignty in particular policy domains because the relevant problems are best addressed at some other level of governance, whether this means empowering (and perhaps creating) smaller units of governance within the polity or resolving collective action problems among polities by elevating decisions to some (new) authority that can bind all the polities under its jurisdiction.

[49] As we saw in the previous section, most citizens will identify with their polity precisely because of the ethno-cultural particularity of its institutions, but such a civic culture should be "thin" enough that it does not alienate (and ideally can be incorporated into the culture of) minority groups within the polity.

[50] Callan (2006, p. 546) addresses this concern as an objection to patriotism.

5.7. Conclusion

People have strong moral reasons to contribute to the democratic polities of which they are citizens. These reasons, grounded in the distinctive opportunities afforded by citizenship, direct each person to play her part in helping to realize her polity's extraordinary potential to generate important moral goods both within and beyond its borders. But, alas, recognition of the moral reasons for civic action, even when supported by considerations of narrow self-interest and by certain habits and tastes, is insufficient to reliably motivate most people. Patriotic love promises to make up some or all of the motivational shortfall, but at a high price: love of one's polity impairs one's capacity to see that polity's weaknesses and faults. *Contra* the orthodox view, this price might be worth paying if patriotic love were the only available solution to the civic motivation problem. But civic identification is a superior alternative.

A citizen who identifies with her polity has increased motivation to contribute to it: she wants to feel pride and to avoid shame (in both the moral and non-moral senses of each of those concepts); she may also feel a degree of responsibility for the polity's acts and omissions; she sees civic actions as important ways in which to express the constitutive significance of her membership in the polity. And, I have argued, civic identification is superior to patriotic love as a solution to the civic motivation problem because it is less of an impediment to critical civic judgment. Although susceptibility to pride and shame about one's polity's actions will regrettably introduce systematic bias and self-deception into one's evaluations of those actions, this is a price worth paying for enhanced civic motivation, in just the same way that susceptibility to feelings of pride and shame about *one's own* actions is a net moral virtue. Widespread and robust civic identification can realistically be achieved without the need for the polity to adopt (or retain) a highly exclusive ethnocultural identity. And civic identification does not constitute an obstacle to morally appropriate reconfigurations of political space at the domestic, regional, or global level. I therefore propose that the best solution to the civic motivation problem is to cultivate civic identification without, as far as possible, arousing patriotic love.

In the conclusion of Chapter 4 I made some suggestions as to how civic education could be designed and delivered to pursue this goal.

But I should close this section of my argument by reiterating my awareness that it may well not be feasible to educate a whole generation of citizens in a mass democracy so that many or even most of them exhibit a high degree of civic identification but little or no patriotic affection. A feasibility constraint of this kind does not negate the practical significance of knowing that identification is always a net good but that affection is sometimes (at least when adequate civic motivation is provided by other sources, and perhaps also in other cases) a net bad. I have no doubt that, in practice, many approaches to fostering civic identification will also generate some degree of patriotic affection. But one need only accept the modest proposition that civic identification and patriotic love do not always have to exist in the same fixed proportion to one another to see the practical significance of evaluating each of these psychological phenomena separately. In other words, if we represent a person's attitudes to a particular polity graphically with identification on one axis and affection on the other, my normative conclusions are likely to be action-guiding (for agents with the power to shape attitudes) unless the set of all feasible points in this two-dimensional space is merely a straight line through the origin. Perhaps it will turn out that societies are not best off aggressively promoting civic identification because the only feasible ways to do so also arouse a great deal of affection for the polity. But there is every reason to believe that institutions and practices of civic education can be improved if they are creatively (re)designed in full awareness of the fact that the expected value of a person's civic contributions is a function that is always increasing in civic identification but sometimes decreasing in patriotic love.

PART III

STATUS QUO BIAS IN CIVIC EDUCATION

CHAPTER 6

Status quo educational bias: its nature and sources

In a democracy, the laws reflect adult citizens' political preferences. This does not mean that citizens' preferences uniquely determine a set of laws. Two impeccably democratic polities whose citizens have the exact same profile of political preferences could have very different laws. These differences would be explained by two factors: institutions and history. As social choice theorists and comparative empirical scholars have long since shown with great sophistication, there is no singular "will of the people" that democratic institutions aim merely to discover: different agenda-setting and decision procedures (including those instantiated by various forms of representative government) generate different political outcomes from the same profile of citizen preferences, and no set of institutionalized procedures is uniquely democratic. In addition, because there are always barriers to, delays in, and costs associated with political change, the laws we observe in a society at time t are partly a function of that society's laws at time $t-1$: a combination of preferences and institutions that is sufficient to *preserve* a particular existing law might not (yet) have been sufficient to *enact* that same law. Nonetheless, given a starting point that is defined by a particular set of democratic institutions and a determinate body of other laws, a polity's future laws (including its future institutions) are very largely a function of the preferences of its current and especially its future adult citizens.

If we treat citizens' political preferences as independent variables, we can ask various interesting descriptive and normative questions about the institutions through which those preferences are expressed and aggregated. But most of the interesting questions about democratic politics do not treat political preferences as independent variables. Citizens' political beliefs and values are not exogenous, immutably given by nature. In particular, we cannot study the *dynamics* of a democratic polity—continuity and change in its laws and political institutions—without attending to the *determinants* of citizens' political preferences. In part, this means studying the ways in which adult citizens form or alter one another's preferences—obviously a subject of central concern for scholars and practitioners of democratic politics alike. But there is a prior question: how are citizens' political preferences shaped during childhood? Intentionally and otherwise, through both private and public decisions, each society educates its children in ways that predictably and lastingly impact their political beliefs and values and therefore help to determine the future laws and political institutions of that society.

This chapter analyzes, and the next chapter evaluates, one especially widespread and important phenomenon in this process of civic reproduction: status quo educational bias. How might schools, parents, and other educational institutions and agents tend to encourage children to believe in the substantive merits of existing political arrangements in the democratic polities of which they are (future) citizens?[1] What forms can such status quo civic educational bias take, what are its sources, and to what extent is it under the control of adult citizens, individually and collectively? These are the questions of the present chapter. In the next chapter I ask how we should *evaluate* status quo biases in civic education; I examine two important objections to such bias before arguing that those objections can be outweighed by the combined force of several diverse reasons to value educational methods that reproduce popular support for particular existing political arrangements.

[1] I shall sometimes refer to the cultivation of such beliefs as (one way of) teaching children to "support" the status quo. This "support" may not be active. In my terms, someone who believes that his polity's major political institutions are excellent "supports" those arrangements even if he takes no action to defend them when they are threatened. The preceding pair of chapters addressed the separate question of whether civic education should aim to instill various motives for civic action. It is one thing to shape a person's beliefs about what a polity should and should not do. It is quite another to motivate that person to act on those beliefs.

The alternative with which I want to contrast status quo bias throughout my analysis and argument is *not* education that is biased against the status quo (and presumably in favor of certain alternative political arrangements) but rather an approach to educating future citizens that is (as far as possible) free of bias. Bias minimization is the preferred approach of what I have called the orthodox view of civic education, according to which our highest priority is to cultivate and preserve children's capacity for autonomous, critical thought about the laws and institutions of their polity.

I am tempted to refer to status quo biases in civic education as "conservative" biases because they encourage the "conservation" of existing arrangements, but the language of conservatism is now so strongly associated with the values of the political right that it is often not possible fully to escape the connotation simply by stipulating that one does not intend it. My subject is educational bias that favors any particular element of the political status quo, regardless of where that element lies on the traditional left–right ideological spectrum or other continuums of political value. And so I do not want to risk confusion by referring to conservative bias when the particular status quo arrangements for which civic education encourages support are, for example, robust civil rights protections and a generous welfare state. But, as we shall see in the next chapter, there are some familiar conservative beliefs (most notably the view that we are more likely to regress than to progress when we overturn institutions of some proven merit) and values (especially stability and the social order that results from widespread compliance with laws) that tend to favor status quo bias even when the arrangements it favors are decidedly to the political left.

There is a host of important practical decisions to be made about status quo civic educational bias. Some examples of these decisions should help to motivate the theoretical exploration that follows. One set of decisions concerns the manner in which children will learn about the constitution of their polity. As we shall shortly see, status quo biases can and usually should be narrowly targeted, so the most salient question is not whether civic education should portray the polity's constitution as a whole in a positive light but rather how each particular provision of that constitution should be presented to children. Take, for example, American children learning about the Bill of Rights. Should American schools celebrate any or all of the

US Constitution's First Amendment, its codified protections for freedoms of religion, speech, press, and assembly? Or should teachers strive to present the First Amendment and the jurisprudential tradition surrounding it simply as descriptive facts about the country and its history? What about the Fourth Amendment (protecting citizens against "unreasonable searches and seizures"), the Fifth (especially its so-called double jeopardy provision and the right not to incriminate oneself), and the Sixth and Seventh (with their guarantees of trial by jury in criminal and civil cases, respectively)?[2]

Moving beyond the Bill of Rights, should American children be taught (explicitly or implicitly) that the institution of judicial review is an important check on the legislative and executive branches, a vital safeguard against tyranny? Or would it be better for these children to be educated in ways that do not predispose them to favor federal courts' having this role (that the US Constitution is now typically understood to afford them)? More generally, if American teachers intend merely to inform their students about the constitutional laws of their polity, should we be troubled if those civics lessons turn out systematically to increase students' support for many provisions of the US Constitution?

It may be natural for American readers to think of status quo educational biases in terms of how American children learn about the US Constitution. And, as I have just illustrated, there are many important issues here. But we should not arbitrarily restrict our attention to constitutional laws, to the federal government, or to the United States. In *any* polity, if existing laws that prohibit hard drugs enjoy overwhelming support among adult citizens, should the next generation nonetheless be encouraged to think through the issue from first principles without any prejudice against the extreme libertarian position? Should societies that pride themselves on having achieved a high degree of gender equality teach their children that a legal right to paid maternity leave is a key component of that equality? What about the legal right to an abortion? Or to use contraception? Is it appropriate for schools in strongly capitalist societies to explicitly or implicitly reinforce the dominant social

[2] I assume, for reasons that will become clear in the next chapter, that American civic education should not be biased in favor of the highly controversial Second Amendment with its "right of the people to keep and bear arms."

message that most goods are rightly viewed by the law as private property and distributed only by consensual transfers in the free market?

To develop a normative theoretical framework with which to address such questions as those I have just posed, we first need to engage in some careful conceptual and descriptive analysis. In particular, we need to define status quo educational bias, identify its various forms and sources, distinguish it from other educational phenomena with which it is liable to be confused, and investigate the costs and feasibility of reducing or even eliminating it. These are the tasks of the present chapter.

6.1. What is status quo educational bias?

I define status quo biased civic education as *education whose expected effect is to encourage a recipient's belief in the substantive merits of existing laws or political institutions, where that effect does not derive solely from an improvement in the recipient's ability and/or an increase in her inclination to engage in autonomous assessment of the best arguments and evidence for and against those laws or institutions.*[3] This definition is, alas, neither succinct nor elegant. But its complexity is necessary to isolate the specific kind of education about which, I shall argue in the next chapter, important normative questions arise.

I should note that by adopting this conception of bias I am operating within the paradigm of the orthodox view whose conclusions I aim to refute in the next chapter. That refutation can therefore be understood as arguing that the orthodox view cannot justify its absolute opposition to status quo educational bias *even when bias is defined in the orthodox view's preferred fashion.* Let me

[3] In Bill Galston's (1989, p. 90) terminology, "civic education" is *defined* by this kind of status quo bias that distinguishes it from "philosophic education" about politics, where the latter merely equips recipients to pursue the truth by the light of their own developed and autonomous reason. I employ a similar distinction, but I prefer different terminology: I think it is confusing to say that civic education is biased by definition, so I shall use the term "civic education" to refer to education about the political arrangements of one's own society whether or not that education evinces status quo bias.

explain this point briefly. Why would one regard civic education as unbiased simply because its impact on recipients' beliefs is fully explained by the fact that it facilitates and encourages autonomous and informed evaluation of existing political arrangements? If civic education expresses the value of forming one's political beliefs in this way, it implicitly encourages recipients to believe in the substantive merits of political institutions that protect, facilitate, and promote precisely this kind of critically autonomous citizenship. That effect looks like educational bias. And, in a society that already has such institutions, education that encourages critically autonomous citizenship therefore appears to be status quo biased.

But, according to the orthodox view, encouraging children to make autonomous and informed civic judgments is a core component of an essential civic educational task, namely, inculcating the basic and universal moral values that constitute liberal democracy. Education that encourages critically autonomous citizenship will indeed shape recipients' beliefs about the merits of certain political institutions, just as teaching children to be tolerant and to believe in the equal moral worth of persons will predictably lead those children to oppose theocracy and slavery. But none of these effects is properly described as educational bias because, as we saw in Chapter 1, basic moral education enhances rather than detracts from the autonomy of its recipients' judgments. When a child is taught liberal democratic principles in a way that does not favor any particular conception of those principles, let alone any concrete institution that instantiates those principles, her education is not biased: she is simply being taught some of the prerequisites for good moral reasoning. So, according to the orthodox view, there is no educational bias to be seen in the fact that encouraging children to *practice* critically autonomous citizenship will dispose them to *favor* political institutions that support this ideal of citizenship over those institutions that do not.

Of course, all of the work in the preceding argument is being done by the claim that critically autonomous citizenship is an unassailable liberal democratic value on a par with tolerance and respect for the moral equality of persons. It is precisely this claim that I have been trying to undermine throughout the book, and I continue that task in Chapter 7, notwithstanding the fact that I am using the orthodox view's conception of bias. In short, and to reiterate, I shall argue that supporters of the orthodox view are wrong to aspire to the minimization of (status quo) educational bias *as they understand that phenomenon.*

6.2. Biases in education and in judgment

When a person's belief in the substantive merits of an existing institution is the product of status quo educational bias, that belief will often be held to some degree as a prejudice, i.e., a belief that exhibits resistance to rational criticism and revision. In other words, status quo biases in *education* often cause status quo biases in *judgment* as these are understood in the fields of cognitive psychology and behavioral economics, namely, as irrational preferences for (or beliefs in the superiority of) the status quo. When education induces a person to hold a belief by any means other than facilitating and/or encouraging the person's autonomous judgment, that belief can be expected to show some degree of nonrational resilience in the face of counterarguments and disconfirming evidence. This is true both when the recipient is capable of making an autonomous judgment but her education wholly or partially bypasses this capacity and when education induces belief prior to the recipients' development of the rational capacities that would be needed to make an autonomous judgment on the proposition in question.

But status quo biased education need neither bypass its recipients' rational capacities nor precede adequate development of those capacities. The educational bias could simply take the form of exposing children to a skewed selection of the available evidence and arguments for and against an existing institution (including evidence and arguments about the existence and merits of alternatives). If I introduce my students to the most powerful arguments and/or evidence for p while failing to do the same with respect to not-p (or q, where q entails not-p), any resulting increase in those students' belief in p is not solely due to increased knowledge and improved reasoning ability. In John Stuart Mill's (1859/1989, p. 38) words, "he who knows only his own side of the case, knows little of that." But recipients of such an informationally unbalanced education might not be impaired in their development of the capacity to engage in autonomous assessment of arguments against the status quo and in favor of alternatives; their education simply does not supply (the best) arguments of these kinds.

Biases in the evidence and arguments to which children are exposed are conceptually compatible with what Bill Galston (1989, p. 89) calls "philosophic education," whose goals are to cultivate "the disposition to seek truth" and "the capacity to conduct rational inquiry." It is likely, however, that early beliefs will prove to be "sticky" regardless of how they were formed. People tend to irrationally discount arguments and evidence that contradict their current beliefs even if those beliefs were originally formed in an impeccably rational fashion.[4] All status quo biased education is therefore likely to encourage status quo biases in judgment simply by increasing the likelihood that citizens' early beliefs will favor the status quo. In what follows, I shall typically assume that status quo biased education generates some degree of status quo bias in recipients' judgment for either or both of the reasons canvassed above.

6.3. Status quo bias: general or particular?

Status quo educational bias could take the form of encouraging children to trust the judgment of those citizens who created and/or preserved *all* the many laws and institutions that now constitute the status quo. Children who learn this kind of trust will apply a (rebuttable) presumption of merit *generally* to existing political arrangements.[5] Such general civic educational bias produces support for the status quo by encouraging future citizens consciously to doubt their own unfavorable assessment of any existing institution, especially one that has withstood the test of time and therefore the judgment of many previous generations. Educators might even try

[4] Psychologists refer to this common phenomenon as "confirmation bias."

[5] Interestingly, as we shall see in the next chapter, if this kind of trust is warranted, it should increase adults' confidence in their own favorable assessments of particular existing laws and could thereby strengthen the case for teaching children to support those particular laws. But we must beware of double-counting. Adults' warranted trust in the merits of the status quo may be sufficient to justify *either* teaching children to share that trust *or* biasing education in favor of particular existing arrangements, but it may not by itself justify adopting *both* these educational measures.

to instill the kind of trust that preempts private judgment, discouraging future citizens from assessing the substantive merits of longstanding and fundamental features of the political status quo. By contrast, education that exhibits *particular* status quo biases *encourages* recipients to judge the substantive merits of *select* existing institutions: it produces support for the status quo by increasing the likelihood that the resulting assessments will be favorable.

As I shall shortly argue, it is extremely valuable for educational bias to be able to be narrowly targeted, and my defense of status quo bias in Chapter 7 is accordingly a defense of particular rather than general bias. But that does not mean that general status quo bias should play no role whatsoever in civic education. It is possible that the best educational strategy is to cultivate a low but non-negligible degree of trust in the status quo as a whole and then supplement this effect with targeted bias favoring select institutions. So it is worth considering the best case that can be made for teaching future citizens to apply some weak presumption of merit generally to existing political arrangements.[6]

We need to distinguish the kind of trust that properly leads citizens to *support* existing laws from the kind that merely provides a reason for *compliance* with those laws. In Chapter 2 I explored trust reasons for *compliance*, whether those trust reasons are *in se*, i.e., believing that the demands of the laws track the reasons for action that one would have in the absence of the laws, or *prohibitum*, i.e., believing that one often fails to perceive or underestimates the force of social coordination reasons to comply with laws. On Rousseau's account, democratic decisions made under appropriate conditions give a dissenting citizen an *in se* trust reason to comply with the resulting law, but should they also inform his judgment the next time he is called upon to vote on the law in question? More generally, if one's vote is supposed to express one's best judgment on the issue at hand, should the results of previous votes on the same issue factor into the judgment one expresses?

[6] I consider here only the argument that trust may improve the accuracy of citizens' beliefs about the substantive merits of existing institutions. As we shall see in Chapter 7, there are also "content-independent" reasons to favor status quo biases in education. In particular, the arguments from stability and compliance lend some support to *general* status quo educational biases.

If the electorate remains the same, the answer is "no." If, since the last vote was taken, I have been persuaded by substantive arguments in favor of the law, of course I should change my vote accordingly. But, if I have not been so persuaded, the virtues of majority voting as an epistemic device are diminished when I allow my vote to be influenced by the mere fact that I was in the minority last time. I am being asked to render my independent judgment: this independence condition is not violated if I base my vote on my trust in someone whom I reasonably regard as a well-motivated expert on the issue at hand, but I must not introduce a feedback loop into the majoritarian decision procedure by using its previous output as one determinant of my input to it on this occasion. This would give extra and undue weight to the judgments of those citizens who happened to be in the majority last time and whose views are unchanged: in addition to casting their votes this time, they would influence the outcome via my deference to the outcome of the previous vote.

In a "repeated game" model of democratic decision-making wherein the citizens remain the same over time, if a society is to maximize its chances of correcting its own errors, each citizen should vote without reference to the results of previous votes on the same issue. A simple example will illustrate this claim. A five-member committee votes on a proposition, then deliberates, then votes again on the same proposition. The first round of voting, in which each member expresses her private judgment of the proposition's merits, comes out 3–2 in favor. During the deliberation, only one person is persuaded to change his judgment by the substantive reasons that are advanced: someone who previously believed in the proposition's merits now regards it as deeply unwise. As a result, three of the five members now privately judge that the proposal is a bad idea. But the second and final round of voting nonetheless comes out 4–1 in favor of the proposition because the two members who were originally dissenters improperly allow their votes in the second round to be swayed by their trust in the result of the first round.

But, of course, in the real-world dynamic game of democratic politics, the electorate changes continually. Citizens die. Citizens come of age. Immigrants acquire citizenship. Indeed, by the time a society revisits a particular law (through, for example, a ballot initiative for repeal or a general election in which that law becomes an especially salient issue), there may be little or no overlap between the old electorate and the new one. Is it still inappropriate for a voter in the second election to be influenced by the fact that a large majority of voters in the first election supported the law in question? It need not be. In addition to evaluating the reasons that were offered in deliberations preceding the previous election and considering the possibility that relevant circumstances may have changed since that time, it can be quite proper to take into account the outcome of that election (including the margin of victory). The dead may have grasped something that the living fail to appreciate. By contrast with an ahistorical form of trust in the laws whereby democratic decisions may offer reasons but only for compliance, this historical form of trust would also be a (defeasible) reason for supporting—i.e., not only believing in the merits of but also voting to retain—the existing laws of one's society.

We may call this historical form "Burkean trust," in reference to Edmund Burke's (1790/1987) exhortation to trust one's ancestors, to assume that the laws and institutions we have inherited from them are good, deferring to their collective wisdom rather than relying exclusively upon one's own independent judgment in one's political participation. Burke did not intend for such trust to be absolute. He believed in both the possibility and the importance of political progress; he just asked for great caution from those contemplating political reform or, heaven forbid, revolution. For our purposes, the defining feature of Burkean trust in the laws is not its strength or weakness but rather its applicability not only to decisions about compliance but also to citizens' reasoning in the democratic process of making, revising, and repealing laws.[7]

Rousseau (1762/1987, p. 195) observes that there is a greater degree of "respect paid to ancient laws," which he attributes to our being impressed that those laws have for so long survived the scrutiny of a sovereign which could "have revoked them a thousand times." Is this respect justified in established liberal democratic societies? Should educators be encouraging children to be impressed by the longevity of laws? I think the answer is a heavily qualified yes.

[7] Of course, Burke was not a democrat: for him, the collective wisdom in which we should trust is the cumulative judgment of political elites across the generations. But the logic is the same.

To the extent that the sovereign, at various points in history, failed to live up to something like Rousseauean democratic standards, its decisions not to revoke particular laws may lack epistemic authority. The defect may have been one of motivation: citizens were pursuing sectional interests rather than sincerely trying to express the general will through their votes. Or the institutional design of the sovereign may have led to decisions being made using incomplete information: because certain classes of adult members of the society were excluded from or underrepresented in the sovereign, some important perspectives were not adequately voiced in the deliberative process. These two defects—motivational and informational—have the same implication: they undermine the assumption that is vital for Condorcet's jury theorem (as discussed in Chapter 3), namely, that each voter was more than 50 percent likely to vote correctly. But we should also be wary of assuming that the sovereign's failure to revoke a law indicated majority support for that law. It is often not true that existing arrangements could and would have been overturned if a simple majority of the electorate opposed them: formal supermajority rules often protect constitutional provisions, and various less formal barriers to political reform frequently mean that a bare majority of like-minded citizens is insufficient to disrupt the status quo.[8]

It is also important to remember that, on Rousseau's or any other plausible account of the "respect paid to ancient laws," respect does not arise suddenly when a law crosses some threshold to become "ancient." Rather, respect is paid to a law in rough proportion to the length of time that the law has been in force. So it would be a serious mistake for the present generation, when deciding how much trust to have in a particular existing law, to reason that each previous generation's decision not to revoke that law expresses a fully independent favorable assessment of its merits, where "independent" means without deference to the judgment of previous generations. As a result, the cumulative significance of the thousand decisions that Rousseau describes is less than it first appears. But, assuming

[8] See Schwartzberg (2003, p. 398) for a discussion of the relationship in Rousseau between trust in established laws and procedural constraints on amendment. I discuss the strategy of entrenchment in the next chapter as an alternative or complement to status quo biased civic education for those who fear rash decisions to overturn existing political institutions.

that each generation's decision not to revoke rests only in (perhaps increasing) part on deference to the judgments of its ancestors, if the democratic standards I describe above were adequately met when at least some of the decisions in that historical sequence were made, we should nonetheless be impressed by the law's longevity and take this into account before voting to overturn the law.

How would one teach children to have Burkean trust in long-standing political arrangements, to believe that the laws they have inherited are not merely old but also venerable? One tactic would be to praise the polity's founders (or those who were responsible for subsequently introducing the laws in question) for their wisdom and political judgment.[9] Popular support for the US Constitution is almost certainly explained in significant part by the fact that Americans have a high degree of Burkean trust in their founding fathers, and that trust is surely encouraged by much of the civic education that Americans receive as children. Another, potentially complementary, tactic to realize general status quo educational bias would be directly to assert the abstract principle of collective wisdom, illustrate and support it with persuasive examples drawn from various domains, and urge children to apply this principle to the decisions made by preceding generations of citizens of their society. Presumably one would also need to tell children that most political problems, or at least the really important ones, are timeless, i.e., that what was a good solution in the past can be expected to be a good solution today.

But it seems likely that an education exhibiting *general* status quo bias will also need to exhibit a good deal of *particular* status quo bias. It is hard to teach children to believe that existing laws often have unperceived or underappreciated merits without teaching those children directly that certain existing laws are good. To the extent that Burkean trust arises as the conclusion of an inductive argument, the way to get future citizens to trust that the existing laws are good, even in cases when their private and independent judgment would not reach that conclusion, is to teach them that lots of particular existing laws are good (in ways that one might easily have missed or underestimated) and to avoid teaching them that (m)any particular existing laws are bad.

[9] In Rousseauean terms, this would mean celebrating the Legislator.

But the preceding observation highlights the great advantage of particular educational biases, which lies precisely in the capacity to pick and choose the institutions that will be favored (and the *degree* of bias in each case). In other words, the great weakness of trust cultivation is that it indiscriminately encourages children to support all established features of the status quo (and especially those arrangements that have been in place for a very long time).[10] General status quo educational bias is a blunt instrument. If it is effective, it is likely to lead citizens to override their negative judgments in many cases when those judgments are fully warranted.[11] The only feasible way to reduce the number of errors of this kind is to reduce the degree of trust that is cultivated so that the presumption of merit is weaker, more easily defeated by the person's private judgment. But then the reverse concern arises: when there is need for a counterweight to private judgment, trust will not figure strongly enough in the formation of a person's evaluative beliefs.

In short, general status quo bias may sometimes be a desirable feature of civic education: it can be appropriate under certain conditions for educators to cultivate in children some low degree of trust in their ancestors and therefore in all the institutions they will inherit. But assuming that, as I shall argue in the next chapter, some of a polity's existing institutions ought to be specially promoted through civic education, the best educational strategy will have to involve targeted bias in favor of those institutions rather than (or perhaps alongside) cultivation of trust in status quo arrangements generally. In the rest of this chapter and throughout Chapter 7, I therefore focus on particular status quo biases.

6.4. The dangers of inferring bias from effects, motives, and intentions

Suppose, not implausibly, that Americans with PhDs are, on average, further to the political left than those without such a degree.

[10] In Chapter 5 I made a similar argument against the "conservative" defense of patriotic love.

[11] By contrast, robust trust reasons for *compliance* (of the kind we discussed in Chapters 2 and 3) are desirable under realistically favorable political conditions because noncompliance is so rarely permissible.

Why might this be? One possible explanation is selection bias: left-wingers are more likely to apply for and/or be accepted into and/or complete PhD programs. But let us assume, for the sake of argument, that this is not the case, or at least that selection bias fails to fully explain the difference we observe. The other (not incompatible) possibility is that there is a causal relationship running in the opposite direction, i.e., the process of acquiring a PhD makes one more left-wing. This putative explanation itself subdivides into two (again, not mutually exclusive) explanations. First, it could be that the process of getting a PhD makes you smarter and that it is smart to be on the political left! On this view, the change in a person's political beliefs and values is due to improvements in that person's knowledge, reasoning, and judgment. Second, it could be that universities directly promote the values and beliefs of the left in their graduate students, perhaps via the influence of an overwhelmingly left-wing faculty and peer group. This effect may or may not be intended by the various individuals that comprise the university or by the university itself conceived as a collective agent. But its defining quality is that the effect is not mediated by an improvement in the affected person's political knowledge, reasoning, or judgment. Only this unmediated effect is rightly regarded as an instance of left-wing educational *bias*.

In just the same way, the mere fact that a program of education systematically leads children to support a particular existing institution does not entail that the education evinces status quo bias. Evenhanded exposure to the best arguments for and against that institution may simply reveal its great merits. The arguments in favor may even be rationally decisive. If so, a high-quality unbiased education should lead recipients to form the same belief that would be encouraged by status quo educational bias.[12] Analogously, if a mathematical principle or scientific claim is and can be known to be true (by logical argument alone or because it is overwhelmingly and unambiguously supported by the evidence), a high quality unbiased

[12] Alternatively, education may induce support for an existing institution without affecting the recipient's private judgment of that institution's merits. The recipient may learn to trust that established institutions often have merits that she fails (adequately) to perceive, or she may be taught in ways that emphasize the costs and risks of political reform: "better the devil you know."

education will lead its recipients to believe the proposition, just as would a program of brainwashing.

Admittedly, beliefs that are the product of educational biases will often be less nuanced than those resulting from autonomous reflection on the strongest arguments and evidence for and against. A fair assessment of a particular law will often lead to the judgment that it warrants support all things considered, notwithstanding certain objections of which one is aware and whose force one does not altogether deny. These objections may highlight costs that are outweighed by the benefits of the law and that cannot be reduced by any feasible redesign of the law without thereby causing a larger reduction in the benefits of the law. Alternatively, one may recognize that a particular law is imperfect while correctly judging that the costs and risks of attempting to remove those imperfections are sufficiently great that it is most sensible simply to retain the law, warts and all. By contrast to these kinds of nuanced support that often result from a balanced assessment of the pros and cons, there is a kind of coarseness of judgment that is often encouraged by status quo biases in civic education.[13] For example, students who are taught to support the First Amendment will often fail to fully appreciate the very real costs associated with robust free speech protections. However, not all forms of status quo educational bias will have this result: a charismatic teacher who carefully and accurately describes the costs associated with a particular law might nonetheless cultivate students' support for that law by urging them to accept his view that those costs are outweighed by the law's benefits.

To recap, the fact that one of a polity's existing institutions is widely endorsed by the citizens of that polity does not by itself indicate that there are status quo biases in that polity's civic education system. It is certainly possible that citizens have autonomously (and with knowledge of the strongest considerations on both sides of the debate) converged on an appreciation of the powerful reasons to support this feature of the status quo. But unbiased education never succeeds in leading *all* of its recipients to the truth, except

[13] Eamonn Callan (1997, pp. 105–8) makes a similar point about certain approaches to teaching history, describing the "coarsening of moral vision" that results when historical figures are presented one-dimensionally as either heroes or monsters.

perhaps when that truth is exceedingly simple and evident. There are always defects both in educators' efforts and in the human materials on which they must work. So, if a society is marked by near unanimous belief in the substantive merits of a particular status quo political institution, we will naturally suspect status quo educational bias. Even if that institution is uniquely best and decisively favored by the balance of reasons, we would not expect such a large proportion of recipients of unbiased education to recognize this fact.[14]

Some readers will be skeptical about the concept of uniquely best political arrangements. But if we grant even the possibility that an existing law is a member of some non-singular "top set" of possible laws that are equally or incommensurably good, we must still be cautious about inferring bias from the observation that a program of civic education leads recipients to support that law. The "top set" of possible laws is defined by the following two conditions: (a) every non-member is inferior to at least one member, and (b) no member is superior to any other member. Condition (b) will typically be explained by incommensurabilities among the various values instantiated by the members of the top set. For example, one might believe that there is a non-singular top set of institutions for administering criminal justice: jury trials may be incommensurable with exclusive reliance on professional judges to determine guilt and innocence because each system is superior to the other on a particular dimension of value and there is no common metric (or other justified decision procedure) by which we could judge that the advantages of one system outweigh (or trump) the advantages of the other. But there can also be a relation of equality (as opposed to incommensurability) between some or all members of a top set: "always drive on the left" and "always drive on the right" are, as far as I know, two equally good ways to realize the values that should be served by traffic laws.

The important point here is that it can be uniquely rational to support an existing law that is a member of the (non-singular) top set given *both* an accurate appraisal of its substantive merits *and* a

[14] And that is precisely why, when adults have a high degree of confidence in the substantive merits of an existing institution, they will be tempted to employ status quo educational bias. In Chapter 7 I make the case that there are conditions under which we should give in to this temptation despite the fallibility of our political judgments.

conscious recognition of the costs and risks associated with disrupting the status quo.[15] The American law requiring motorists to drive on the right is surely such a case. The reasons to retain that law are decisive.[16] We can say this boldly in part because we are so confident that left-handed traffic laws are not intrinsically superior to right-handed laws. That confidence derives from the fact that we regard the two possible laws as equally good, not incommensurable with one another. It is always harder to have a high degree of confidence in one's judgment that two possible laws are incommensurably good. Having said that, I believe that there often are several incommensurably good ways to legislate on a given issue. And, I would argue, if an existing law is not intrinsically inferior to any alternative, it is usually foolish to change it.

Precisely because status quo bias cannot reliably be inferred from the fact that a particular educational program or practice systematically encourages support for an existing political arrangement, it also cannot reliably be inferred from the motive of the educator (or policy-maker). Biased teaching may not be necessary to generate the desired effect. Even when I evenhandedly expose children to both sides of the debate about an existing law, my motive for teaching (or prescribing) this lesson may be to increase support for the law. I would not teach in this way (or require others to do so) if I did not confidently foresee this effect. Analogously, it is perfectly possible *both* that a person's motives for being a doctor prominently include the enjoyment she derives from seeing patients naked *and* that this person will never conduct a medically unnecessary or inappropriate physical examination. She works as a doctor in significant part because she gets to see people naked. If this were not a part of the job, she would do something else for a living. But she does not need to abuse her position in order to satiate her desire to see people naked, and so her professional decisions are guided exclusively by the goal of maintaining and restoring patients' health.

[15] I shall argue in Chapter 7 that our limited capacity to appreciate and be motivated by these costs and risks of change underpins one content-independent reason for status quo educational bias.

[16] Of course, some polities will *not* have decisive reasons to retain their existing laws dictating on which side of the road to drive. The costs of change will always be significant, but they can be outweighed by the long-run efficiency benefits of harmonizing with one's neighbors and/or with the overwhelming majority of polities worldwide.

Although, as we have seen, there are many hazards involved in inferring status quo bias from the fact that civic education increases support for some existing political arrangement, status quo biased education is nonetheless defined solely by its effects on recipients' beliefs. More precisely, it is defined by its *expected* effects. This refinement explains why there is no contradiction in the statement: "John's civic education was biased in favor of judicial review, but it didn't affect his beliefs about the merits of judicial review." The first half of this statement is true if and only if the civic education John received has (or would have) a general tendency to encourage recipients (by some means other than enabling and encouraging autonomous assessment of the best arguments and evidence) to form and/or retain positive evaluative beliefs about judicial review. This general tendency is fully compatible with John's not having been personally affected in this way. A biased education is one that can be expected to generate certain effects (even if it does not do so in any particular instance).

It should be clear from the preceding discussion that I am using the language of civic education's "*expected* effects" much as statisticians and probability theorists use the language of "expected value." There are at least two other ways in which one might use the term "expected effects." It may be helpful to articulate those alternative meanings so as to clearly distinguish them from the phenomenon to which I refer. First, "expected effects" might be used to denote beliefs about the consequences of a particular civic educational practice, regardless of whether those beliefs are true or false. This use of the term is far indeed from my subject: civic education is not status quo biased simply by dint of the fact that people erroneously believe that it will dispose recipients to support existing political arrangements. Second, "expected effects" could be used to refer to a subset of civic education's actual effects, namely, all and only those effects that were accurately foreseen. By contrast, the effects that I call "expected effects" need not be foreseen by anyone: we could all be surprised when a retrospective study reveals the true consequences of a particular civic educational practice. Indeed, my account of status quo educational bias does not even require that the defining effects be foreseeable.[17]

[17] Needless to say, however, there is little to be gained by dwelling on the possibility of unforeseeable consequences.

In similar fashion, my definition of status quo bias does not hinge in any way on the educator's (or policy-maker's) intention.[18] It is neither necessary nor sufficient for bias that an educator intends to shape students' beliefs. Unintended bias is a hugely important and prevalent phenomenon: it will be discussed at length in the next section. But first I want to take a moment to emphasize and justify the other way in which my conceptual account of educational bias focuses on expected effects to the exclusion of intentions. On my view, an adult who zealously but incompetently tries to indoctrinate a child may not have biased that child's education in any way.[19] Attempts to bias someone's education are precisely that: *attempts*. Whether one *actually* biased that person's education depends only on whether one's actions would be expected to shape the person's beliefs (as distinct from helping the person to form and revise her own beliefs in an autonomous and informed fashion).

Of course, we will often care about an educator's intentions both because they are indicative (albeit imperfectly) of the expected effects of his actions and because they are relevant to our evaluative judgments of the educator (as distinct from his actions). But notice that the desirability of an intention to produce status quo educational bias will not always track the desirability of the educational bias itself. Ordinarily, to be sure, if it is undesirable for civic education to be status quo biased then it is undesirable for an educator to intend that effect. But this will not always be so. In some cases, status quo educational biases may be less likely to arise precisely when they are intended by the educator. This counterintuitive relationship will obtain when three conditions are met. First, the educator's intentions are apparent to her students. Second, the students are more strongly motivated and better able to resist (and perhaps

[18] For a somewhat contrasting view, see Snook (1972), whose definition of indoctrination (which is a stronger concept than educational bias) includes intention as a necessary condition but then unhelpfully broadens the concept of intention to include all effects that are both foreseen and avoidable. If it would be costly to avoid a particular foreseen effect, one cannot infer that the effect was intended from the fact that the agent allowed it to occur.

[19] She may have biased the child's education in some unintended way. For example, children may tend to recognize and react against this adult's blatant attempts at indoctrination: without assessing the relevant evidence and arguments, children can be expected to align themselves firmly with a position that is directly opposed to the one that was being pressed upon them.

even react against) influences on their beliefs when they perceive that an educator is trying to influence them. Third, the educator's attempts to transmit civic knowledge will be marked by significant status quo biases even if she does not intend any such influence. I do not know how often these three conditions will all be met, but I would speculate that the trifecta—students who resent and resist perceived efforts to shape their beliefs (even to the point of contrarianism) and a teacher who is both short on guile and unwittingly portrays her polity's major institutions in a positive light—is not wildly uncommon.

So, when the effects that constitute educational bias are undesirable, it may sometimes paradoxically be preferable for educators to intend those effects. Conversely, when certain effects that constitute status quo educational bias are desirable, it may be preferable to rely on unintended bias. In part this is for the same reason we just saw: children may tend to identify and successfully resist efforts to shape their political beliefs. But, in other cases, deliberate efforts to shape belief will tend to generate *more* bias than the educator intends. If this is so, and assuming that educators aim at the optimal range and degree of status quo bias, the result will be an excess of such bias. For reasons that I explore in the next section, we adults will often not be aware of all the unintended status quo educational biases that attend our interactions with children. And even when we are aware of a bias we will tend to underestimate it. Analogously, it may be both prudent and justifiable for a skilled driver to drive ten miles per hour above the speed limit, but *aiming* to do so may not be a good strategy if, unbeknownst to the driver, the car's speedometer underestimates its speed by ten miles per hour. Or, to extend the analogy, perhaps the driver knows that the speedometer systematically underestimates the car's speed but falsely believes that it does so by only three miles per hour.

6.5. Unintended and unavoidable biases

Status quo educational bias can be and often is unintended. When an educator intends merely to describe the status quo, he may inadvertently express his evaluation of it: a stray word or turn of phrase can easily betray his normative position. More radically, it is not clear that the concept of "mere description" is coherent. All descriptions of political arrangements are selective and rely upon contestable empirical judgments: the selections and judgments that educators make will always be influenced by their values. In addition, there is the danger that children will not grasp the distinction between statements that are intended to be merely descriptive of the political status quo (and perhaps also the history that led to it) and those that are meant to express endorsement of it. It would be exhausting, impracticable, and probably ineffective for a teacher to attach an explicit disclaimer to every statement she makes in civics class: "...and I'm not saying that's a good thing." Merely by spending more time describing the institutions of one's own polity than one does relating alternatives (existing, historical, or hypothetical), one is likely to cause children to feel more comfortable with the arrangements they know and understand best: familiarity, in this instance, seems more likely to breed approval than contempt.[20]

Additional sources of unintended educational bias arise when one moves beyond the attempt "merely" to describe a status quo institution to the more ambitious task of trying to evenhandedly introduce children to arguments about that institution's substantive merits. I may earnestly intend to present both sides of the debate in their strongest light but fail for one of two reasons. First, unintended bias may result from the limits of my knowledge: I am well versed in the arguments on one side, but I am unaware of or do not properly understand the best arguments on the other side (including the most important objections to the arguments that I know well). Second, the educational biases may flow from biases in my judgment: I know both sides of the debate equally well but am nonetheless unable to present one side as compellingly as the other because I am either unaware of or unable to overcome the biases in my own judgment. I inadvertently make weak reasons sound highly persuasive when they support the position I favor, and powerful objections to that position always seem oddly lifeless in my articulation of them, no matter how hard I try. Notice that educational biases can be both foreseen and unintended by the educator: for this to be true,

[20] Psychologists refer to this well-documented phenomenon as the "mere exposure effect."

it must be the case that the educator is either unable to eliminate the bias or unwilling to accept the costs of elimination.[21]

Importantly for our purposes, the various sources of unintended educational bias cannot be expected to produce random "errors" and therefore to cancel themselves out in the aggregate. In particular, within a given democratic polity the effects of educators' limited knowledge and biased judgment can be expected systematically to favor the status quo. At least, this will be true as long as education in that polity is controlled and delivered predominantly by its own citizens rather than by outsiders. Citizen educators, like all citizens, can be expected to know their own society's institutions and the arguments for them better than they know the alternatives (existing in other times or places or merely in theory) and the arguments for these alternatives. And citizens' judgment is likely to be systematically status quo biased for two mutually reinforcing reasons that operate in opposite causal directions from one another. First, because political preferences are often somewhat adaptive, we can expect to observe nonrational beliefs in the merits of status quo arrangements, whatever those arrangements are. Second, because the laws of a democracy reflect the political preferences of its citizens and those preferences are importantly shaped by biases in citizens' judgment, we can expect the status quo to reflect the systematic biases in citizens' judgment, whatever those biases are. In other words, citizens' (and therefore citizen educators') biases in judgment will systematically favor the status quo both because the status quo shapes the bias and because the bias shapes the status quo.

Although citizens whose judgment biases are opposed to the status quo will be in a minority, it is theoretically possible that these citizens could wield disproportionate influence within the education system. In almost all societies, immediate authority over children's formal education resides disproportionately with a small subset of adults: professional educators and education policy-makers. In so far as these teachers and educational elites enjoy the freedom of not being directly and frequently accountable to the masses, their actions and decisions can diverge significantly from

[21] Strictly speaking the first explanation is just a special case of the second one: the only way in which the educator can eliminate bias on a given topic is to avoid that topic altogether, and she is unwilling to accept that cost. I shall shortly discuss this drastic strategy for eliminating unintended biases.

those that the majority would prefer. In particular, if the group that controls the education system has political preferences (and associated judgment biases) that differ from those of the adult citizenry as a whole, the unintended biases of that system might not always favor the status quo.[22] And it is often said (in the United States, the United Kingdom, and probably elsewhere) that professional educators as a group do indeed have political preferences that differ systematically from those of the larger population. But, if this is true, it is typically because the professionals tend to the (moderate) political left rather than being radical opponents of the status quo. For example, British teachers may well on average favor somewhat more redistributive taxation than currently exists in the UK, but very few have radically egalitarian or anti-capitalist economic commitments. Similarly, there may be a higher proportion of republicans (i.e., opponents of the monarchy) in the UK teaching profession than in the UK population as a whole, but British teachers are unlikely to be critics of the UK constitution more generally: I assume that very few will be opposed to trial by jury or the parliamentary system, for example.

So we should not mistake a cadre of mildly leftist teachers for a force that will encourage revolutionary ideas in children even without trying to do so. Furthermore, to the extent that formal education is directly subject to democratic authority—i.e., curricula, policies, textbooks, criteria for teacher certification and recruitment, and the like are chosen collectively using a roughly majoritarian procedure—we would expect the pro-status-quo judgment biases of the majority of citizens to exclude the influence of the dissenting minority's biases, amplifying the net unintended status quo bias of the education system compared to the alternative scenario in which each citizen fully controls her own child's formal education.[23] In the United States, with its

[22] It is obviously also possible that teachers and educational elites might *intend* to bias children's education against certain aspects of the status quo.

[23] Perhaps—it hardly seems likely—the citizenry as a whole could be so alert to the pervasiveness of unintended bias and so committed to reducing status quo biases in schooling that it would democratically decide to recruit teachers disproportionately from outside the mainstream, encouraging and favoring candidates from ideological and cultural groups whose unintended biases are less likely to favor the status quo. But there may be few if any citizens whose biases do not favor certain political institutions that are very widely accepted within the society. And, even if such citizens exist in sufficient numbers and can reliably be identified, they may not be willing to become professional educators and/or they may lack the other qualifications to do so.

strong tradition of locally and democratically controlled public schools, it hardly seems likely that the education system could be disproportionately controlled by those few citizens who want to see the US Constitution radically overhauled. Recall also that education should be understood in its broad sense, which includes parenting. I see no reason to believe that the minority of citizens whose judgment biases systematically and profoundly oppose the status quo have more than their proportional share of offspring! But even if these radically dissenting adults are extraordinarily fecund, they constitute such a small share of a polity's population that their aggregate influence on the civic upbringing of that polity's children cannot be very great.

It is no doubt possible to select and train professional educators (and especially those who will teach civics, history, social studies, human geography, politics/government, economics, sociology, etc.) such that they possess, in comparison to other citizens, superior knowledge of the leading alternatives to status quo institutions and the best arguments for those alternatives. It may also be feasible to help these teachers to reduce the (predominantly status quo) biases in their political judgment, or at least to identify and acknowledge these biases: once I am conscious of my tendency not to give a fair hearing to certain kinds of political argument, I may be able to adapt my pedagogy to reduce the extent to which my bias will affect my teaching. But teachers are only human, so we will never be wholly successful in eliminating their propensity to deliver unintentionally status quo biased education.

And, even if we could somehow conceive of a profession of superhuman educators who do not bias their students' civic education, we surely could not imagine all parents successfully eliminating unintended status quo bias from the upbringing they give to their children. Moreover, the mass media and popular culture will realistically always impart a net status quo bias to children's education. And, as we shall discuss in Chapter 7, Harry Brighouse (2000, p. 77) notes that "weak conditioning of consent [to the existing political order] is . . . a predictable consequence of many proper activities of the liberal state." No system of formal education could entirely counteract or insulate children from the effects of parenting and these other social and political institutions that dispose them to favor the status quo.[24] As Mill (1859/1989, pp. 82–83) notes, it is inevitable that children's minds will be shaped to some degree by society's received opinions.

It might be possible to eliminate status quo bias from schooling simply by eliminating all mention of politics from schools. But this drastic measure would probably increase rather than reduce the overall status quo bias of children's education. Schools seem likely, or at least have the potential, to be the venues in which civic education is less status quo biased, more successful at encouraging critical and evenhanded political debate, than it is in other social institutions that influence children's political beliefs and values.[25] And even if

[24] George Counts (1932, pp. 24, 54) argued that the role of schools in a liberal society is to serve as progressive counterweights to these inertial influences, actively teaching children that their polity is flawed in various fundamental ways. On Counts' analysis, schools will (only) be able to play this role if we resolutely protect the autonomy of educators so that they cannot be punished for failing to transmit majority opinion or for educating children in ways that threaten the dominant, especially capitalist, interests in society (pp. 28–30). But, as I have discussed, although the typical educator in capitalist societies may be more progressive than the average citizen, he will still have many political preferences that favor fundamental features of the status quo. Therefore, *contra* Counts, guaranteeing the professional autonomy of teachers will not be sufficient to create schools that systematically push back against the forces that favor the status quo. Teachers would have to engage in continual devil's advocacy and successfully overcome their susceptibility to unintended status quo educational bias. It is, in short, extremely hard to imagine radically anti-status-quo education being successfully institutionalized on a large scale.

More promisingly, Counts' argument suggests the potential value of immigrant parents' giving their child a biased upbringing that favors the very different (but still liberal democratic) institutions of the parents' native country over the status quo arrangements in the country in which the family now resides. Ex hypothesis, these parents do not just want their child *exposed* to the arguments for alternative institutions—they want to teach their child to embrace a particular alternative. Provided that such parents do not insulate their child from competing messages, it could be that the biases will roughly cancel one another out, that the net effect of such parental teachings and the influence of other social institutions that reinforce the locally dominant political beliefs might approximate some form of education for autonomous and informed civic judgment, especially if the child's formal schooling cultivates the capacity and inclination for critical reasoning.

[25] If we wish to reduce status quo bias in formal education, the case for doing so simply by avoiding all mention of politics is strongest with young children, those whose reasoning capacities are insufficiently developed to engage in an autonomous assessment of existing political arrangements. It would still be regrettable that these children would not be acquiring civic knowledge, but at least we would not be losing an opportunity to stimulate critical thinking about the status quo.

eliminating civic education from schools would reduce the overall status quo bias in children's education, opponents of such bias should think twice before signing on to that proposal. As we saw in Chapter 1, an important function of civic education is to transmit knowledge about the polity's existing institutions, and schools are especially well suited to serve this function. It seems most unlikely that we should stop using schools to transmit political knowledge even if this transmission tends to bias children's attitudes in favor of the status quo in ways that we regard as regrettable.[26]

Finally, I should acknowledge that all education that shapes its recipients' beliefs and values presupposes (whether explicitly or implicitly) some premises that recipients are not invited, encouraged, or empowered to critically evaluate. When these presuppositions are implicit, the educator herself may not be conscious of them. One can argue about whether these presuppositions should be made explicit to students, whether the educator should always be conscious of them, and what their content should be. But it would be incoherent to regret the inescapability of presuppositions in education. Just as science education presupposes the validity and merits of certain methods and principles that constitute scientific practice as it is currently conceived, civic education must presuppose some empirical, normative, and/or methodological premises that are not themselves subject to critical scrutiny in the educational process. The fact that education involves presuppositions is a conceptual necessity as distinct from a psychological inevitability.

Assuming that civic education is directed and conducted by insiders, its presuppositions will typically be propositions that are widely accepted in the society. These presuppositions need not all constitute status quo biases. As we saw in Chapter 1, teaching

[26] More moderately, one could imagine civic education courses in which children are taught only about the least normatively and empirically controversial features of their polity, with educators declining even to describe significantly contested laws and institutions, never mind trying to present children with all the conflicting views on these arrangements. If my arguments in the next chapter are correct, the status quo biases that would accompany such restricted civic education would often be desirable. But we would be missing the chance to increase children's knowledge and understanding of precisely those features of their polity about which they are most likely to be called upon to reflect, deliberate, and decide. This, I would suggest, is too high a price to pay in the cause of limiting the range of status quo biases in formal education.

children basic and universal moral values actually enhances their capacity for autonomous reasoning, and we can say the same about teaching children the precepts of logical reasoning and sound statistical analysis, for example. But some of the presuppositions in any civic education—especially the empirical and methodological premises that are presupposed by educators' attempts to describe political institutions and their effects—will indeed detract from the autonomy of children's political beliefs and will therefore constitute educational biases, most of which will favor the status quo.

6.6. Conclusion: controlling status quo bias

We may conclude, without any great surprise, that perfectly unbiased civic education is a mirage and, in particular, that biases favoring the status quo could only be eliminated if a society took the extraordinary step of entrusting the education of its children to the citizens of another society with very different political institutions.[27] Is my qualified defense of status quo biased education in the next chapter therefore an elaborate and unnecessary justification of the kind of education to which there is no feasible and remotely attractive alternative? Am I simply making a virtue out of the psychological inevitability of unintended status quo biases? Am I making the weak claim that status quo biases are justified only insofar as the conceptual necessity of presuppositions makes some bias inescapable in all education? The answer to all three questions is no.

Civic education will realistically always exhibit some status quo biases, but the range and degree of those biases are very largely under the control of citizens, individually and collectively.[28] We must decide whether, when, and how to expose children to (what

[27] Taking this approach to children's formal civic education would be very costly and challenging. And extending the approach to children's informal civic education is barely conceivable: children would have to be raised (presumably by some agent other than their parents) outside of the polity to which they will return as adult citizens.

[28] As the analysis in this chapter should have made abundantly clear, it will often be difficult for anyone to *determine* (and even more difficult for people with different political views to *agree*) where a particular civic educational practice lies on the continuum from most to least status quo biased.

we take to be) the most powerful critiques of and significant alternatives to our existing political order.[29] We must decide whether to use particular educational practices whose effects include biasing children's judgment to nonrationally reject challenges to the status quo. And, if we are sensitive to the premises that particular approaches to civic education presuppose, we can make conscious choices about how "thick" or "thin" these presuppositions should be: they certainly need not be so concrete, determinate, and value-laden as to favor particular political institutions over most or all alternatives.

Perhaps no civic education can avoid explicitly or implicitly prejudging questions about the rival merits of contemporary political arrangements in the US and North Korea, and if so it would scarcely be controversial to say that American children should be educated in ways that favor the US Constitution over the North Korean one. As I argued in Chapter 1, inculcating the basic values underlying liberal democracy is fully compatible with, and indeed promotes, the development of children's capacity for autonomous and informed political judgment. But it is not conceptually necessary for a civic education to take sides as between the contemporary political arrangements of, say, Germany and the US, and it is by no means obvious that American children's education should encourage the belief that the US Constitution is superior to the German one. Teaching American children to believe in the right to a fair trial is *not* status quo biased, but teaching them that jury trials are fairer than (or for some other reasons preferable to) inquisitorial procedures *is* status quo biased. In the next chapter, I argue that, notwithstanding two powerful objections, some robust civic educational biases favoring the local status quo have much to recommend them and should not lightly be eschewed or discarded.

[29] The most defensible forms of status quo educational bias will rarely involve shielding children from knowledge of alternative political arrangements. Such knowledge is often an important element in truly understanding one's own polity's institutions; the contrast is instructive. When some measure of status quo bias is desirable, it is usually better for it to arise through the manner in which alternatives are presented rather than through suppressing knowledge of their existence.

CHAPTER 7

A qualified defense of status quo bias

In the previous chapter I argued that status quo biases in civic education, although not realistically eliminable, are substantially amenable to control by citizens acting individually and collectively. That conclusion clears the way for the normative question that I take up in this chapter: when, if ever, are status quo biases in civic education desirable?

In a very general sense, all educational bias stands in need of justification. In other words, there is a presumption against bias in education. Some reason must be given to justify adults in using their (individual or collective) power over children in ways that—foreseeably, avoidably, and often intentionally—shape those children's substantive beliefs rather than simply equipping children to make their own independent judgments based on the best information and arguments available. Of course, if the bias would be costly to eliminate (which, as we saw in the last chapter, will often be the case with unintended biases) and is relatively harmless, avoiding the cost of elimination might be a sufficient reason. But, if the bias could be eliminated without significant cost (often because it is intentional), it does not constitute a justification for adults to say: "I want (or am happy for) these children to believe p, so I shall present them with skewed information, bypass their rational capacities, or induce belief before they are capable of making an autonomous judgment about p." Inducing belief in one of these ways will sometimes be justified, to be sure, but it will never be justified by adults' mere preferences (as distinct from adults' warranted beliefs about p's truth value or about the beneficial consequences of the children's believing p).

I shall argue that status quo biases in civic education can be and often are justified. But justifying any particular instance of such bias requires doing much more than merely overcoming the aforementioned general presumption against educational bias. Status quo biases in civic education are vulnerable to two more specific objections: I refer to these as the *fallibility* and *legitimacy* objections, and I spend the first part of this chapter both describing them and attempting to convey their considerable force. But, since I do not believe that these objections are always decisive, I devote the rest of the chapter to exploring the various arguments that could jointly defeat them in particular cases. I show the possibility of constructing compelling *content-dependent* reasons for status quo bias, i.e., reasons that invoke widespread beliefs about the substantive merits of existing institutions, notwithstanding the fallibility objection. And I identify four *content-independent* reasons, i.e., reasons that appeal not to the substantive merits of the institutions favored by status quo bias but merely to the fact that those institutions are the status quo: I refer to these as the arguments from *stability*, *contentment*, *compliance*, and *civic identification*.

I conclude that status quo educational biases have much to recommend them. The combined force of content-dependent and content-independent reasons will sometimes outweigh the fallibility and legitimacy objections to particular instances of status quo bias. Therefore, the best civic education will typically include significant elements of such bias. But, to reiterate an important point that I made back in Chapter 1, my claim is *not* that most civic education in the world today is lacking in status quo bias. Rather, I claim, *contra* the orthodox view, that a significant degree of avoidable status quo bias is justified and desirable in civic education. Much actual civic education may already contain at least this much bias.

7.1. Objections to status quo bias

There are two principal objections to status quo bias in civic education. First, the *fallibility* objection argues that status quo biases in civic education are barriers to political progress. A democratic society's prospects for seeing and correcting its own mistakes are diminished if each new generation of citizens is taught to believe in the status quo. Status quo educational bias distorts or even short-circuits what ought to be an ongoing debate about the substantive merits of existing political arrangements, even those that today's adult citizens overwhelmingly regard as just and wise. In recognition of the fallibility of their collective judgments, adult citizens should equip and encourage the next generation to reevaluate without prejudice all the laws and institutions that they will inherit.[1] As we saw in the previous chapter, this involves not only promoting the capacity and inclination for autonomous, critical thinking about political arrangements but also making children aware of significant alternatives to the existing order and exposing them fair-mindedly to the strongest arguments and evidence in favor of those alternatives.

The fallibility objection owes much to John Stuart Mill's arguments for freedom of speech and discussion and his fear of excessive state control of education in Chapters 2 and 5 respectively of "On Liberty" (1859/1989).[2] But Mill's concerns were narrower. He argued against giving the state monopoly power over children's education and more generally against both formal and informal exercises of social power over individuals that threaten to homogenize opinion throughout society. The tyranny of the majority, whether it operates through the coercive machinery of the democratic state or via the insidious and even more effective power of individuals and groups deploying sanctions of disapproval and avoidance, is a relentless force for conformity not only in actions but also in beliefs. But, although Mill was deeply worried about *society's* power over belief formation, he did not object to allowing *parents* to mold their children's beliefs through education. Mill's concerns would therefore be satisfactorily taken into account by measures that preserve the freedom (from social sanctions both formal and informal) of individual parents (and the professional educators who, on Mill's view, should serve as their agents). But such measures would not evade the force of the fallibility objection.

[1] A variant on the fallibility objection observes that an existing law, although justified in current conditions, may be ill-suited to the conditions that the next generation of citizens will face. In such cases, status quo educational bias is a barrier not to progress but to appropriate flexibility.

[2] Mill also warns us that certain attempts to deploy status quo educational bias could be self-defeating: I return to this point at the end of the chapter.

If parents all decide to exercise their freedom by heavily biasing their children's civic education in accordance with their beliefs, status quo political arrangements that enjoy overwhelming support among adult citizens can be expected to enjoy similarly high levels of support in the next generation even if they are, in fact, deeply flawed in ways that might be apparent to citizens whose education was far less biased.

It is not hard to generate examples of deeply unjust laws whose survival across many generations was almost certainly explained in large part by powerful and pervasive biases in children's civic education. Indeed, it is hard to think of (or even imagine) an unjustified regime of legal discrimination against a particular subset of a polity's members whose intergenerational perpetuation did not (or would not) rely on teaching children to believe that the laws in question are justified. Status quo educational bias preserves unjustly discriminatory institutions by making it harder for *both* beneficiaries and victims to perceive the injustice, either by concealing the costs to the victims or by misrepresenting those costs as morally permissible. As Mill makes devastatingly clear in his "The Subjection of Women" (1869/1989), the many British laws that for centuries systematically subordinated women depended for their continued support on formal and especially informal educational institutions propagating the views that women are profoundly different from (and in many respects inferior to) men and that these sex differences necessitate various forms of legal discrimination.

I am no expert on apartheid South Africa, but can anyone seriously doubt that the education of white children (and at least the state-provided education of black children) in that society was systematically designed to foster the belief that apartheid was not only legitimate but also essential, an expression of the natural order of society? A third prominent example of the perpetuation of gross political injustice through this kind of misuse of education would be the historic use of schools (and other educational institutions) to encourage children to believe both that homosexuality is morally wrong and that the state ought to reflect that wrongness by not only criminalizing same-sex intercourse but also discriminating (and permitting private discrimination) against homosexuals in a wide range of contexts (such as employment, family law, civil rights, etc.).

The second major argument against status quo bias in civic education is the *legitimacy* objection, whose central premise is that the permissibility of state coercion depends (to some degree) upon citizens' giving their autonomous and informed consent to the institutions by which they are governed (Brighouse 2000, 1998).[3] Consent does not confer legitimacy if it is manufactured. "Consent should not simply be caused by the state itself, through mechanisms that have nothing to do with the appropriateness of the [existing political] arrangements" (Brighouse 2000, p. 76). A state that indoctrinated its children to believe in the goodness of its laws would be a "political perpetual-motion machine" (Arons 1983, p. 203), and such a state would be illegitimate *even if* all its laws were in fact uniquely best. Status quo educational bias, even when it falls short of outright indoctrination and even if it operates only through the selection of evidence and arguments to which children are exposed (and therefore may not bias their *judgment*), poses precisely this threat to the legitimacy of the state. And the threat arises even when the state is not the agent of the biased education (Callan 2000, p. 152).[4] Only if children's education permits[5] them to form independent political beliefs and make up their own minds about political values can their future endorsement of their society's political institutions be expected to be both autonomous and informed and therefore to confer legitimacy on the state.[6]

Readers can be forgiven (and should probably also be congratulated) if they have a sense of déjà vu at this moment. We have indeed encountered this legitimacy concern before. In Chapter 1,

[3] Ackerman (1980, Chapter 5) also offers a version of this argument from liberal legitimacy; for the sake of simplicity and brevity, I focus on Brighouse's formulation.

[4] In addition to eschewing bias in the schools it operates, Callan argues, the state may therefore also need to regulate private and home schools. It may even be possible for the state to lack legitimacy simply because non-school educational influences thwart the efforts of schools to cultivate future citizens' autonomy.

[5] I would add that education should *encourage* the development and exercise of autonomy, but Brighouse (2000, pp. 80–2) disclaims this further step as a violation of character neutrality. I argued against character neutrality in Chapter 1.

[6] Given that we are born into particular political communities and that emigration is costly, John Rawls (1993/1996, p. 222) argues that citizens' considered, rational, and informed endorsement of political principles must play the role of consent to political authority in liberal accounts of legitimacy. "We may over the course of life come freely to accept, as the outcome of reflective thought and reasoned judgment, the ideals, principles, and standards that specify our basic rights and liberties, and effectively guide and moderate the political power to which we are subject."

I considered the argument in its most radical form, namely, as the claim that the liberal principle of legitimacy paradoxically and perversely prohibits inculcating the basic moral values upon which a liberal polity depends. I argued that the radical argument should be rejected because it rests upon impoverished views of autonomy and moral reasoning: teaching children to be tolerant and respectful of others as their moral equals does not detract from the cultivation of children's autonomy and therefore does not imperil the state's legitimacy. But this concern for political legitimacy recurs and has considerable force when it is interpreted as a more moderate claim. Status quo biases in civic education *by their very definition* threaten the legitimacy-conferring qualities of citizens' consent to the particular political arrangements they inherit from their ancestors.

Let us summarize the case against status quo biases in civic education. Such biases run directly counter to the goal of enabling (and perhaps encouraging) future citizens to be *autonomous* and *informed* participants in the democratic process of reauthorizing, revising, or repealing the laws by which they are governed. Political participation that exemplifies these two qualities is of civic value both *intrinsically* (because it confers legitimacy) and *instrumentally* (because it contributes to discovering and correcting the defects in our political institutions). My question in the remainder of this chapter is whether the legitimacy and fallibility objections to status quo biased civic education are always decisive. By exploring the strongest arguments in favor of a degree of status quo bias when educating future citizens about certain existing institutions, I aim to show that status quo bias is often a justifiable component of the best civic education.

We can divide the various reasons to favor status quo biased civic education into two broad categories: those reasons that appeal to (widespread beliefs about) the substantive merits of existing institutions and those that appeal merely to their being the status quo. Let us call reasons of the former type "content-dependent" and those of the latter "content-independent." As we shall see, it is hard to imagine that status quo bias could be successfully defended without invoking content-dependent reasons, and any such reasons must confront the fallibility objection. But the various content-independent reasons are also important and can play a significant auxiliary role, especially in counterbalancing (as opposed to refuting) the fallibility and legitimacy objections.

7.2. Content-dependent reasons for status quo bias

One might think that there is an obvious reason to bias children's education in favor of certain existing institutions: namely, that those institutions are good. We worry that children who receive a minimally biased education will not reason their way to supporting good laws, and we believe that we can increase the number who do so by judicious use of educational bias. So, should we simply conclude that there are content-dependent reasons for a particular instance of status quo educational bias if and only if the institution that it favors is good? This would be a singularly unhelpful conclusion. The problem we face is epistemological: we do not know which of our political institutions are good. Often we disagree. And, even when we agree, we can be wrong. This is precisely the force of the fallibility objection.

Would it help to "raise the bar" by saying that we have content-dependent reasons to bias education in favor of only those institutions whose substantive merits it would be irrational or unreasonable to deny?[7] No, it would not help: the epistemological problem recurs. Assuming that this higher standard can be met, how do we know whether any of our existing institutions meet it? We can be wrong about such second-order judgments just as we can be wrong about the first-order question, namely, the merits of an existing institution. We may fail to recognize the admissibility of certain arguments against the status quo, and we may wrongly regard other arguments as admissible. We are especially prone to error when applying the concept of reasonableness. It is one thing to say that an argument is unreasonable if it cannot be reconciled with the basic moral values underlying liberal democracy; it is quite another to try to determine in a particular case whether all the arguments against an existing political institution meet this standard. The fallibility objection strikes again.

So, much as Ronald Dworkin (1985, p. 106) proposes a "*working* theory of civil disobedience" whereby the permissibility of disobedience does not depend on "which side is right in the underlying

[7] Here I follow Rawls (1993/1996) and Scanlon (1982, 1998). The idea is that one may judge the balance of arguments to be in favor of a particular institution without claiming that it would be irrational or unreasonable to think otherwise.

controversy," we need a working theory of civic education whereby the permissibility of status quo bias does not depend on the actual substantive merits of the existing law or institution for which educators would be encouraging children's support. The theory should guide our educational policy and practice using only our *beliefs* about the substantive merits of our political arrangements, including not only the *content* of those beliefs but also their *distribution* across citizens and the *conditions* under which they were formed. A working theory should take the beliefs themselves, and not their truth or falsity (to which we do not have direct access), as its inputs.[8] The fallibility objection rightly insists that we not confuse a belief, even a widely and strongly held belief, with the truth of that belief. But it is one thing to recognize the fallibility of our inferences from widespread belief to truth; it is quite another never to draw and act upon such inferences in the design of children's education. The fallibility objection highlights one important concern, namely, that an institution favored by status quo bias may be imperfect, perhaps even seriously unjust or unwise. But we should not overlook the opposite danger, namely, that by eschewing status quo educational bias we increase the chance that future citizens will overturn the good institutions we currently have (and perhaps replace them with decidedly inferior alternatives).

To get an intuitive sense of the case for status quo biases in civic education, it may help to draw an analogy to science education. If children are taught to autonomously assess the arguments and evidence for and against evolution, many will form a belief in evolution. But more children will form that belief if their science teachers omit arguments against and/or assert the truth of evolution. As a result, many educators do not favor purely unbiased education about evolution: if one has a very high degree of confidence in the truth of evolution, one may believe that evenhanded exposure to the best arguments for and against evolution both unacceptably increases the chance that children will (irrationally) form false beliefs

[8] One might therefore argue that, on a working theory, our reasons are never truly content-dependent. I don't think anything of substance hangs on the choice of label. I prefer to call these reasons content-dependent to highlight the fact that the beliefs they depend on are beliefs about the *substantive* merits of the laws, by contrast with the reasons I label content-independent.

and consumes educational time and resources that could have been better used. Indeed, it is surely tempting for biology teachers to treat the theory of evolution as a presupposition of the subject they are teaching.

For the political analogue, consider constitutional laws mandating that the judicial function be separated from and meaningfully independent of the legislative and executive functions of government. If the institution of a separate and independent judiciary is presented to children without bias, I imagine that more than a few would endorse it as an important safeguard against tyranny (and, more generally, against government action that is arbitrary and/or fails to treat citizens with equal respect). But would enough of a polity's future citizens form this view, and would they give it sufficient weight in their reasoning, to preserve the institution from the many threats it inevitably faces in the rough-and-tumble of democratic politics? If adult citizens have great confidence in the merits of judicial independence, they may see it as irresponsible and foolishly risky not to design children's civic education to encourage this belief. Even if one believes that, in a hypothetical world of infinite time, every feature of the status quo should be reevaluated without prejudice by the rising generation of citizens, in the real world there is surely a strong case for presenting certain issues to children as settled in order to encourage those children to focus their critical energies on debates about institutions whose merits are much more contestable.

But don't these examples simply ignore the force of the fallibility objection? We could be wrong to believe in evolution, and we could be wrong to believe that an independent judiciary (or any other particular existing law or institution) is a good way to realize the basic values of liberal democracy. Under what circumstances might we have content-dependent reasons for biasing education in favor of an existing law notwithstanding the ever-present possibility that we have overestimated the substantive merits of that law? In other words, when should we have confidence in our belief that a law is good? I would argue that when all the members of something like the following set of conditions are met for law X in society Y we have strong content-dependent reasons to bias education in Y to some degree in favor of X.

1) An overwhelming majority of Y's adult citizens[9] believe that X is a good law.[10]
2) Y's citizens are permitted to express opposition to X, organize against it, etc.
3) Today's adult citizens of Y were not themselves educated in such a biased fashion that an overwhelming majority would be expected to believe that X is good regardless of its merits.[11]
4) If X is to the disadvantage of some citizens of Y, a majority of those citizens nonetheless believe that it is justified (and those citizens' education must have been no more biased in favor of X than was the education of their peers).[12]
5) The law has been on the books for at least a generation, and conditions 1–4 were all satisfied one generation ago.

An interesting dilemma arises in cases where adult citizens overwhelmingly believe that an existing law is justified on its substantive merits but disagree on what those justifying merits are. By way of a simple example, citizens may be united in their support for laws prohibiting the use of hard drugs but deeply divided in their reasons. Some citizens believe that the laws are and can only be justified paternalistically: these citizens appeal to the grave harms that users

[9] I assume that the society in question presumptively includes all of its permanent adult members in the demos and employs defensible standards to justify any exceptions.

[10] By analogy with the issue of teaching evolution, perhaps we should look for a consensus among experts rather than among all adult citizens. But who are the experts on normative political questions? Plato has an answer to that question. But it is not compatible with democracy. If there is an identifiable subset of the population whose normative political judgments are epistemically more reliable than those of the masses, we should defer to their judgments not only in the design of civic education. We should also let them rule.

[11] When conditions 2 and 3 are both met—that is, citizens enjoy significant autonomy in the formation and maintenance of their political beliefs—some status quo educational biases will typically be justified even in polities that are riddled with imperfections and injustices. Notwithstanding their many defects, such polities are likely to have some laws and institutions that meet conditions 1, 4, and 5. But, even in polities whose political arrangements are predominantly good, status quo biased education will be extremely hard to justify if certain illiberal conditions undermine the epistemic reliability of a strong consensus among adult citizens that a given law is good.

[12] X may disadvantage these citizens relative to the *absence* of law on the relevant issue or when compared to a possible *alternative* law on that issue.

of hard drugs do to themselves. Other citizens are outraged by such paternalistic arguments but believe that prohibition is justified as the only practicable way to prevent the unacceptable costs that users of hard drugs predictably impose on others in their society. We might also consider some examples in which more than two grounds for supporting a law are commonly invoked. Overwhelming support for incarceration of violent criminals may mask disagreements as to whether the justification is deterrence, retribution, or incapacitation. And public subsidies for mass transit can be supported for a host of different reasons: environmental benefits, economic development, redistributive justice, reduced commuting times, a partial antidote to the privatization of citizens' lives, and even aesthetic preferences.

If status quo educational bias is appropriate in cases such as these, we shall obviously want to use educational tools that do not encourage children to adopt any particular position in the disagreement that underlies adult citizens' consensus. But, more fundamentally, one might ask whether a shallow consensus of this kind really constitutes a valid content-dependent reason for biasing children's education. I think it does. Although it is admittedly unsettling when, as will sometimes be the case, each putative justification is rejected by a majority of adult citizens, we can nonetheless take comfort in the existence of multiple justificatory strategies and the fact that very few people reject all of these. In particular, when citizens' starkly different lines of reasoning converge on support for a law it is very unlikely that the consensus rests heavily on one false belief that is widely shared, which is often the fear that prompts us not to dismiss the concern about fallibility as a mere philosopher's objection even when a consensus is numerically overwhelming.

Some readers may believe that the five conditions I propose are too demanding, that they concede too much to the ignorance, prejudice, and selfishness that explain much opposition to existing laws. To these readers I would emphasize that although I regard the five conditions as jointly sufficient to justify status quo educational bias, I do not think that they are individually necessary. Even when these conditions are not all fully met, we may still have content-dependent reasons that, when combined with the content-independent reasons I shall soon describe, are strong enough to outweigh the fallibility and legitimacy objections to status quo bias. I do not think it is possible to precisely articulate necessary conditions for justified educational bias: an instance of bias that falls far short of meeting one of my five conditions may nonetheless be justified if it clearly satisfies the other four and is also strongly favored by content-independent considerations. Moreover, as I noted above, it will sometimes be prudent to present a political issue to children as settled in favor of the polity's current practice, notwithstanding the existence of cogent reasons to prefer an alternative practice, as part of a larger educational strategy to focus the finite resources of those children's capacity for critical reflection on important issues about which there is still a raging debate within the polity. As with many decisions in this complex domain, these are matters for contextual judgment and practical wisdom rather than algorithmic resolution.

One might also worry that the aforementioned conditions are not demanding enough in some key respects. Longstanding but imperfect political arrangements may meet the conditions because hardly anyone thinks to reevaluate them. Or, perhaps more troublingly, discriminatory laws might meet condition 4 because many of the victims have adaptively accepted the bad reasons offered to justify the discrimination. In response to this second objection, I should note that the formulation of condition 4 aims to strike a balance between two opposing concerns. I do not require supermajority support among those disadvantaged by the law (as condition 1 does among citizens generally) because selfishness will often lead at least a sizeable minority of those disadvantaged by a just and good law to oppose that law. On the other hand, condition 4 requires the support of more than a significant minority of those disadvantaged because of the worry about adaptive belief formation.[13] Having said this, I am certainly open to tinkering with the criteria for assessing the strength of the content-dependent case for educational bias. My main goal is simply to illustrate the important point that we can have strong content-dependent reasons for implementing or retaining status quo biased education when conditions render the fallibility objection much less potent than it often is.

Of course, demanding as the above five conditions are, the fallibility objection is not entirely defused even when they are fully met.

[13] On this last point, see Wingo (2003, p. 82).

Even under the most favorable circumstances, the overwhelming majority of adult citizens could be wrong: epistemic reliability is not infallibility. Status quo educational bias, even if used sparingly and judiciously, will lead to the formation of some false beliefs that would have not have been formed by recipients of unbiased education.[14] But the interesting question is not whether status quo bias induces some errors. Unsurprisingly, it does.[15] We need to ask whether unbiased education is less likely to lead to errors. After all, even the highest-quality unbiased education is no guarantee that its recipients will arrive at sound political beliefs: following Oakeshott (1962, p. 7), we must reject the view that "unhindered human 'reason' (if only it can be brought to bear) is an infallible guide in political activity."

We must be careful to make the comparison in a way that is fair to unbiased education. Status quo biased civic education is not justified by the commonplace observation that *young* children's assessments of political institutions are likely to be more accurate if they have been biased in accordance with the above conditions than if these children simply exercise their own embryonic independent judgment to decide between the best arguments for and against. We do not grant eight-year-olds the right to vote, so it matters very little that people's political beliefs at age eight should closely track the merits of political institutions. Since the quality of a citizen's political beliefs really starts to matter at the age of majority, the relevant question is whether the strong consensus of adults under (something like) the above conditions is epistemically more reliable than the judgment of the average eighteen-year-old who was educated as far as possible without status quo bias. I would argue that it is.

The grounds for preferring the adults' judgment are not simply the mathematical fact that it is the view of an overwhelming majority and

[14] As we saw in the last chapter, it is often impossible entirely to eliminate the biases from civic education, and some unintended biases can be removed or reduced only at a cost that is realistically prohibitive. "Unbiased education" should therefore be understood as shorthand for "education whose biases have been minimized given reasonable budget constraints."

[15] If political progress is to be possible across the board, status quo educational bias, even where it is strongly justified, must therefore not render citizens entirely incapable of discovering flaws in the institutions it favors. I return to this point in the conclusion.

the greater maturity and experience of the average citizen compared to an eighteen-year-old. There is also reason to believe that each adult citizen inherited some accumulated political wisdom through her own education's status quo biases. We assume that a considerable degree of status quo bias has been the norm in civic education throughout a society's history. In any generation, the political beliefs of a randomly selected member of the adult population are therefore a function of both the (predominantly status quo) biases contained in her education and her own independent reasoning. Throughout much of the society's history, its status quo educational biases probably did not come close to meeting the above five conditions. And, once that society has developed to the point where it has the potential to meet the five conditions with respect to some of its existing laws, its citizens may regard many of the political arrangements that were previously supported by those status quo educational biases as deeply unjust; perhaps the most obvious examples are political institutions that denied equal rights to women and the members of various racial, ethnic, religious, and cultural groups. But if we believe that independent reasoning tends to improve the quality of our inherited beliefs (on average, although obviously not in all cases), then we should expect each generation of adults to have better beliefs than the previous generation. (If one doesn't have this kind of faith in human reason, the fallibility objection has no force.) The cumulative effect of such improvement is the so-called wisdom of ages: each generation, on average, makes an incremental improvement on the beliefs of the previous generation (Burke 1790/1987).

To deny the superiority of adults' judgment under suitably demanding conditions (and therefore to reject altogether the content-dependent arguments for status quo biased education) requires an unrealistic faith in the capacity of each person's undirected reason to fully appreciate the accumulated wisdom of her ancestors.[16] "We are afraid to put men to live and trade each on his own private stock of reason, because we suspect that this stock in each man is small, and that

[16] Even when one is not capable of *appreciating* the political wisdom of one's ancestors it may be possible to improve the quality of one's political beliefs by *trusting* their judgment. But, as we saw in Chapter 6, this kind of indiscriminate trust will also generate a great many errors, especially if it establishes more than a slight presumption in favor of the status quo.

the individuals would do better to avail themselves of the general bank and capital of ages" (Burke 1790/1987, p. 76); "the work [of politics] requires the aid of more minds than one age can furnish" (p. 149).

Note also that citizens need not overwhelmingly believe that a particular political arrangement is *uniquely best* in order to have content-dependent reasons for promoting it through education. Content-dependent reasons for status quo biased civic education can be grounded in the belief that an institution is (either no worse than or exactly) a member of the top set or even good but imperfect. A related observation helps to further defuse the fallibility objection: even if we wrongly believe that some institution is uniquely best, it may nonetheless have considerable substantive merit, and education that promotes this institution may be the best way to promote to children an important political value that the institution (perhaps imperfectly) realizes.

Similarly, an imperfect law that we wrongly believe to be in the top set may nonetheless have much to recommend it, and teaching children to support it may do more good than harm. This observation is important if, as I suspect, we are often too quick to conclude that a law is in the top set. Recall that the members of a top set are by definition neither superior nor inferior to one another. This relationship of being neither superior nor inferior must take one of two forms: equality or incommensurability. It is very rarely the case that two laws are equally good. The only obvious sources of such equality are pure coordination problems such as choosing sides of the road on which to drive, but pure coordination problems are very unusual. Even in the world of traffic-flow management, which might seem a promising source of pure coordination problems, it is usually unwise to assume that the various possible solutions are of equal value: when dealing with intersecting roads, for example, it is most unlikely in any given case that stop signs, roundabouts, and traffic lights will all be equally good options. Admittedly, these three options will sometimes be incommensurable with one another. But among those citizens with some (intuitive) grasp of the concept of incommensurability there is a tendency to overuse that diagnosis, too quickly dismissing the possibility of discovering decisive reasons to prefer one option to another. The claim that two alternative institutional solutions to a political problem are incommensurable with one another sometimes captures an important truth, but often it simply expresses unwillingness to grapple with the arguments for and against each option.

In short, most good laws are not uniquely best, and many are straightforwardly imperfect. A classic conservative argument presents itself at this juncture. If we decline to bias education in favor of an existing institution, we increase the chance that future citizens will abandon or dramatically reform that institution. When the status quo has considerable merit—the institution in question, although not uniquely best, is a member of the top set or good but imperfect—there is a grave danger that any such change will be for the worse. Status quo biased education may indeed be a barrier to progress, as the fallibility objection warns us, but it is also a bulwark against regression. A "great leap forward" often proves to be quite the reverse. And notice that the fallibility objection draws no force from the possibility that a law is not uniquely best but nonetheless a member of the top set: since such a law is not inferior to any alternative, its supporters are not barriers to progress.[17]

In addition, civic education that is biased in favor of an existing law or institution that is not (and sometimes is not even believed to be) uniquely best might help instill the values that underpin that political arrangement, albeit at the cost of making future citizens less inclined and/or able to fair-mindedly consider 1) other, perhaps even better, ways to instantiate those values (see Carr 1991, pp. 380–81) and 2) competing values (or rival conceptualizations of the same values). Some political values—for example, the substantive and procedural values of liberal democracy—may be best taught by securing children's allegiance to concrete local institutions and practices that are particular, contestable, and perhaps imperfect ways of instantiating those values.[18] This is why the consensus

[17] Of course, the legitimacy objection still has force in a case of this kind. We hope that citizens will collectively select one of the laws in the top set, but increasing the chances that they will do so by biasing education in favor of the existing law calls into question the polity's moral right to coerce its citizens.

[18] Oakeshott (1962, pp. 118–30) defends a more extreme position. He argues that political values do not exist in the abstract and therefore can only be understood in the form of a concrete practice. By contrast, I claim only that children will more readily learn political values that are introduced in a concrete form. Many citizens may not ever (fully) abstract the values from the concrete instantiation through which they were learned, but it is conceptually possible to do so.

required to justify status quo biased *civic* education, unlike the consensus that justifies biases in *science* education, need only be internal to the polity, local rather than global.[19]

So, for example, it seems likely that American children should be taught to believe in limited government and individual rights by being taught to support the practice of judicial review and the Fourth Amendment's prohibition on "unreasonable searches and seizures," notwithstanding the existence of important critiques of both these institutions. Or consider John Dewey's (1927) view that although democracy is first and foremost an idea, it cannot exist in the world without institutional embodiment. Adapting Dewey, the most effective way to teach children to value democracy as an idea may be to teach them to value a concrete set of institutions that (imperfectly) embody the idea. And if we teach children to support the (imperfectly) democratic institutions that currently exist in their own society, we also establish a bulwark against regression as well as promoting various goods that are unrelated to the merits of those institutions, as I shall shortly discuss.

It is hard to see how one could realize the goal of cultivating children's commitment to liberal democracy as a concept without endorsing a particular conception or at least favoring some conceptions over others.[20] Nonetheless, we may be more amenable to the promotion of children's support for existing laws and institutions if we understand this as a way of teaching the fundamental values of liberal democracy[21] but less so to the extent that we perceive the education as promoting one particular and contestable conception of liberal democracy. In many instances, the laws and institutions for which children's support is cultivated through status quo biased civic education will be particular and contestable ways of instantiating liberal democratic values. Most features of the constitutions and electoral systems of existing liberal democratic countries will fall into this category. Even if we set aside the conservative concern that any change to such arrangements might well prove to be for the

[19] This is true even if all political values are universal: I return to this theme later in the chapter.

[20] Here I follow Hart (1961, pp. 155–59) and Rawls (1999/1971, p. 5) in my distinction between a concept and a conception.

[21] I defended the inculcation of such values in Chapter 1.

worse, it is not clear that we should strive to minimize status quo educational bias. When should we prioritize inculcating the underlying values over preserving and expanding children's capacity to see different, perhaps even better, ways of conceptualizing or institutionalizing those values? I do not propose an algorithmic answer to this question: I merely draw attention to the trade-off to highlight another potential reason to value civic education that is biased in favor of institutions that are not uniquely best.

One might think that it is possible to have one's cake and eat it: first teach young children to support the particular form in which liberal democracy is instantiated in their society; then, as the children mature, introduce them as evenhandedly as possible to the arguments that favor alternative (real and/or hypothetical) understandings and instantiations of those principles. (Compare the ways in which science teachers periodically tell students that the things they were previously taught to believe are not in fact true but rather simplifying assumptions.) But there are (at least) two potential problems with this optimistic "no trade-offs are necessary" view. First, it is not clear that all, or even most, children can be expected to reach the level of formal education at which the less biased and more comparative approach is most appropriately employed. And, second, even if citizens stay the full civic educational course, it is likely that the status quo bias of the early-years education will never be fully undone; citizens educated according to this two-stage formula may predictably retain, even after the second stage, the preference for (or belief in the superiority of) status quo institutions that was inculcated in them during the first stage. As I noted in my Chapter 6 discussion of biases in judgment, early beliefs typically exhibit a degree of nonrational resilience, even when they were originally formed in an impeccably rational manner.

If status quo educational bias were justified only as a means to the end of inculcating abstract liberal democratic values, it would be regrettable that we cannot fully undo its effects on recipients' beliefs about concrete institutions. But, as I have already argued and will soon adduce further reasons to believe, often we should not wish to undo these effects, even when the institutions in question are significantly imperfect. Indeed, it turns out to be a blessing that educationally-induced biases in judgment are persistent. This fact enables us to retrospectively draw people's attention to the status quo biases that were present in their education without fear of undoing the salutary effects of those biases.[22] And, I now want to suggest, there are good reasons to practice this kind of retrospective disclosure.

We want adult citizens to be aware of the biases in their own education so that they can make informed decisions about the extent to which they will deploy or permit these and other biases in the education they deliver to the next generation of citizens. Unintended and unperceived status quo educational biases could easily ratchet up to excessive levels if each generation fails to recognize the ways in which the previous generation knowingly biased their education. Admittedly, one solution to this problem is to concentrate educational authority in an elite few: the masses need never become cognizant of the biases in their own education if they will not be making decisions about their children's education. But this elitist solution is barely practicable in the case of informal education (including parenting). And it is open to powerful objections as a recipe for distributing authority over formal education. Retrospective disclosure of status quo educational biases enables us to preserve a broad measure of democratic control over formal education without risking steady escalation of unconscious educational bias from each generation to the next.

Having now concluded my exploration of the content-dependent reasons for status quo bias in civic education, I should note that although these reasons function primarily as direct responses to the fallibility objection, they also provide a partial riposte to the legitimacy objection because the permissibility of state coercion is in part a function of the justice of the polity's institutions. I shall make this argument more fully in the conclusion of the present chapter. However, my response to the legitimacy objection has a second dimension, namely, that enhanced legitimacy does not trump all the competing values that can be promoted by status quo biased education. To see these other values, we need to turn our attention now to the content-*independent* reasons for status quo educational bias.

[22] Indeed, spontaneously disclosing educational biases might *safeguard* the effects of those biases against the potentially angry reaction of a person who discovers for herself the ways in which her civic education was biased.

7.3. Content-independent reasons for status quo bias

In this section, I shall consider four content-independent reasons for status quo biased civic education, i.e., arguments whose force does not depend upon (our beliefs about) the substantive merits of the existing institution for which children's support is cultivated.[23] These reasons will rarely if ever suffice, even in combination, to justify status quo biased civic education. Rather, they will complement content-dependent reasons, adding weight to the argument for teaching children to support laws that we believe are good (notwithstanding the ever-present possibility that we are mistaken in this belief) and helping to counterbalance the legitimacy objection. Each of the four content-independent reasons draws our attention to a different benefit that flows from status quo biases in civic education whether or not the political arrangements favored by that bias are good.

7.3.1. Stability

The first content-independent reason for status quo biased education invokes the value of political stability. Political experimentation and change are not costless. Social order depends upon citizens' compliance with the demands made by their political institutions, and people are motivated to comply partly out of reverence for long-established institutions. "Far from growing weak, the laws continually acquire new force in every well constituted state. The prejudice in favor of antiquity each day renders them more venerable" (Rousseau 1762/1987, p. 195). Political reform weakens or destroys these affective and trust motives for compliance and thereby threatens social order. And this is not the only way in which change undermines compliance.[24] "Law has no strength with respect to obedience apart from habit, and this is not created except over a period of time. Hence the easy alteration of existing laws in favor of new and different ones weakens the power of law

[23] As we shall soon see, the argument from compliance is not entirely content-independent, but it will often have force even when we have severe doubts about (or straightforwardly deny) the merits of the law in question.

[24] We shall shortly see that status quo educational bias often also promotes compliance more directly.

itself" (Aristotle 1984, Book 2, Chapter 8, p. 73). Aristotle overstates the case, but there is no denying that, when the laws change, some particular habits that used to support law-abiding conduct will no longer do so.[25]

Additionally, citizens make plans based on the existing political order—tax and inheritance laws provide obvious examples—and those plans are disrupted by political reform. A climate of continual legal change discourages certain forms of socially valuable investment.[26] And there are various transactional and transitional costs associated with changing laws: negotiating about and securing agreement on the exact changes to be made, propagating the new laws to all citizens, retraining public officials, designing and implementing new systems to execute the laws, etc. For reasons such as these, it might seem desirable that future citizens be educated to support the status quo (albeit not to such a high degree that they are blind to its defects when they are clear, severe, and readily remediable).

Perhaps, under various pessimistic assumptions about the risks and costs associated with attempts at significant political reform, the value of political stability could suffice to justify using education to bolster support for a society's existing laws and institutions even if their substantive merits are gravely in doubt (or straightforwardly absent). Like Marcus Aurelius, whom Mill (1859/1989, p. 29) portrayed as reluctantly accepting the need to suppress Christian doctrine in a society built around belief in traditional Roman gods, one might promote belief in very flawed political institutions simply because one could not "suffer society to fall to pieces." But I shall consider the force of the argument from stability only in cases when there are also significant content-dependent reasons to bias education in favor of the status quo. As we have already seen, if there are strong grounds to believe that a particular existing political institution belongs to the top set, which is to say that it is not inferior to

[25] As I argued in Chapter 2, the fact that laws will (and sometimes should) change highlights the value of *general* habits of compliance.

[26] Strictly speaking, the subset of stability's benefits that flow from predictability do not require the persistence of status quo institutions. If everyone knew that the laws will change in specified ways every ten years, we would have predictability without stability. Planning would be more complex, but at least there would be no uncertainty.

any alternative, one reason to promote that institution's virtues to the next generation of citizens is to reduce the risk that they will abandon it for some inferior alternative. But the argument from stability highlights the fact that there are costs associated with any change, even if the institution is replaced by another member of the top set. And, since any movement within the top set does not (by definition) constitute an improvement, there is no gain[27] that could potentially outweigh these costs.[28]

One might think that educators should limit themselves to teaching children to see the value of political stability itself, to be open to supporting existing laws and institutions simply for the sake of avoiding turbulence, rather than (also) teaching them that existing arrangements are superior to the various alternatives on their substantive merits. The former approach has the considerable advantage of being fully candid and transparent to children—we do no more than introduce them to the very same content-independent reasons that we ourselves have for favoring the status quo. I have no doubt that we should educate children to appreciate the value of stability. But such teachings may not, as an empirical matter, be as effective as we think they should be: it is possible that the costs and risks associated with political reform will seem so abstract and remote to children (and the young adults they will shortly become) that they give insufficient weight to arguments from stability. If children cannot be sufficiently moved by content-independent reasons to preserve the status quo, those very same reasons may also justify adults in delivering status quo biased education.

One noteworthy feature of the argument from stability is that it favors status quo biased civic education more strongly when there is more domestic opposition to the status quo. The threat to political stability (and therefore the need for the stabilizing effects of status quo biased education) arises most urgently when citizens are divided over the merits of laws and institutions by which they are presently governed. By contrast, as we have seen, if one's focus is on

[27] Here I bracket the potential efficiency benefits of harmonizing one's laws with those of other polities. I noted this possibility in Chapter 6.

[28] Admittedly, one might still maintain in such a case that the value of the legitimacy that is conferred by autonomous and informed consent outweighs the costs of change. I shall return to the legitimacy objection shortly.

the content-dependent reasons to promote the existing political order, one will generally be inclined to reason to the opposite conclusion: if there is more opposition to some feature of the status quo, one will be less inclined to promote it through education because one thinks that it is less likely to be justified on its substantive merits—we have confidence in the judgment of the overwhelming majority, less so in the judgment of a slim majority or even a minority.

Of course, status quo biased civic education is not the only measure that might be recommended by the content-dependent and political stability reasons for increasing the probability that existing institutions will persist across the generations. As an alternative or complement to educational strategies that cultivate belief in the substantive merits of the status quo, there is the constitutional strategy of entrenching certain political arrangements by introducing procedural obstacles (such as supermajority requirements) to amendment. Entrenchment increases the odds that existing institutions will survive by (partially) insulating them from public opinion. Compared to the educational strategy, entrenchment is more liberal but less democratic: we do not interfere with the next generation's capacity to form autonomous and informed judgments on the merits of the status quo, but we deny that a mere majority of those judgments is sovereign. This makes entrenchment especially pernicious in those cases where the entrenched arrangements unjustly favor a minority that is large enough to block reform efforts. By contrast, the educational strategy without any entrenchment respects the majority principle for the exercise of political power but represents, critics might say, a kind of tyranny over the developing minds of the next generation. As we have seen, this tyranny may be objectionable on grounds of liberal political legitimacy even if we stipulate that the beliefs it supports are true. But entrenchment is also vulnerable to a version of the legitimacy objection: the polity's authority to coerce its citizens in accordance with a particular law is highly questionable if that law would have been repealed but for its entrenchment, especially if the popular opposition to the law expresses beliefs that are both autonomous and informed.

One might think that there is never likely to be a shortage of forces tending to preserve existing political arrangements. After all, when a majority of citizens favors some change to the status quo, they are typically confronted by many barriers besides those constituted by any formal supermajority rules that may exist. It is costly and difficult for citizens to organize collectively, especially when the majority that favors change is drawn from different political parties. And vested interests often possess various forms of power to resist popular reform movements. Barriers of this kind make almost *all* popular political reforms significantly more difficult and should therefore be lowered where possible. But even as these barriers inevitably continue to exist, we would be unwise to rely exclusively on them for the long-run preservation of institutions that meet (or even approximate) the aforementioned five conditions under which, I have argued, we should have a very high degree of confidence in an institution's merits.

It is important to note that several of the reasons favoring status quo educational bias do not depend upon its increasing the probability that an existing institution will persist across the generations. This is true of the aforementioned argument that status quo biased education can be justified as a way of inculcating fundamental liberal democratic values that an existing institution imperfectly realizes. Indeed, if recipients of such an education act on the values it taught them by replacing the institution with one that does a better job of realizing those values, this consequence paradoxically vindicates the decision to bias education in favor of the institution that has now been discarded. In similar fashion, the forthcoming arguments from contentment, compliance, and civic identification all treat the increased probability that existing institutions will persist as an inevitable (but not necessarily desirable) byproduct of a process that is independently justified: it is good for citizens to be content with the political institutions that structure their lives, to comply with legally enshrined schemes of social coordination, and to contribute to the civic life of their polity, and one way to promote these goods also happens to increase the probability that existing institutions will persist. Indeed, these content-independent arguments may actually have *greater* force when the survival of existing institutions would be near certain even in the absence of status quo educational bias.

7.3.2. Contentment

A second content-independent reason to encourage children to believe in the merits of their polity's existing political arrangements is that doing so may promote their subjective well-being. Citizens whose education exhibited significant status quo biases are less likely to experience the discontent of being opposed to and potentially therefore feeling alienated from the institutions by which they are governed. Most children who are educated in a particular polity will live their entire life in that polity (given the significant costs associated with emigration). The polity's (fundamental) political arrangements are unlikely to change dramatically from their current form. And people are generally happier living under institutions that they support.

This argument evidently highlights the potential for a kind of collective action problem in civic education. Whether a democratic polity's institutions are likely to change significantly in the decades to come is very largely a function of how its children are educated. As an individual parent or other educator, how do I best promote the subjective well-being of the children over whom I have educational authority? If I believe that most children will receive a status quo biased civic education, the argument from contentment supports giving my children a similar education. When there are strong grounds to believe in the merits of existing institutions, this concern for my children's subjective well-being dovetails nicely with the content-dependent case for status quo educational bias. But even if I have grave and justified doubts about the virtues of my polity's existing institutions, I may rightly worry that by unilaterally eschewing status quo educational biases for my children I am setting them up for a lifetime of alienation from what will remain the dominant political culture of their society.

The collective action problem arises when most adult citizens reason in this fashion. Given the widespread belief that most others will opt for status quo educational bias, it seems prudent to do the same, even if one would prefer to change the overall tenor of the education system, to give most or all children a far less status quo biased civic education in the interests of facilitating change through the democratic process.[29] One virtue of binding collective decision-

[29] But note that adults who see imperfections in the status quo might nonetheless oppose a system-wide reduction in status quo educational biases. As we have just seen, there are significant risks and costs associated with political reform, so it could happen that a majority of citizens are dissatisfied with some aspect of the political

making about formal education is that it enables resolution of these kinds of collective action problems: the parent who wants to see major political reform can vote in favor of reducing the range and degree of status quo biases in civics textbooks and courses safe in the knowledge that this reduction will happen for all children or for none. But, interestingly, the force of this argument depends upon educational authority being centralized in the polity whose institutions one wants to see changed. Parents in ("The People's Republic of") Cambridge, Massachusetts or Provo, Utah ("the most conservative city in America") may believe that children who are liberated from status quo biases in their formal civic education will readily see the grave injustices in the contemporary United States of America,[30] but those parents should also recognize that these injustices are unlikely to be corrected by the rising generation of citizens if it is only the school district of Cambridge or Provo that moves towards unbiased civic education.

7.3.3. Compliance

A third content-independent reason to inculcate children's support for laws is as a way of encouraging their compliance with those laws. When status quo educational bias takes the form of promoting reasons to believe in the merits of the favored law, some of those reasons will also be reasons to comply. If I teach my children that there are sufficient *in se* (usually moral) reasons for acting as this law directs and that it does not exceed the polity's legitimate authority,

status quo but still prefer not to see their polity embark upon reform. "Better the devil you know," these citizens might say as they reflect on both the failings of the status quo and the costs and uncertainties of initiating a change. If, ex hypothesis, these citizens are right to prefer the familiar devil, would it be best for the children of that polity not to learn to see him as a devil, never to acquire the autonomous and informed political perspective that will lead them to feel dissatisfied with an existing order that they nonetheless rightly prefer to retain rather than rolling the dice of political change?

[30] This example is obviously highly stylized. It seems likely that the parents I describe do not want to minimize the biases in their children' schooling; rather, they want (and may already have achieved) bias that favors their own political beliefs and values. Of course, it is also very likely that much of the bias these parents would like to see would be unintended: they would not recognize it as bias because of the gaps in their own knowledge and the biases in their own judgment. I discussed these issues in Chapter 6.

I am encouraging those children not only to support but also to comply with the law. Alternatively, if I teach children to believe that a particular law promises to deliver an efficient and just solution to a social coordination problem, I am (implicitly, at least) also cultivating a *prohibitum* reason for compliance, namely, the moral reason to play one's part in realizing such a good solution. And even when education leads children to believe in the merits of a law without providing them with any reason for that belief, it will still arouse trust reasons for compliance. Furthermore, simply by increasing support for (and moderating opposition to) a law, status quo educational bias decreases the prevalence and intensity of one particular strategic reason for noncompliance, namely, to pursue repeal of the law through an act of civil disobedience. And, in addition to all these ways in which status quo educational bias cultivates *reasons* for compliance (and diminishes one possible *reason* for noncompliance), it will also diminish the prevalence and intensity of a basic *nonrational* motive for noncompliance: people derive expressive satisfaction from acts of noncompliance with laws that they oppose (even when their noncompliance is not part of any strategic effort to repeal the law).

As we saw in Chapter 3, it is often desirable for education to cultivate nonautonomous motives for compliance with laws. When status quo bias favors a law that is good, the benefit of increased compliance comes in addition to the benefit of decreasing the chance that the law will be repealed through the democratic process. Indeed, even when educational bias would not be needed to ensure that the next generation of citizens will support the law in sufficient numbers to secure it against any movement for repeal, such bias will still be valuable if it helps to reduce levels of unjustified noncompliance. But it is important to note that increased compliance can and often will be desirable even when the law is bad. This is the important sense in which the argument from compliance is content-independent.[31]

As we saw in Chapter 2, there are often moral reasons to comply with a bad law. Laws arouse expectations about behavior, and we

[31] Unlike the other arguments I consider in this section, the argument from compliance is not *fully* content-independent. Compliance with bad laws is not always morally desirable, let alone morally obligatory. But there will be many cases in which increased compliance (due to status quo educational bias) is desirable despite the fact that an increased likelihood that the law will persist (also due to this same bias) is undesirable.

usually have moral reasons not to violate those expectations. Sometimes these reasons are strong enough to render noncompliance *malum prohibitum*.[32] But these kinds of *prohibitum* reasons for compliance, even when they are (normatively) sufficient to establish that noncompliance is impermissible, may nonetheless not be sufficient to *motivate* compliance with a law to which one is opposed. Citizens whose education was biased in favor of a (bad) law are more likely to support that law and therefore both to (falsely) perceive additional reasons for compliance and to lack an expressive motive for noncompliance. For example, rates of tax evasion will be lower if more citizens have been educated to (falsely) believe that the tax code is efficient and just. Assuming that citizens are morally obligated to pay their assessed taxes (even if the tax code is both inefficient and unjust), any reduction in tax evasion is a good thing.

None of the above is meant to imply that educators should knowingly mislead children in order to boost their motives for compliance. As I argued in Chapter 2, while it is certainly desirable to promote children's compliance with (bad) laws when such compliance is morally required for *prohibitum* reasons,[33] it is considerably more important to avoid inducing false beliefs about the merits of existing political arrangements.[34] Therefore, as with the arguments from

[32] Compliance with a bad law can also be obligatory for *in se* reasons: this will be the case when a law prohibits an action that is *in se* impermissible but lies beyond the legitimate authority of the polity. Laws against adultery are an example. But, holding constant the belief that adultery is morally wrong, I doubt that people would be significantly less likely to commit adultery if they regarded the law prohibiting it as legitimate.

[33] It will often also be desirable to increase rates of *supererogatory* compliance with bad laws, but, as noted in Chapter 3, supererogatory compliance is not always a good thing.

[34] In his darker moments, Galston sounds as if he may not accept this comparative judgment. For example, he warns (1989, p. 90) that "philosophic education can have corrosive consequences for political communities in which it is allowed to take place. The pursuit of truth... can undermine structures of unexamined but socially central belief." Perhaps Galston here means only to oppose shining the unforgiving light of historical accuracy on a nation's "pantheon of heroes" (p. 91). But his general proposition might seem to suggest that status quo bias in civic education may constitute a net good if it sustains high levels of morally requisite compliance with a law that ought to be repealed notwithstanding the fact that this same educational bias reduces the chances that the law in question *will* eventually be repealed through the democratic process. Such a view very heavily discounts the long-run good of increasing the chances that bad laws will be repealed versus the short- and medium-run benefits of increased morally-requisite compliance with laws.

stability and contentment (and the forthcoming argument from civic identification), the argument from compliance will usually be of practical significance only when it adds weight to a case that is built on content-dependent reasons. It is important to remember that the four content-independent reasons function primarily in this auxiliary role, counterbalancing fallibility and legitimacy objections that might be decisive if they only had to defeat the content-dependent reasons for status quo educational bias. The combined force of the four content-independent reasons is considerable, but status quo educational bias is nonetheless very unlikely to be justified unless the institution that it would favor enjoys overwhelming popular support that meets (or at least approximates) the aforementioned conditions under which the fallibility objection is relatively weak. Content-independent reasons can tip the scales towards status quo educational bias by highlighting some significant benefits of such bias, benefits that will be realized even if we are mistaken about the merits of the institution favored by the bias.

7.3.4. Civic identification

Let me now turn to the fourth and last content-independent reason for status quo bias. Teaching children to believe in the substantive merits of at least some of their polity's laws and institutions—especially those that are fundamental to its identity—may be justified in part as one component of an educational strategy to foster children's identification with the polity. Stronger and/or more widespread civic identification would be a valuable byproduct of status quo biased civic education because, as we saw in Chapter 5, civic identification is a central element in the best solution to the civic motivation problem.

It is certainly possible to promote civic identification without shaping children's evaluative beliefs about the polity's laws and institutions. I argued in Chapter 4 that children can learn to feel pride and shame in response to a polity's actions simply by being immersed in a community of people who express such feelings. But I went on to argue (in Chapter 5) that children are *more likely* to identify with their polity and to feel that identification strongly if the polity has at least some distinctive cultural features with which they identify. In much the same way, although one need not think well of a polity in order to identify with it,[35] civic identification can be expected to be both more prevalent and more intense among citizens who support their polity's basic laws and institutions. Combining these two observations, we may conclude that the goal of fostering civic identification will be greatly advanced if children are both encouraged to believe in the merits of the polity's fundamental institutions and acculturated such that they are familiar and comfortable with the cultural norms that give these institutions their distinctive "flavor."

It may be instructive to compare and contrast my position here to that of Eamonn Callan. Callan and I agree that one legitimate and important goal of civic education is to cultivate civic motivation. And, although I advocate pursuing this goal by promoting civic identification as distinct from the patriotic love that Callan defends, he and I also agree that the goal is more likely to be achieved by an education that encourages children to think at least somewhat well of their polity. In light of this, Callan (1997, pp. 115–21) argues that children in countries whose history is marked by severe injustice should be taught to view that history with "emotional generosity," understanding their ancestors' moral lapses in context rather than simply recoiling in horror from a country that once did such things. More generally, and with greater relevance for my questions about status quo educational bias, Callan urges educators to help children find what is best in the political tradition that they have inherited. But he is at pains to distinguish his position from cruder prescriptions for encouraging children to think well of their polity. He specifically rejects the propagation of patriotic myths, "fictions of purity and political vice" (Callan, 1997, pp. 105–108).

How should we interpret Callan's calls for helping children to find the best of their polity's tradition? Do they amount to an acceptance that some (perhaps small) degree of status quo educational bias is a necessary evil, the inescapable price we should be willing to pay for the cultivation of civic motivation? Callan himself evidently thinks that he is making no such concession. He (1997,

[35] Michael Hand (2011) makes the analogous claim about patriotic love. Love, he argues, is an emotion that descriptively does not require, and normatively need not be warranted by the truth or justifiability of, any underlying belief about the merits of the object that is loved.

p. 121) explicitly rejects as a "false dilemma" the proposition that we are "compelled to choose between sentimental civic education and a pedagogy that liberates critical reason at the cost of political alienation." He insists that his prescription for arousing patriotism does not compromise on its "exacting commitment to reason." In other words, Callan believes that none of his approved pedagogical and curricular strategies detracts from what he takes to be civic education's core mission, namely, equipping citizens to use critical reason to make autonomous political judgments that are informed by all the relevant facts and arguments.[36] I suspect that the success of his strategies for cultivating patriotism will in fact depend upon their deviating from this mission, albeit not necessarily in such drastic ways as lying to children or brainwashing them. At any rate, I have argued *contra* Callan that the promotion of civic motivation (via civic identification) is one of several goals that can jointly justify deviating from the orthodox view of civic character education by skewing the information to which children are exposed, bypassing their critical reason, and/or inducing beliefs before children have the capacity to critically evaluate them.

Even when combined with the values of stability, contentment, and compliance, the benefits of enhanced civic identification are most unlikely to outweigh the harms that would result from teaching children to support a fundamental law that is seriously unjust or deeply unwise. But when we have content-dependent reasons for biasing civic education in favor of a particular fundamental political institution, and even when those reasons face a significant challenge from the fallibility objection, the content-independent argument from civic identification adds weight to the case for status quo bias. It is sometimes more important to encourage the kind of civic participation that sustains what we reasonably believe to be a good regime than to refrain from teaching children to support one of that regime's fundamental laws because of the possibility that the law in question is imperfect or even unjust.

[36] However, as I discussed in Chapter 5, Callan has now departed from the orthodox view of civic character education by acknowledging that patriotism itself (as distinct from the strategies used to cultivate it) impairs critical judgment and nonetheless advocating cultivation of patriotism.

Just as with the content-dependent reasons for biasing education in favor of institutions that contestably and perhaps imperfectly instantiate liberal democratic values, one might think that a two-stage educational solution enables us to have our cake and eat it. Young children's identification with the polity could be encouraged in part by teaching them to believe in the merits of its fundamental political arrangements. As the children grow up, they could be encouraged to reflect critically on these beliefs. And, one might hope, their identification with the polity would remain intact even after the bias towards its existing institutions has been overcome (and, most importantly, even among those citizens whose critical reflection led them to abandon their early-childhood beliefs). But the likelihood is that this bias will *not* be fully overcome: *both* effects of early-years bias—civic identification *and* nonautonomous support for the status quo—will prove to be somewhat enduring. Of course, this is an empirical claim: if a second stage of education can fully undo the effects of early-years bias on future citizens' beliefs about the substantive merits of existing institutions without any loss of civic identification, then the argument from civic identification will not favor programs of civic education that allow status quo biases in citizens' judgment to persist and/or fail to correct the skewed information that was provided to citizens as young children.[37] The argument from civic identification, unlike the arguments from stability, contentment, and compliance, only contingently requires higher levels of support for existing institutions among *adult* citizens.

7.4. Justified parochialism for universalists

The four content-independent arguments—from stability, contentment, compliance, and civic identification—significantly bolster the content-dependent reasons for teaching children to believe in the merits of particular local institutions that instantiate liberal

[37] More generally, all the content-independent arguments for status quo biased civic education rest on various empirical premises. These premises all strike me as intuitive, but I do not attempt to test them. That would take me, far beyond my expertise, into developmental psychology and elsewhere.

democratic values in ways that may be (and that we may even believe to be) incommensurable with or even inferior to alternatives. In particular, these content-independent reasons help to substantiate a claim that may initially seem counterintuitive, namely, that two countries with different and incompatible political institutions could both be justified in biasing their systems of civic education in favor of their local status quo. For example, my arguments suggest that civic educators in America might well be justified in cultivating children's belief in the merits of jury trials notwithstanding the fact that German civic educators are justified in promoting the merits of relying instead on expert judges. Similarly, it might be desirable both for German civic education to encourage support for that country's particular proportional representation electoral system and for American civic education to emphasize the virtues of the less proportional US system.

As Galston (1989, p. 90) has argued, civic education—unlike, say, science education—is not "homogeneous and universal. It is by definition education within, and on behalf of, a particular political order." And this is true not only when we impart knowledge and skills but also when we shape character. How can such educational parochialism be justified? One strategy would be to claim that certain values properly apply only to particular societies: when each polity is judged by the particular values that are applicable to it, different educational biases will prove to be justified in different polities. But that has not been my strategy. I have defended educational parochialism with arguments that are grounded in avowedly universal values. This may seem odd. Once one accepts the notion that "truth is one and universal" (Galston, 1989, p. 90), it can be hard to see the force of a popular consensus that exists only here and now. John Stuart Mill (1859/1989, p. 21) derided the parochialism of the man who derives great confidence in his beliefs from the fact that they are part of such a consensus, even when he knows that contradictory beliefs have commanded a similar consensus in other times and places. This man "devolves upon his own world the responsibility of being in the right against the dissentient worlds of other people; and it never troubles him that mere accident has decided which of these numerous worlds is the object of his reliance."

Mill is surely right that this kind of parochialism greatly hinders the search for truths that are universal. Indeed, the Millian concern was reflected in my specification of the conditions under which widespread belief among a polity's citizens in the merits of one of their political institutions constitutes a valid content-dependent reason to bias education in favor of that institution. But, as we have seen, status quo bias in civic education can be justified without any need to make a preposterous inference from today's local consensus supporting law X to the proposition that law X is uniquely best for all polities at all times. Under the right conditions, that same consensus can constitute strong evidence for the much weaker proposition that X is one good way to instantiate a universal value (albeit there may well be alternatives that are equally or incommensurably good, and there may even be superior alternatives). We have seen how this weaker proposition can serve as a content-dependent reason for status quo educational bias. And the case for such bias is strengthened when the four content-independent arguments, themselves grounded in universal values, are given their full weight. All this still leaves open the possibility that some parochial educational biases can be justified by invoking values that are particular to the polity in question; I explain this possibility further below. But my main concern is to make clear that a good deal of educational parochialism can be warranted without embracing value particularism.

In any content-dependent argument for status quo biased civic education, we need to distinguish between universalist and particularist claims of value: when one says that a certain law is (believed to be) uniquely best, a member of the top set, or good but imperfect, is one appealing to supposedly universal standards of value (such that one's claim is intended to be applicable in all times and places) or is one instead making a more localized claim about the values of a particular community at a particular time? Communitarian reasoning is premised on the view that the proper way to evaluate (certain) political arrangements is by gauging their fit with the best (most accurate and/or authentic) interpretation of the values found in the relevant community's tradition or culture.[38] Thus, from a

[38] As is often pointed out, the leading political theorists who are typically viewed as "communitarian" rarely self-identify as such, but I follow standard practice by using the term to refer to the family of theorists whose most celebrated (and criticized!) members include Michael Walzer, Alasdair MacIntyre, and Michael Sandel.

communitarian perspective, one might argue that teaching children to support our laws and institutions is justified when those political arrangements instantiate our political values, i.e., values that are right for us because they are (partly) constitutive of us given our membership in the community.

Universalists believe in and appeal to a realm of political values that supposedly transcend the boundaries of any particular community, whether these are the values of liberal democracy, the political implications of the one true religion, or any other source of alleged universal normative authority. It is worth noting that the universal/particular cleavage cuts across (or at least is conceptually orthogonal to) all disagreements about substantive values. If I invoke a conception of liberal or democratic rights to show the merits of an existing law that I propose to teach children to support, I do not thereby necessarily adopt a universalist position: I may believe that liberal democratic values are right for our community only because they are deeply embedded in our political culture.[39] One might, for example, believe that discrimination against homosexuals should be illegal in (contemporary) America not because such discrimination is morally wrong everywhere (and always) but rather because it is inconsistent with some of (contemporary) America's fundamental values: individual liberty and equality before the law. And, of course, just as liberal values can be and often are advanced without claiming universal authority for them, many universalists are deeply illiberal in their values. Religion has been and sadly remains one prominent source of such illiberal universalism.[40]

I mean to describe the universalist and particularist perspectives on value so as to leave open the possibility that each expresses part of the truth about value. If there are universal values, as I believe there surely are, contradictory claims from a particularist perspective cannot be true: where they exist, universal values necessarily trump all competition. But there may be questions of value that have no definitive answer from the universal perspective; if so, these questions may, perhaps, properly be answered from a particularist perspective. To borrow the language of Joseph Raz (1986,

[39] This is one reading of the later work of John Rawls.

[40] These observations make clear that the so-called liberal-communitarian debate is only one form in which the universal-particular debate can arise.

pp. 345–57), some incommensurabilities may be "constitutive": several alternative political institutions may be incommensurable with one another, and no more can be said about their relative value from the universalist perspective, but the fact that one of them is ours, partially constitutive of us, renders it appropriate for us to support it.[41] That institution is uniquely best for us, although not for everyone. One could, therefore, regard civic education as a means by which political communities properly aim to reproduce themselves not merely as liberal democracies that uphold certain universal values but also as entities with a distinctive civic–political culture and traditions whose justification does not lie solely in an appeal to universal principles.

For example, imagine that our political community provides generous public funding to the arts: this may be a practice that helps to define us as a people and is therefore right for us despite the fact there is no decisive reason for a different community to adopt the same policy. Alternatively, perhaps we have always had a bicameral legislature, and that arrangement is best for us not because it is universally the best way to institutionalize liberal democracy but rather because it is our way. These kinds of communitarian arguments could operate within a framework of universal values: particularist moral reasoning may complement the universalist arguments I have offered to justify political communities in a limited use of their systems of civic education to transmit their political values as expressed by their distinctive laws and institutions, encouraging students' commitment to a local political tradition.

My goal in the preceding four paragraphs was *not* to endorse the claim that there are good value-particularist arguments for status quo biased civic education. I intend merely to show what such arguments would look like, principally in order to highlight the contrast between them and the various universalist arguments I have offered. My central claim is that value univeralism leaves ample scope for parochial biases in civic education. The universally valuable goal of reproducing and improving a recognizably (but inevitably always imperfect) liberal democratic regime is not best

[41] I mean this argument to be distinct from content-independent arguments grounded in the universal values of political stability and civic identification, as discussed earlier.

served by the least parochially biased education that adults can provide to the next generation of citizens. Critical autonomy is not the only civic virtue that universalists can and should acknowledge. We should recall Edmund Burke's (1790/1987, pp. 7–8, 28) admonitions to those purveyors of abstract reason whose words threaten to weaken people's support for established institutions that serve them well, albeit not perfectly.

7.5. Conclusion: two cheers for status quo bias

I have argued that there are conditions under which the fact that a polity's adult citizens overwhelmingly believe in the merits of one of their political institutions constitutes a strong content-dependent reason for civic education in that polity to be biased to some degree in favor of the relevant institution. The Millian fallibility objection to status quo bias is important, but it is not conclusive,[42] especially when we attend to the content-independent reasons that complement arguments grounded in our beliefs about the substantive merits of the status quo. The fact that we could always be wrong in our assessments of existing institutions does not warrant setting aside those assessments when we educate the next generation of citizens. Current adult citizens are indeed fallible, but members of the next generation are even more likely than their parents to err if they are raised in ways that scrupulously avoid even the most defensible forms of status quo bias.

But what about the legitimacy objection? Again, this is important but not conclusive. Although Brighouse is right—*contra* Matthew Clayton (2006, pp. 133–34)—to say that it is *a* liberal value that citizens should autonomously endorse their political institutions, it is not the supreme liberal value.[43] As we saw in Chapter 1, Brighouse

[42] Perhaps this is not surprising: Mill's concern, after all, was to avoid the systematic *suppression* of dissenting opinions, which is different from, despite raising many of the same issues as, status quo educational bias.

[43] It may seem odd that I assert the intrinsic value of autonomous *consent* to laws given that I am agnostic (as we saw in Chapter 3) on the issue of whether there is intrinsic value to autonomous decisions about *compliance* with laws. Why do I respond differently to these two claims that autonomy has intrinsic value? The claims differ fundamentally in the kind of (intrinsic) value they ascribe to

himself observes that the state's legitimacy is a function of more than one variable; (actual) autonomous consent certainly matters, but so does hypothetical consent: "it must be true that [the laws and institutions of the state are such that] citizens would give their consent if they were reasonable, informed, and not overly self-interested" (2000, p. 76). It is appropriate to trade off citizens' capacity to give autonomous consent against the values that are served by status quo biased education, not least because some of these values—those associated with the intergenerational preservation of good and just institutions—help the state to pass the test of hypothetical consent and thereby contribute to the state's legitimacy.

Moreover, Brighouse (1998, pp. 727, 736) is quick to acknowledge that the capacity to give free and authentic consent is always a matter of degree, never absolute. He emphasizes the ways in which the autonomy of this consent is frequently undermined by exercises of state power that are perfectly appropriate and often morally essential: "even the most conscientiously self-limiting state is unlikely to refrain entirely from encouraging consent in ways that bypass or preempt [citizens'] rational scrutiny." Merely by acting through and demanding citizens' compliance with the particular political institutions available to them, states will implicitly give their imprimatur to those institutions. More generally, as I explained in Chapter 6, unintended status quo biases will always realistically be a feature of children's civic education, both within and especially outside of schools. The autonomy of citizens' political beliefs and values is a matter of degree, and more is certainly better from the standpoint of liberal political legitimacy, but there are other potentially conflicting goods with which the legitimizing properties of autonomy must compete. If civic education induces

autonomous choices. If autonomous compliance decisions are intrinsically valuable, their value is prudential: a person's life goes better, *ceteris paribus*, to the extent that her decisions (including her compliance decisions) are made autonomously. I am agnostic about assertions that autonomy has such intrinsic prudential value. But the claim that autonomous consent confers legitimacy is a moral claim about (one of) the conditions under which coercion is permissible. I am not agnostic about such assertions that autonomy has intrinsic moral value. I believe that this particular assertion is true. Of course, if I am wrong about this, Brighouse's objection has no force and the case for status quo biases in civic education is correspondingly stronger.

stronger and more widespread belief in the merits of (particular) liberal democratic arrangements at some cost to the autonomy of those beliefs, this cost will often be worth paying in our quest to transmit important values, preserve good political institutions, and promote stability, contentment, compliance, and civic identification.

It is important to emphasize that my qualified defense of status quo bias leaves considerable scope for civic education that prepares children to be vocal and active critics of many of their polity's arrangements. When children (typically adolescents) are strongly opposed to one of their polity's many existing laws or institutions that should *not* be favored by civic educational bias, it is usually permissible (and may often be desirable) for educators to facilitate and even encourage those children's (peaceful, respectful, and usually lawful) expression of their opposition. Dissent, contestation, protest, and even occasional civil disobedience are vital elements of the political culture of a liberal democracy, and civic education should help to reproduce those elements[44] at the same time that it encourages support for certain fundamental laws and institutions.

Even when the arguments for status quo bias are strongest, educators should stop short of the kinds of indoctrination or propaganda that threaten to extinguish the capacity for critical reflection altogether.[45] Civic education of this extreme type is a grave threat to the polity's legitimacy. Moreover, some views that now strike citizens as profoundly mistaken were once among the least controversial beliefs of their society,[46] so it would be hubristic for us to assume that we do not need to preserve at least some degree of receptivity to arguments that challenge the sacred cows of our political–moral culture. And, as Mill warns us, the most heavy-handed attempts at status quo educational bias may tend to be

[44] For a recent book-length paean to education for dissent, see Stitzlein (2012).

[45] In this vein, Wingo (2003) claims that the "veils" used to flatter our institutions must be "translucent." Interestingly, if educators do not heed this warning they will undercut the justification for employing or allowing status quo educational biases in the future. Recall that adult citizens' widespread belief in the merits of an existing law will not constitute a valid content-dependent reason to bias education in favor of that law if those citizens were themselves educated in such a biased fashion that an overwhelming majority would be expected to believe that the law is good regardless of its actual merits.

[46] Although rarely would the aforementioned conditions 2, 3, and 4 all have been met with respect to these beliefs.

self-defeating: if future citizens are taught the supposed merits of existing institutions as "dead dogma" (Mill, 1859/1989, pp. 37–46), with arguments and evidence to the contrary either omitted entirely or presented so unfavorably that they serve as mere cannon fodder, citizens' understanding of and commitment to those institutions are both likely to suffer.[47] So, for example, American schools may justifiably teach children to believe in the merits of electing the head of state, but they should not do so in a way that entirely blinds children to the force of arguments that, within a framework of liberal democratic values, favor a hereditary and constitutional monarch.

My arguments in this chapter are fully compatible with the claim that children (should) have a (legal) right to express opposition to any and all of the political arrangements through which their polity instantiates liberal and democratic values. Even when a particular element of the status quo is properly favored by civic educational bias, it is a further and very different question whether, when, and where children should nonetheless be permitted to speak freely in opposition to that element. My focus in Part III of this book has been on the ways in which educators could and should try to shape children's beliefs about existing political arrangements rather than on how children with dissenting beliefs should be permitted to behave. Admittedly, these two issues are not entirely unrelated. One could try to promote a particular set of beliefs in the next generation of citizens in part by restricting the freedom of children to articulate contrary views. But I am not inclined to support such restrictions. And I rather doubt that they would, in fact, be effective instruments of status quo educational bias.

Intentional status quo bias may well have a part to play in the best civic education. And unintended status quo bias certainly need not be relentlessly rooted out and minimized. This is not to deny that status quo educational bias can be (and probably often is) both

[47] Burke precisely contradicts Mill's claim about the motivational efficacy of reason: "prejudice, with its reason, has a motive to give action to that reason, and an affection which will give it permanence. Prejudice is of ready application in the emergency; it previously engages the mind in a steady course of wisdom and virtue and does not leave the man hesitating in the moment of decision skeptical, puzzled, and unresolved" (Burke, 1790/1987, p. 76). More recently, Wingo (2003, pp. 47, 130) sides with Burke in this debate. I discussed Wingo's position in Chapter 1.

excessive and worth combating, especially when we take into account the influence of non-school forces on future citizens. Indeed, my argument in this chapter is consistent with the view that *schooling* should generally be as free from status quo bias as is reasonably possible,[48] but that is not my view. The objections to status quo bias should be taken seriously, but they must not be overstated. Status quo educational bias is an important means by which well-functioning liberal democratic states reproduce themselves, and no apology is needed for this fact. Admittedly, as I discussed above, both the fallibility and legitimacy objections caution against using education to promote a singular and contestable conception of liberal democracy. But, given that competing conceptions may be incommensurable, that it is hard to transmit liberal democratic values without favoring some conceptions over others, and that there are weighty content-independent reasons to cultivate children's support for their society's fundamental institutions, it is also possible to err by abstaining from or eliminating valuable status quo bias: this is the mistake that adherents of the orthodox view of civic education will systematically make.

How might we apply my analysis in practice? What would be the signs that we had erred in one direction or the other? Taking the fallibility objection seriously precludes answering this second question by saying: "civic education has too much status quo bias if it leads children to embrace bad laws, and it is too unbiased if it leads them to reject good ones." But, for practical purposes, we would know that we have erred in the direction of status quo bias if we are producing citizens who, for example, believe that there is nothing to learn from the examples of other polities or who do not find fault with any significant component of the status quo in their own polity.

[48] George Counts (1932, pp. 24, 54) offers an even more radical proposal: schools should not only eliminate biases that favor the (capitalist) status quo but also promote an alternative (socialist) political order. In Chapter 6 I expressed skepticism about the feasibility of this proposal. Setting aside the feasibility issue, I grant that it may often be appropriate for a school to focus on exposing its students to alternatives and challenges to the status quo, trusting that informal education will supply the status-quo-reinforcing messages. But schools' best response to social forces that excessively bias children's *judgment* in favor of the status quo is not to fight bias with bias: rather, it is to help children autonomously assess the arguments and evidence they encounter.

By contrast, we would know that we have erred by providing too little status quo bias if we are producing citizens who reject long-standing features of the political order that meet the conditions outlined above without a well-reasoned and compelling basis for their rejection or who are so disenchanted with and alienated from their polity that they will not contribute to its maintenance and betterment. One could argue that these are symptoms not of insufficient status quo bias in children's education but rather of, respectively, insufficiently high-quality unbiased education and failure to find other ways to cultivate robust civic identification. Similarly, one might argue that status quo bias is unnecessary if children are taught to consciously appreciate both the risks of instability associated with political reform and the *prohibitum* reasons for compliance with laws.

But the argument of this chapter is that status quo biased civic education will sometimes be justified precisely by the practical limitations of these other methods for promoting important and universal values. Admittedly, if all children could successfully be raised with a very high degree of philosophic sophistication in their approach to politics and an appropriate sensitivity to the value of political stability and *prohibitum* reasons for compliance, and if citizens who are opposed to their polity's fundamental institutions could nonetheless reliably be expected to identify strongly with that polity and be content living in it, it is hard to see why we would endorse any status quo biases in education. But if the values that such biases can serve are genuine values, as I think they are, and if other approaches to education cannot by themselves fully realize those values, which seems very likely to be the case in practice, then some significant degree of intentional status quo bias in civic education may be justified, and some unintended bias will be desirable, notwithstanding the attendant costs and risks.

CHAPTER 8

Conclusion: citizenship and the limits of autonomy

This book is my response to a view of civic education that has become orthodox among contemporary political and educational theorists. On that view, education for civic character, although essential for the reproduction of a healthy liberal democratic polity, should not extend beyond inculcating in children the basic and universal moral values that constitute the ideal of liberal democracy itself. In particular, civic education should not cultivate nonautonomous motives for compliance with laws, it should not lead children to feel a special emotional connection to their polity or its actions, and it should not be biased in favor of that polity's existing institutions. These three traditional goals and functions of civic education must be rejected because they compromise the ideal of critically autonomous citizenship.

I have argued that this orthodox view of civic education, with its associated ideal of citizenship, makes unrealistic demands of the human capacities for autonomous reasoning and moral motivation. If, as seems mercifully improbable, the orthodox view ever became as popular among parents and educational professionals as it is among academic theorists, and if (even less probably) all people with significant influence over children's character formation assiduously adopted the most effective means to the promotion of critically autonomous citizenship, the results (one generation later) would not be pretty. We would see increased rates of law-breaking that is morally impermissible, selfish, and/or imprudent. Voluntary civic participation would reach pitifully low levels: an epidemic of free-riding would severely undermine democratic institutions and the important values that they exist to promote. Citizens would be much too quick to support radical proposals for political change, hastening to overturn arrangements that have long served their polity well. And those same citizens' understanding of and commitment to core liberal democratic values would be weak because the values were taught to them as abstractions, which are both harder to grasp and less motivationally powerful than concrete instantiations.

At the same time as faulting the extremism of the orthodox view, I have acknowledged throughout the book that critically autonomous citizenship does have a lot to recommend it and that our departures from this ideal should therefore be judiciously chosen. In our eagerness to embrace more traditional forms of civic character education, we certainly do not want to create a citizenry that is chronically unable to engage critically with political authority. In such a polity, deeply flawed and often unjust political institutions would persist across the generations because each new crop of citizens would lack the dispositions, skills, and information that are required to discover the need for change. Even the good political arrangements in this polity would lack the moral legitimacy that flows from the informed and autonomous consent of the governed. Citizens' ardent love for their country would blind them to its misdeeds at home and abroad. And we would observe many instances of overcompliance with laws: citizens abetting injustice by their compliance with truly noxious laws, sacrificing their own legitimate interests to comply with laws whose demands were unreasonable, slavishly abiding by good laws even when circumstances warranted noncompliance, and declining to participate in important campaigns of civil disobedience.

Does liberalism's dependence on civic education that detracts from citizens' critical autonomy show that liberalism is an inherently unstable, self-defeating, or even internally incoherent political doctrine? No, it does not. It is a mistake to regard autonomy as a master value within liberalism, a binding constraint on the actions of civic educators (including but not limited to those acting on behalf of the liberal state itself). Autonomy is indeed an important value within liberalism, as I have explored throughout this book, but it should not always be preferred to other important values in cases of conflict. When the path to maximizing citizens' autonomy diverges from the educational measures that are best suited to reproduce and improve liberal democracy, it is often perfectly appropriate to sacrifice autonomy to some degree, and there is nothing illiberal or paradoxical about acknowledging this.[1] A liberal polity must prize autonomy but should not die for it, both because liberalism rightly recognizes other values and because autonomy's long-run survival prospects look bleak outside of a flourishing liberal democratic regime.

I have tried, in the preceding six chapters, to explain how civic education can steer a good path between excesses and deficiencies of critically autonomous citizenship. I certainly do not claim to have identified the one best path: as I noted in Chapter 1, it strikes me as fanciful to propose that there is a uniquely correct answer to the complex and multi-dimensional question of how to shape children's civic character. In large part, therefore, my contribution has been to identify and explore the many competing values that are at stake in this domain, clearly and precisely specifying the various trade-offs that are entailed by particular educational policies and practices. But I have also argued for some more determinate conclusions. Educators should strive to promote civic identification without arousing patriotic love because the former yields much-needed civic motivation without distorting civic judgment as severely as the latter does. The intergenerational survival and flourishing of liberal democracy is often best served by educating children in ways that dispose them to support some of their polity's existing institutions, notwithstanding the fact that there are other, equally or incommensurably good (and perhaps even better) ways to instantiate liberal democratic values. And, under realistically favorable political conditions, educators have a responsibility both to strategically manipulate children's prudential values and to cultivate habits of and trust reasons for compliance with laws in order to compensate for the inadequacies of individuals' moral motivation and autonomous judgment when deciding whether to comply.

For several important reasons that I shall soon restate, the conclusions of this book do not constitute concrete prescriptions for educational policy and practice. And I have been concerned

[1] As I noted in Chapter 1's discussion of value pluralism, no algorithm or mechanical decision procedure can determine for citizens exactly how they should trade off autonomy against competing values.

throughout with education conceived very broadly to include far more than formal schooling. But it is possible, and I have periodically attempted, to identify some likely implications of my view for classroom pedagogy and curriculum design. It may be helpful here to draw together and expand a little upon these thoughts regarding application of my theory.

The analysis in Chapter 4 strongly suggests some techniques that professional educators could and should use to encourage civic identification while teaching children about the history of the country to which they belong as residents and citizens. Teachers should routinely use the language of "our country" and should probably also speak of what "we" did when describing the country's actions. Classroom exercises and field trips should be designed in ways that encourage children to experience appropriate emotional reactions to their country's past actions: pride and shame, and probably also feelings of responsibility. Teachers can and should model these emotional reactions for their students. And children should also be exposed to appropriate expressions of civic pride and shame by (other) compatriots with whom they (more) strongly identify and whom they aspire to emulate. To combat any tendency for such educational practices to arouse patriotic affection (and its associated biases in civic judgment), educators should ensure that children learn about (and feel the emotional force of) plenty of their country's shameful episodes in addition to its finest hours. And schools should eschew the kinds of imagery, music, rhetoric, ritual, and other tools for shaping children's emotions that would cultivate positive sentiments towards the country itself (as distinct from arousing feelings of pride at some of the country's specific actions).

Given my contention (in Chapter 5) that robust civic identification is unlikely to be developed and maintained in the absence of some significant degree of identification (or at least familiarity) with the culture of the polity in question, children's education in language, literature, and the arts should include substantial components that are focused on the cultural elements that give those children's country its distinctive identity. In practice, this usually means that education best serves its civic purposes when it creates citizens who are fluent in and comfortable with the dominant culture within the country, the culture of its *staatsvolk* (O'Leary, 2001). To be clear, following this recommendation does *not* entail total neglect of other cultures and their products. There are both civic and, of course, many non-civic reasons for children to learn about the diversity of cultures that exists both within their country and beyond its borders. But, given the motivational value of civic identification and the difficulty of achieving such identification without cultural affinity, there are strong grounds to object to an education that fully immerses a child in a culture (and sometimes also a language) that does not characterize the political institutions and practices of the country to which that child belongs. Recall that I am using the term "education" here, as I have throughout the book, in a very broad sense. When a child's *schooling* does not have enculturation effects that foster civic identification, other aspects of her education (including her familial upbringing, her exposure to mass media, and her interactions elsewhere in civil society) may perhaps make up the shortfall. But there are important civic grounds to be concerned about the educational practices of immigrant and other minority cultural groups whose children are comprehensively sequestered from the culture of their country.[2]

I argued in Part III that civic education should not aspire to unbiased presentation of the rival merits of different institutional embodiments of liberal democratic values. The orthodox view holds that all children would ideally be exposed evenhandedly to the debates between supporters of parliamentary government and those who prefer presidential systems, between defenders and critics of the use of juries in criminal (and civil) trials, and between those who believe that the right of free expression entails legal protection for hate speech and those who maintain conversely that such speech should be prohibited in the name of liberal democratic values. In each of these cases, I have argued that it is usually best to expose children predominantly to perspectives that favor the status quo in their polity.[3]

[2] Failure to foster civic identification is not the only concern one might legitimately have about the civic effects of such educational arrangements. One might also worry that children educated in this way will not acquire the *knowledge* and *skills* that they need to participate fully and effectively in the life of their polity. And, of course, one might worry about the *non-civic* effects of lacking access to and understanding of the dominant culture in a society (Kymlicka, 1995).

[3] Predominantly does not mean exclusively. Exclusivity might well be warranted with young children, but adult citizens should possess (and therefore schools presumptively should provide to their older students) some familiarity with the strongest arguments against their polity's political institutions and in favor of alternative ways to instantiate liberal democratic values.

As I noted in Chapter 7, it is possible for a child's *informal* civic education to favor the local status quo so strongly that her school would ideally not add to (and might even need to counteract) such bias. But I doubt that this is often the case. I am therefore inclined to believe that civics courses in American schools should dispose their students to favor presidential systems of government, extensive use of trial juries, and strong legal protection for hate speech. Schools in Germany should present each of these issues in a rather different light. Liberal democracy gains more than it loses from this type of parochialism. When Michael Gove, the UK's Secretary of State for Education, recently proposed rules to ensure that "all [British] schools actively promote British values" (Gove, 2014), he was right in two important respects. First, all British schools should seek to instill in their pupils the fundamental and universal liberal democratic values to which the UK is and should remain committed. Second, as the Prime Minister subsequently emphasized in staunchly Burkean fashion (Cameron, 2014), it is often best for British schools to pursue this goal by promoting the particular British institutions and political traditions in which these universal values are embodied.

To some degree, therefore, my conclusions support traditional approaches to civic education that celebrate the constitutional and other fundamental political arrangements of an established liberal democratic society. But I diverge from these traditional approaches by insisting that civic educational status quo bias can and should be narrowly targeted in accordance with the criteria I outlined in Chapter 7. Citizenship education in the United Kingdom should emphasize the merits of the parliamentary system of government, notwithstanding the existence of legitimate alternatives to and critiques of that system, but children in the UK would ideally not be taught in ways that dispose them to favor their country's longstanding "first past the post" system for electing Westminster MPs because this electoral system is a subject of active political controversy within the country. Similarly, civic education in the United States should be biased in favor of the First Amendment (by which I mean to refer both to forty-five words in the Bill of Rights and to the jurisprudential tradition and political culture that those words have spawned) but should not dispose children to favor the hotly contested Second Amendment, let alone the US Constitution as a whole.

Now that I have sketched some apparent practical implications of my conclusions concerning civic identification and status quo bias, I shall briefly do the same for the promotion of law-abidingness. Children should routinely be exposed to stories and examples that portray acts of compliance with the law as ordinary, wise, and admirable, while illegal acts are depicted as exceptional and almost always as imprudent, deviant, and/or morally wrong. The function of such exposure is to cultivate and reinforce norms, habits, and instincts of law-abidingness as well as trust-based reasons for compliance and probably also the belief that there is a *prima facie* moral duty to obey the law.[4] These are all motives that do not require forming one's own judgment either about the merits of particular laws or about the particular circumstances in which one must decide whether to comply with those laws. Stories and examples of this kind might usefully shape children's prudential values by cultivating the specific type of conformism that I identified in Chapter 2: the desire to conform to a society's norms as expressed through its laws (and thereby to avoid the disapproval commonly directed at those who violate such norms). Indeed, education for this type of conformism not only discourages its recipient from breaking the law but also typically encourages that person to feel and express disapproval of others who do break the law (and thereby strengthens the social stigma that helps to deter acts of noncompliance).

Needless to say, the disapproval of one's fellow citizens is not the only sanction for noncompliance with laws. Polities impose material penalties on convicted law-breakers through their criminal justice systems; as I noted in Chapter 2, one potentially powerful way in which to promote compliance is to heighten children's aversion to incurring these penalties. How this can best be done is a question about which further empirical research is needed. In particular, the efficacy of "Scared Straight" programs, which take children on visits to prisons in an effort to make vivid the unpleasant nature of life behind bars, has recently been called into doubt (Petrosino et al., 2013). This example aptly illustrates the dangers of relying upon "common sense" assumptions about the effects of particular educational techniques. So I should stress that my thoughts about the

[4] See my discussion in Chapter 2 of the worry that teaching children to perceive such a duty may constitute instilling a false belief.

practical implications of my theoretical positions are all tentative precisely because they rely on little more than such common sense. I have systematically defended the adoption of several civic educational goals that conflict with the cultivation of critical autonomy, but I have neither the expertise nor the data to reach any authoritative conclusions about how best to realize these goals.

In this same spirit, and lest any reader is tempted to put down my book and immediately attempt to apply its findings, I want to close by reiterating some of the cautionary remarks that I made in Chapter 1. To ward off one especially dangerous misunderstanding: my target throughout this book has been an *ideal* that is presently very popular and influential among political and educational theorists. Although I suggested in Chapter 1 that this ideal of critically autonomous citizenship does have some significant currency beyond the ivory tower, I have not assessed and therefore am not critiquing the educational policies and practices of any particular existing society. A reader could agree with my overall conclusion that optimal civic education diverges significantly from maximization of critical autonomy while nonetheless believing that most of the education she observes in her polity unduly neglects the importance of producing social and political critics. (Analogously, one could believe that the institutions of a perfectly just society would allow more inequality than those advocated by most contemporary political philosophers while nonetheless believing that one's own polity is insufficiently egalitarian.)

In addition to restating the target of my critique, I should remind readers one more time of the substantial gap that exists between my normative theoretical arguments and any concrete prescriptions for educational policy or practice. My conclusions in this book should always be understood to have the following form: it would be desirable for *education* to have certain *effects* on the ways in which its recipients will think and act *as citizens*. I have italicized three parts of that formula in order to highlight three important limitations of my analysis. First, since I conceptualize education broadly as the totality of influences on a child's learning and development, the implications of my conclusions for schooling (or for any other single aspect of a child's education) cannot be known without knowing the various other forces that are shaping that child's character. Second, my focus is on educational outcomes. I have said little about how best to realize the outcomes that I would like to see. Any consideration of educational means must be attentive to costs, side-effects, and the probability of success, not merely to the desirability of the intended effects. This leads me to the third limitation of my analysis. I have focused on the effects of character education on its recipients' behavior as citizens, their engagement (or lack thereof) with the polity, but we should obviously also be concerned with its effects on recipients' purely private lives. It is certainly possible that particular character traits that are desirable for the ways in which they influence civic behavior will prove also to be undesirable for their impact on private choices and psychological well-being. If and when this is the case, tradeoffs will have to be made, and those choices may be hard. So, although I believe that educators (broadly conceived, as ever) and citizens more generally can gain a lot from attending to the benefits of "civics beyond critics," I do not claim to have provided a comprehensive account of the costs and risks that may be associated with this approach to education.

REFERENCES

Ackerman, Bruce. 1980. *Social Justice in the Liberal State.* New Haven: Yale University Press.

Appiah, Kwame Anthony. 1996. "Cosmopolitan Patriots." In *For Love of Country*, ed. Joshua Cohen. Boston: Beacon Press.

Aristotle. 1984. *The Politics*. Transl. Carnes Lord. Chicago: University of Chicago Press.

Arons, Stephen. 1983. *Compelling Belief: The Culture of American Schooling*. New York: McGraw-Hill New Press.

Barber, Benjamin. 1996. "Constitutional Faith." In *For Love of Country*, ed. Joshua Cohen. Boston: Beacon Press.

Berger, Ben. 2011. *Attention Deficit Democracy: The Paradox of Civic Engagement*. Princeton: Princeton University Press.

Berlin, Isaiah. 1958/2002. "Two Concepts of Liberty." In *Liberty*, ed. Henry Hardy. Oxford: Oxford University Press. 166–217.

Brighouse, Harry. 1998. "Civic Education and Liberal Legitimacy." *Ethics* 108 (4): 719–45.

Brighouse, Harry. 2000. *School Choice and Social Justice*. Oxford: Oxford University Press.

Brighouse, Harry, and Adam Swift. 2009. "Legitimate Parental Partiality." *Philosophy and Public Affairs* 37 (1): 43–80.

Bull, Barry. 2006. "Can Civic and Moral Education be Distinguished?" In *Civic and Moral Learning in America*, ed. Donald Warren and John Patrick. New York: Palgrave MacMillan. 21–31.

Burke, Edmund. 1790/1987. *Reflection on the Revolution in France.* Indianapolis: Hackett Publishing Company.

Callan, Eamonn. 1997. *Creating Citizens.* New York: Oxford University Press.

Callan, Eamonn. 2000. "Liberal Legitimacy, Justice, and Civic Education." *Ethics* 111 (1): 141–55.

Callan, Eamonn. 2006. "Love, Idolatry, and Patriotism." *Social Theory and Practice* 32 (4): 525–46.

Cameron, David. 2014. "British values aren't optional." http://www.dailymail.co.uk/debate/article-2658171/DAVID-CAMERON-British-values-arent-optional-theyre-vital-Thats-I-promote-EVERY-school-As-row-rages-Trojan-Horse-takeover-classrooms-Prime-Minister-delivers-uncompromising-pledge.html.

Carr, Wilfred. 1991. "Education for Citizenship." *British Journal of Educational Studies* 39 (4): 373–85.

Citizenship Foundation. 2012. "What is citizenship education?" http://www.citizenshipfoundation.org.uk/main/page.php?286.

Clayton, Matthew. 2006. *Justice and Legitimacy in Upbringing*. Oxford: Oxford University Press.

Counts, George. 1932. *Dare the Schools Build a New Social Order?* New York: John Day Co.

Crick, Bernard. 1998. *Education for Citizenship and the Teaching of Democracy in Schools. Final Report of the Advisory Group on Citizenship.* London: Qualifications and Curriculum Authority.

Crittenden, Jack. 2002. *Democracy's Midwife: An Education in Deliberation*. Lanham, MD: Lexington Books.

Curren, Randall. 2000. *Aristotle on the Necessity of Public Education.* Lanham, MD: Rowman & Littlefield.

Curren, Randall, and Muna Golmohamad. 2007. Review of Sigal Ben-Porath's *Citizenship Under Fire*. *Theory and Research in Education* 5 (1): 119–23.

Dagger, Richard. 1997. *Civic Virtues: Rights, Citizenship, and Republican Liberalism*. New York: Oxford University Press.

Deigh, John. 1988. "On Rights and Responsibilities." *Law and Philosophy* 7 (2): 147–78.

Dewey, John. 1927. *The Public and Its Problems*. Columbus, OH: Swallow Press.

Dworkin, Ronald. 1985. *A Matter of Principle*. Cambridge, MA: Harvard University Press.

Dworkin, Ronald. 1986. *Law's Empire*. Cambridge, MA: Harvard University Press.

Ebels-Duggan, Kyla. 2014. "Autonomy as Intellectual Virtue." In *The Aims of Higher Education*, ed. Harry Brighouse and Michael MacPherson. Chicago: University of Chicago Press.

Edmundson, William. 2006. "The Virtue of Law-Abidance." *Philosophers' Imprint* 6 (4): 1–21.

Elkins, Zachary, and John Sides. 2007. "Can Institutions Build Unity in Multiethnic States?" *American Political Science Review* 101 (4): 693–708.

Estlund, David. 2008. *Democratic Authority: A Philosophical Framework.* Princeton: Princeton University Press.

Feinberg, Joel. 1980. "The Child's Right to an Open Future." In *Whose Child?*, ed. William Aiken and Hugh LaFollette. Totowa, NJ: Rowman and Littlefield.

Flanagan, Constance A. 2013. *Teenage Citizens: The Political Theories of the Young*. Cambridge, MA: Harvard University Press.

Flathman, Richard. 1996. "Liberal versus Civic, Republican, Democratic, and Other Vocational Educations: Liberalism and Institutionalized Education." *Political Theory* 24 (1): 4–32.
Frey, Bruno, and Reto Jegen. 2001. "Motivation Crowding Theory." *Journal of Economic Surveys* 15 (5): 589–611.
Fuhrman, Susan, and Marvin Lazerson, eds. 2005. *The Public Schools.* New York: Oxford University Press.
Funder, David. 1987. "Errors and Mistakes: Evaluating the Accuracy of Social Judgment." *Psychological Bulletin* 101 (1): 75–90.
Galston, William. 1989. "Civic Education in the Liberal State." In *Liberalism and the Moral Life*, ed. Nancy Rosenblum. Cambridge, MA: Harvard University Press.
Galston, William. 1991. *Liberal Purposes: Goods, Virtues, and Diversity in the Liberal State.* New York: Cambridge University Press.
Galston, William. 2002. *Liberal Pluralism.* Cambridge: Cambridge University Press.
Gauthier, David. 1986. *Morals by Agreement.* Oxford: Oxford University Press.
Gerber, Alan, Donald Green, and Christopher Larimer. 2008. "Social Pressure and Voter Turnout: Evidence from a Large-Scale Field Experiment." *American Political Science Review* 102 (1): 33–48.
Gilbert, Margaret. 1997. "Group Wrongs and Guilt Feelings." *Journal of Ethics* 1 (1): 65–84.
Gilbert, Margaret. 2009. "Pro Patria: An Essay on Patriotism." *Journal of Ethics* 13 (4): 319–46.
Goodin, Robert. 1988. "What is So Special about Our Fellow Countrymen?" *Ethics* 98 (4): 663–86.
Gove, Michael. 2014. "Birmingham Schools: Secretary of State for Education's Statement." https://www.gov.uk/government/speeches/birmingham-schools-secretary-of-state-for-educations-statement.
Greenstein, Fred. 1965. *Children and Politics.* New Haven: Yale University Press.
Guinier, Lani. 1994. *The Tyranny of the Majority: Fundamental Fairness in Representative Democracy.* New York: The Free Press.
Gutmann, Amy. 1987. *Democratic Education.* Princeton: Princeton University Press.
Gutmann, Amy. 1996. "Democratic Citizenship." In *For Love of Country,* ed. Joshua Cohen. Boston: Beacon Press.
Gutmann, Amy. 1999. *Democratic Education* (revised edition). Princeton: Princeton University Press.
Habermas, Jurgen. 1992. "Citizenship and National Identity: Some Reflections on the Future of Europe." *Praxis International* 12 (1): 1–19.

Habermas, Jurgen. 2000. *The Inclusion of the Other: Studies in Political Theory*, ed. Ciaran Cronin and Pablo De Greiff. Cambridge, MA: MIT Press.
Habermas, Jurgen. 2001. *The Postnational Constellation: Political Essays.* Transl. and ed. Max Pensky. Cambridge, MA: MIT Press.
Hand, Michael. 2011. "Should We Promote Patriotism in Schools?" *Political Studies* 59 (2): 328–47.
Hargreaves, David. 1994. *The Mosaic of Learning*. London: Demos.
Hart, H. L. A. 1955. "Are there Any Natural Rights?" *Philosophical Review* 64: 175–91.
Hart, H. L. A. 1961. *The Concept of Law.* Oxford: Oxford University Press.
Hayward, Clarissa. 2007. "Democracy's Identity Problem: Is "Constitutional Patriotism" the Answer?" *Constellations* 14 (2): 182–96.
Hobbes, Thomas. 1651/1994. *Leviathan*, ed. Edwin Curley. Indianapolis: Hackett Publishing.
Holmes, Richard. 1986. *Acts of War: The Behavior of Men in Battle.* New York: The Free Press.
Holmes, Stephen. 1995. *Passions and Constraints: On the Theory of Liberal Democracy.* Chicago: University of Chicago Press.
Jollimore, Troy. 2011. *Love's Vision.* Princeton: Princeton University Press.
Kahne, Joseph, and Susan Sporte. 2008. "Developing Citizens: The Impact of Civic Learning Opportunities on Students' Commitment to Civic Participation." *American Educational Research Journal* 45 (3): 738–66.
Kahne, Joseph, and Joel Westheimer. 2003. "Teaching Democracy: What Schools Need to Do." *Phi Delta Kappan* 85 (1): 34–40, 57–66.
Kant, Immanuel. 1795/1983. "To Perpetual Peace: A Philosophical Sketch." In *Perpetual Peace and Other Essays*, ed. Ted Humphrey. Indianapolis: Hackett Publishing.
Kateb, George. 1992. *The Inner Ocean: Individualism and Democratic Culture*. Ithaca, NY: Cornell University Press.
Keller, Simon. 2005. "Patriotism as Bad Faith." *Ethics* 115 (3): 563–92.
Keller, Simon. 2008. "How Patriots Think, and Why It Matters." In *Patriotism: Philosophical and Political Perspectives*, ed. Igor Primoratz and Aleksandar Pavkovic. Aldershot: Ashgate.
Kellett, Anthony. 1982. *Combat Motivation: The Behavior of Soldiers in Battle*. Hingham, MA: Kluwer-Nijhoff.
Kinsella, David. 2005. "No Rest for the Democratic Peace." *American Political Science Review* 99 (3): 453–57.
Kymlicka, Will. 1995. *Multicultural Citizenship: A Liberal Theory of Minority Rights*. New York: Oxford University Press.

Lazar, Seth. 2010. "A Liberal Defence of (Some) Duties to Compatriots." *Journal of Applied Philosophy* 27 (3): 246–57.

Lefkowitz, David. 2007. "On a Moral Right to Civil Disobedience." *Ethics* 117 (2): 202–33.

Leising, Daniel, Julia Erbs, and Ulrike Fritz. 2010. "The Letter of Recommendation Effect in Informant Ratings of Personality." *Journal of Personality and Social Psychology* 98 (4): 668–82.

Levine, Peter. 2007. *The Future of Democracy: Developing the Next Generation of American Citizens.* Lebanon, NH: Tufts University Press.

Levine, Peter. 2012. "Education for a Civil Society." In *Making Civics Count*, ed. David Campbell, Meira Levinson, and Frederick Hess. Cambridge, MA: Harvard Education Press.

Levinson, Meira. 1999. *The Demands of Liberal Education.* New York: Oxford University Press.

Levinson, Meira. 2012. *No Citizen Left Behind.* Cambridge, MA: Harvard University Press.

List, Christian, and Robert Goodin. 2001. "Epistemic Democracy: Generalizing the Condorcet Jury Theorem." *Journal of Political Philosophy* 9 (3): 277–306.

Losito, Bruno, and Heinrich Mintrop. 2001. "The Teaching of Civic Education." In *Citizenship and Education in Twenty-eight Countries: Civic Knowledge and Engagement at Age Fourteen*, ed. Judith Torney-Purta, Rainer Lehmann, Hans Oswald, and Wolfram Schulz. Amsterdam: IEA.

Macedo, Stephen. 1990. *Liberal Virtues: Citizenship, Virtue, and Community in Liberal Constitutionalism.* New York: Oxford University Press.

Macedo, Stephen. 2000. *Diversity and Distrust: Civic Education in a Multicultural Democracy.* Cambridge, MA: Harvard University Press.

MacIntyre, Alasdair. 1981. *After Virtue.* Notre Dame: University of Notre Dame Press.

MacMullen, Ian. 2007. *Faith in Schools? Autonomy, Citizenship, and Religious Education in the Liberal State.* Princeton: Princeton University Press.

Madison, James. 1788. Speech to the Virginia Ratifying Convention. http://press-pubs.uchicago.edu/founders/documents/v1ch13s36.html

McConnell, Michael. 1996. "Don't Neglect the Little Platoons." In *For Love of Country,* ed. Joshua Cohen. Boston: Beacon Press.

Mill, John Stuart. 1859/1989. "On Liberty." In *On Liberty and Other Political Writings*, ed. Stefan Collini. Cambridge: Cambridge University Press.

Mill, John Stuart. 1861. *Considerations on Representative Government.* http://www.gutenberg.org/ebooks/5669.

Mill, John Stuart. 1869/1989. "The Subjection of Women." In *On Liberty and Other Political Writings*, ed. Stefan Collini. Cambridge: Cambridge University Press.

Miller, David. 2007. *National Responsibility and Global Justice*. Oxford: Oxford University Press.

Miller, David. 1995. *On Nationality*. Oxford: Oxford University Press.

Morse v. Frederick. 2007. 551 U.S. 393.

Muller, Jan Werner. 2007. *Constitutional Patriotism*. Princeton: Princeton University Press.

Murphy, James. 2004. "Against Civic Schooling." *Social Philosophy and Policy* 21 (1): 221–65.

Murray, Sandra, John Holmes, and Dale Griffin. 1996. "The Benefits of Positive Illusions: Idealization and the Construction of Satisfaction in Close Relationships." *Journal of Personality and Social Psychology*, 70 (1): 79–98.

Nathanson, Stephen. 1989. "In Defense of 'Moderate Patriotism'." *Ethics* 99 (3): 535–52.

Nathanson, Stephen. 1993. *Patriotism, Morality, and Peace*. Lanham: Rowman and Littlefield.

National Council for the Social Studies. 1997. "Fostering Civic Virtue: Character Education in the Social Studies." *Social Studies Review* (Fall/Winter): 23.

National Council for the Social Studies. 2013. "Revitalizing Civic Learning in Our Schools." http://www.socialstudies.org/positions/revitalizing_civic_learning.

Niemi, Richard G. 2012. "What Students Know about Civics and Government." In *Making Civics Count*, ed. David Campbell, Meira Levinson, and Frederick Hess. Cambridge, MA: Harvard Education Press.

Nord, Warren. 2003. "Moral Disagreement, Moral Education, Common Ground." In *Making Good Citizens: Education and Civil Society*, ed. Diane Ravitch and Joseph Viteritti. New Haven: Yale University Press.

Nozick, Robert. 1974. *Anarchy, State, and Utopia*. New York: Basic Books.

Oakeshott, Michael. 1962. *Rationalism in Politics and Other Essays*. London: Meuthen & Co.

O'Leary, Brendan. 2001. "An Iron Law of Nationalism and Federation? A (Neo-Diceyian) Theory of the Necessity of a Federal Staatsvolk, and of Consociational Rescue." *Nations and Nationalism* 7 (3): 273–96.

Petrosino, Anthony, Carolyn Turpin-Petrosino, Meghan Hollis-Peel, and Julia Lavenberg. 2013. "'Scared Straight' and Other Juvenile Awareness Programs for Preventing Juvenile Delinquency." *Cochrane Database of Systematic Reviews*, Issue 4. Art. No.: CD002796. DOI: 10.1002/14651858.CD002796.pub2.

Poole, Ross. 2008. "Patriotism and Nationalism." In *Patriotism: Philosophical and Political Perspectives*, ed. Igor Primoratz and Aleksandar Pavkovic. Aldershot: Ashgate.

Primoratz, Igor. 2008. "Patriotism and Morality: Mapping the Terrain." In *Patriotism: Philosophical and Political Perspectives*, ed. Igor Primoratz and Aleksandar Pavkovic. Aldershot: Ashgate.

Rawls, John. 1964. "Legal Obligation and the Duty of Fair Play." *Law and Philosophy*, ed. Sidney Hook. New York: New York University Press.

Rawls, John. 1971/1999. *A Theory of Justice*. Cambridge, MA: Harvard University Press.

Rawls, John. 1993. *Political Liberalism.* New York: Columbia University Press.

Raz, Joseph. 1979. *The Authority of Law.* Oxford: Clarendon Press.

Raz, Joseph. 1986. *The Morality of Freedom.* Oxford: Clarendon Press.

Rousseau, Jean-Jacques. 1762/1979. *Emile: or On Education.* Transl. Allan Bloom. New York: Basic Books.

Rousseau, Jean-Jacques. 1762/1987. "On the Social Contract." In *The Basic Political Writings*, translated by Donald Cress. Indianapolis: Hackett Publishing Company.

Scanlon, T. M. 1982. "Contractualism and Utilitarianism." In *Utilitarianism and Beyond*, ed. Amartya Sen and Bernard Williams. Cambridge: Cambridge University Press. 103–28.

Scanlon, T. M. 1998. *What We Owe to Each Other.* Cambridge, MA: Belknap Press.

Scheffler, Samuel. 2001. *Boundaries and Allegiances.* New York: Oxford University Press.

Schrag, Francis. 2010. "Moral Education in the Badlands." *Journal of Curriculum Studies* 42 (2): 149–63.

Schwartzberg, Melissa. 2003. "Rousseau on Fundamental Law." *Political Studies* 51 (2): 387–403.

Scorza, Jason. 2007. *Strong Liberalism: Habits of Mind for Democratic Citizenship.* Lebanon, NH: Tufts University Press.

Sherman, Lawrence W. 1993. "Defiance, Deterrence and Irrelevance: A Theory of the Criminal Sanction." *Journal of Research in Crime and Delinquency* 30: 445–73.

Shils, Edward, and Morris Janowitz. 1948. "Cohesion and Disintegration in the Wehrmacht in World War II." *Public Opinion Quarterly* 12 (2): 280–315.

Shklar, Judith. 1989. "The Liberalism of Fear." In *Liberalism and the Moral Life*, ed. Nancy Rosenblum. Cambridge, MA: Harvard University Press.

Simmons, A. John. 1979. *Moral Principles and Political Obligations*. Princeton: Princeton University Press.
Simmons, A. John. 2005. "A Duty to Obey and Our Natural Moral Duties." In *Is There a Duty to Obey the Law?* ed. Christopher Heath Wellman and A. John Simmons. Cambridge: Cambridge University Press. 93–196.
Smith, M. B. E. 1973. "Is There a Prima Facie Obligation to Obey the Law?" *Yale Law Journal* 82: 950–76.
Snook, I. A. 1972. "Indoctrination and Moral Responsibility." In *Concepts of Indoctrination*, ed. I. A. Snook. London: Routledge and Kegan Paul. 152–61.
Spragens, Thomas. 1999. *Civic Liberalism: Reflections on Our Democratic Ideals*. Lanham, MD: Rowman & Littlefield.
Stilz, Anna. 2009. *Liberal Loyalty: Freedom, Obligation, and the State*. Princeton: Princeton University Press.
Stilz, Anna. 2011. "Collective Responsibility and the State." *Journal of Political Philosophy* 19 (2): 190–208.
Stitzlein, Sarah. 2012. *Teaching for Dissent: Citizenship Education and Political Activism*. Boulder, CO: Paradigm Publishers.
Swaine, Lucas. 2012. "The False Right to Autonomy in Education." *Educational Theory* 62 (1): 107–24.
Tamir, Yael. 1993. *Liberal Nationalism*. Princeton: Princeton University Press.
Tan, Kok-Chor. 2002. *Justice Without Borders: Cosmopolitanism, Nationalism, and Patriotism*. Cambridge: Cambridge University Press.
Taylor, Charles. 1979. "What's Wrong with Negative Liberty?" In *The Idea of Freedom*, ed. Alan Ryan. Oxford: Oxford University Press. 175–93.
Thompson, Janna. 2008. "Patriotism and the Obligations of History." In *Patriotism: Philosophical and Political Perspectives*, ed. Igor Primoratz and Aleksandar Pavkovic. Aldershot: Ashgate.
Tocqueville, Alexis de. 1850/2006. *Democracy in America*. New York: Harper Perennial.
Tyler, Tom. 1990. *Why People Obey the Law*. New Haven: Yale University Press.
UK Department for Education. 2013. "Citizenship." https://www.education.gov.uk/schools/teachingandlearning/curriculum/secondary/b00199157/citizenship.
Vaughan, Geoffrey. 2005. "The Overreach of Political Education and Liberalism's Philosopher-Democrat." *Polity* 37 (3): 389–408.
Vernon, Richard. 2010. *Cosmopolitan Regard: Political Membership and Global Justice*. New York: Cambridge University Press.

Waldron, Jeremy. 1999. *Law and Disagreement.* New York: Oxford University Press.

Wellman, Christopher Heath. 2000. "Relational Facts in Liberal Political Theory: Is There Magic in the Pronoun 'My'?" *Ethics* 110 (3): 537–62.

Wellman, Christopher Heath. 2001. "Toward a Liberal Theory of Political Obligation." *Ethics* 111 (4): 735–59.

Wellman, Christopher Heath. 2005. "Samaritanism and the Duty to Obey the Law." In *Is There a Duty to Obey the Law?* ed. Christopher Heath Wellman and A. John Simmons. Cambridge: Cambridge University Press.

White, Patricia. 1996. *Civic Virtues and Public Schooling: Educating Citizens for a Democratic Society.* New York: Teachers College Press.

Williams, Melissa. 2003. "Citizenship as Identity, Citizenship as Shared Fate, and the Functions of Multicultural Education." In *Citizenship and Education in Liberal-Democratic Societies*, ed. Walter Feinberg and Kevin McDonough. New York: Oxford University Press.

Wingo, Ajume. 2003. *Veil Politics in Liberal Democratic States.* Cambridge: Cambridge University Press.

Young, Iris. 2004. "Responsibility and Global Labor Justice." *Journal of Political Philosophy* 12 (4): 365–88.

INDEX